FALLING IN LOVE
WITH WISDOM

FALLING IN LOVE WITH WISDOM

American Philosophers Talk about Their Calling

EDITED BY

David D. Karnos
Robert G. Shoemaker

New York   Oxford
OXFORD UNIVERSITY PRESS
1993

Oxford University Press

Oxford   New York   Toronto
Delhi   Bombay   Calcutta   Madras   Karachi
Kuala Lumpur   Singapore   Hong Kong   Tokyo
Nairobi   Dar es Salaam   Cape Town
Melbourne   Auckland   Madrid

and associated companies in
Berlin   Ibadan

Copyright © 1993 by Oxford University Press, Inc.

Published by Oxford University Press, Inc.
200 Madison Avenue, New York, New York 10016

Oxford is a registered trademark of Oxford University Press, Inc.

Library of Congress Cataloging-in-Publication Data
Falling in love with wisdom : American philosophers talk about their calling /
edited by David D. Karnos, Robert G. Shoemaker.
p. cm.   ISBN 0-19-507201-4
1. Philosophers—United States.   2. Philosophy.
I. Karnos, David D.   II. Shoemaker, Robert G.
B851.F35   1993
191—dc20   92-21965

The publisher gratefully acknowledges receiving permission to reprint from
the following publishers:
Angela Davis, from *Angela Davis: An Autobiography*, published by
Random House, Inc. Copyright © 1974, 1988 by Angela Davis. Reprinted
by permission of Angela Davis.
Willard V. Quine, from *The Time of My Life* reprinted by permission of
the MIT Press.
Huston Smith, "Huston Smith's Story" reprinted from *Primordial Truth
and Postmodern Theology*, edited by Huston Smith and David Ray Griffith,
by permission of the SUNY Press.

1 3 5 7 9 8 6 4 2

Printed in the United States of America
on acid-free paper

Preface

On a warm fall afternoon in sunny San Antonio, Texas, in the backyard of a mutual friend, after sharing our own stories, our own "creation myths," we wondered out loud about how other philosophers described their own stories, their own origins—what caused them to become "philosophical," inquisitive, fascinated with the questions and issues which define philosophy. It was not long before the notion took hold that an organized collection was desirable. Such accounts, in any event, would be interesting in themselves, quite apart from any patterns that might emerge, and collecting a few dozen of them into a single volume was an idea worth pursuing.

The following material is the fruition of that project. We make no claims concerning the adequacy of the sampling method or its representativeness. We contacted friends, and then other colleagues whose names at least were known to us professionally. Still others were approached on a relatively "blind" basis. The range of responding colleagues by geography, gender, area of philosophical interest, age, and type of institution was largely un-contrived. At best, such matters were handled intuitively. But we were modestly pleased with the representation. We wish a higher percentage of those contacted had been able to contribute, but such is the nature of things. Although we have arranged the essays we received into very general headings and groupings, the reader will notice easily that there are many more echoes, cross references, similarities, connections, and typologies contained in the material that go unmentioned. The truth is that most of these stories overlap in one way or another, and hence the task of making clear and informative groups out of them is difficult. Still, as will be seen, there were obvious family connections in some cases, several vignettes that focused on learning a religious "catechism", stories of enchantment with the writings of Nietzsche and existentialism generally, encounters with or concerning death, extremely significant mentors, and so forth.

We hope that not only our colleagues in the field for whom these essays will no doubt be entertaining and interesting—particularly when acquaintances are involved—but others outside philosophy as well will find the material informative and thought-provoking. If there is any truth at all to the intuition that philosophers are perceived in our society as remote, incomprehensible, æthereal, and eccentric eggheads, then we trust that many of these vignettes will exhibit the "human" side of the story. We are confident that students will also find these accounts enlightening, both for educational reasons, and because of the sheer delight in glimpsing the insides of those "odd birds" effusively extolling in class the virtues of equally odd but ordinarily dead "wise ones."

Perhaps a general reader picking up this collection out of sheer curiosity will discover something interesting, entertaining, and even fascinating about these people from coast to coast who are called "philosophers."

For their often enormous contributions to this project with encouragement, friendship, editorial and other practical work and assistance, we wish to thank the following: Cathy Goodwin, Eileen McKie, Pat Wood, Robert E. Bergmark, Ewing and Zsusa Chinn, Nell Doyle, Carleen Leggett, Jerry Blackburn, Pam Zimmerman, David Barrett, and especially our editor, Cynthia Read, and our secretary, Connie Billquist.

Conway, Ark.   R. G. S.
Nye, Mont.   D. D. K.
July 1992

Contents

III   FROM CATECHISMS TO MISSIONS

IV   FROM STRANGE CAUSES TO STRONG CAUSES

V   FROM LOGIC TO ART

VI   OF PLACES AND PASSAGES

FALLING IN LOVE
WITH WISDOM

Introduction

Human identities are perhaps not exclusively, but at least importantly, a collection of stories. These stories portray and delineate the special characteristics of a self or personal identity (who "I" am), of a family (my ancestors, my heritage), of a nation, of a social, cultural, or intellectual tradition, of an institution, and even of a profession or academic discipline. It would be naïve to suppose that these stories or "scripts" are simply "given" to us, or in some way dictated to us by the world of events. Clearly, there are significant senses in which we construct these accounts and memories, manipulate them to fit subjective or ideological preconceptions and purposes, and choreograph them for dramatic impact. This is not to suggest, however, that these stories are therefore misrepresentations of reality. In many ways they can be truer and more enlightening than mere recitations of dates, milestones, and documentary evidence.

From wherever drawn, and however assembled, these stories, epics, legends, histories, accounts, biographies, and autobiographies are crucial to self-understanding. Indeed, it might be urged, they are crucial to self-creation. We *are* our stories, our memories, our encoded renditions of who we once were and how we became who we are now, including the subsequent senses of meaning, purpose, industry, and destination. Historians need not apologize for their dependence on interpretation of artifacts, for the artifacts and other remains of a culture themselves embody the stories, tales, myths, epics, interpretations, accounts, and histories of their own times.

We construct ourselves from our memoirs, in fact and artifact. Our predecessors lived in their own imaginative concoctions, just as much as we today still do. They interpreted their ancient origins, their own becomings, the histories of their families, and the exploits of their heroes in the same ways as we do—with dramatic and instructive sagas for the purpose of directing mind and body in a contemporary world.

As individuals we constantly remind ourselves, through our malleable memories, of the "kind of person" we are—our strengths and weaknesses, values, beliefs, and genealogies. We reminisce about past loves, struggles, triumphs, occasional failures (along with, of course, the lessons to be learned from them), heroic deeds, "notable people we have met," special tutors, and inspirational idols. We surround ourselves with plaques, diplomas, photographs, art, architecture, and other tangible tokens attesting to these events. We both create and learn our identities from these texts and tales and puppydog trails.

Philosophy also finds its identity, value, and purpose in its myths of origin, in its biographies, and in its accounts of conceptual development and purposive endeavor. From the beginning, philosophers have exhibited a tendency to indulge in historical interpretation, both for personal and other (social, political, religious) reasons. Ideas, like people and turnips, need roots. Thus, we find philosophy, as a collective consciousness, struggling to find its boundaries, its voice, its message, and, these days, perhaps its medium, in the autobiographical tracks and tracings of its great practitioners. For example, we find Aristotle discovering the sources of his own questions in an encyclopedic recounting of previous thinkers and the puzzles resulting from their attempts at explanation. Plato depicts the Socratic quest for self-knowledge and moral integrity arising from the dictum of an oracle. The Stoic drift toward inner peace and Augustine's writhings leading to his conversion to the Christian doctrine of salvation also link philosophizing to autobiography—a tradition carried on by a succession of writers from Descartes to Kierkegaard, Sartre, and others.

These are now classic accounts. But what can be said of more recent times? How does philosophy today write its self-defining scripts? Are there uniquely American cultural rhythms, for example, that have shaped the contours of American philosophizing? How do contemporary philosophers explain themselves and their discipline to others? What youthful experiences are said to have led to the philosophical character, the philosophical attitude, style, method, or career? What makes philosophers a breed of wonderers, puzzlers—bulldoggish analyzers of life, meaning, value, truth, human endeavor, art, science, society, knowledge itself, and the discipline of puzzlement itself? Do philosophers manipulate personal memories of childhood and adolescence to fit their current views of what philosophy is or should be? Or, conversely, do they construct stories of what philosophy is in order to be able to consider themselves philosophers?

Have philosophers in this century had anything like what earlier religious thinkers would call "conversion experiences"? Epiphanies? Enlightenments? Having their hearts "strangely warmed" (perhaps by Descartes' stove)? Realizations? Unchainings? Did something fundamentally important happen to American society and culture, and thus to American philosophy, as a result of World War II? In the decade of the 1960s?

Were philosophers kicked, prodded, inspired, captivated, beguiled, enflamed, seduced, tricked, or nudged into the kind of relentless inquiry they generally suppose philosophy to be? Is being a philosopher an enamorment?

A passion? Or is it more like a dark enchantment, which is not necessarily a pleasant captivity? Or is becoming a philosopher something rather more like what becoming pretty much of anything is—not a sudden thing at all, and not necessarily good or bad, but like the subtle drops of chemical accretion that occur in an experiential titration process? Over the longer course, gradual changes in the total balance of acid–base (or, in our simile, the balance of beliefs, values, perspectives, commitments, and the like) are going on, such that at some precise moment a "sea change" occurs, and the Whole becomes visibly, consciously, and behaviorally a different color (i.e., idea or value).

In the case of philosophy as the organized study of a body of knowledge and literature, today's educational system ordinarily defers its introduction until students are somewhere along the line in college. There are exceptions, naturally, but on the whole, seeking the explicit origins of a "philosophical bent" in childhood is somewhat forced. Still, this does not prevent a philosopher from creatively "discovering" those predispositional roots in early experiences and happenstances. Nonetheless, depending upon the specificity and focus of the question, we often express our "awakening" to puzzlement, wonder, or philosophical inquiry as an event or series of events that took place later, in a college course, or under the inspiration and tutelage of some particular teacher of philosophy. Such references are most often the content of stories that we tell each other in the context of specific acts of veneration.

As often as we tell these stories to others, and as often as it happens that the stories which others share with us seem to possess certain themes in common with our own tales, most of us most of the time probably wish we were more comfortable with the conclusion that philosophy has "kid-nabbed" us all in very similar ways. There are, after all, many differences in the stories we hear. Some of them emphasize religious backgrounds and the implications of those carefully feathered nests for philosophic destiny. But even in the instances with that common thread, for example, there appear to be at least two totally disparate tracks or patterns of "ascent" to philosophy. In particular, some colleagues tell us that their early religious training and the accompanying exposure to significant issues in metaphysics and ethics led them directly into the (more abstract, less reverential) realm of philosophical inquiry. Others, however, tell a story of rebellion, of indoctrination that ultimately "failed to take," and of passages through some sort of intellectual and occasionally personal or psychological crisis to the life of perpetual inquiry.

Some colleagues tell stories of movement from scientific pursuits to philosophy, while others speak of departures from art, literature, and mathematics. There are also descriptions of parental influences, mentors, friends and lovers, places, strong emotions, decisions, loyalties, and logic.

The question, therefore, inevitably arises: What, if anything, is genuinely common to these stories about "becoming a philosopher"? Or should we, after the fashion of William James, be satisfied with the irreducible pluralism of variety?

Of Fortune
and Friends

*"Master," I said, "Tell me—now that you touch on this Dame For-
tune—what is she, that she holds the good things of the world within
her clutch?"*

>   (DANTE TO VIRGIL, *Commedia I*, CANTO VII, CIRCLE 4,
>   67–69)

"What is a friend? A single soul dwelling in two bodies."
>   ARISTOTLE, *Diogenes Laertius*, BK. V, SEC. 20

In the Beginning...

ARTHUR K. BIERMAN
San Francisco State University

My friend and colleague, Professor Peter Radcliff, pointed out to me that the number of professional philosophy teachers and philosophers (hereinafter "philosophers") who were born and raised in Nebraska was surprisingly large and probably exceeded the proportion of philosophers to general population that prevails in other states of the Union.

Given the Radcliff hypothesis and the fact that I was born in Nebraska, a world-soul metaphysician would be tempted to explain why I became a philosopher by positing a fecund Nebraska philosophic-state-of-mind, or by claiming that, contrary to Hegel's expectation, his Absolute did not mature in Prussia, but culminated in Nebraska, spreading philosophers upon its great length like manna or droppings. Your estimate of which it spread depends in part on your Hegel Quotient. When you consider, however, that it is also true that the proportion of Nebraska-born-and-bred movie/entertainment stars to general population probably exceeds that which prevails in other states of the Union, these explanations lose plausibility—unless you divine a deep kinship between philosophers and public entertainers.

Even if such generic explanations were plausible, they could not satisfy our desire for the unique set of particulars from which individual philosophers sprout: "What's *your* story, Kitty Duvall?," asks the philosopher in Saroyan's "The Time of Your Life." My philosophical story begins in my early encounter with religion, as I suspect many another's story does.

During my youth (1923–1940), Nebraska was a state of small towns, with the third largest having 12,000 souls. Each town was endowed with enough churches to hold most of the town's faithful—a set almost identical to its citizens—at well attended Sunday Services. Both the Catholic and the Lutheran (Missouri Synod, my synod) churches had parochial schools where pupils had their daily lessons in Bible and doctrine. If Hegel's Absolute didn't descend on Nebraska, at least its churches' absolutes did; few escaped the fishers' wide-cast nets.

For adolescents with a nagging curiosity, a thirst for answers to the "Big Questions," a spirited skepticism, and an insatiable appetite for consistency, religion is tempting foreplay to philosophy. For such youths, what is more satisfying than confounding the keepers of the temple who pander spavined answers? What more daring way to impress your peers? It's the first flight from closure—out and up. Thus is born an adolescent love of wisdom.

Nebraska's Future Philosophers of America were a smaller but more adventuresome breed than its Future Farmers. It wasn't difficult to reject the Future Farmers option. In my sixteenth year I was shocking oat bundles with Delbert Meisinger, a slightly older friend, on a relentlessly hot, 110° F August day, with a 20° heat reflection factor as the sunshine bounced off the oat stubble. He vowed to do anything to escape farm drudgery. It was easy to agree.

But for what else was I suited? High school oratorical contests, debating, and a verbally contentious nature made me a candidate for college pre-law, according to some teachers and my lawyer speech coach, John Kerrigan. His law books smelled seductive and his second-story office over the post office was decidedly cooler than a summer oat field; I preferred his suits to my overalls. Besides I enjoyed delivering day-long speeches to the U.S. Senate, a place most likely reached by a man of the law in our state, as I cultivated endless, indistinguishable rows of corn, addressing the rising and falling rumps of the draught horses in false stentorian tone.

A term in the University of Michigan Law School was subsequently enough to show me that the legal profession would not hold my interest for a lifetime. The law curriculum shunned the philosophical interest religion had kindled but not satisfied. I transferred to the liberal arts school and took up philosophy classes to collar "the hound of heaven" (and to get my BA).

Philosophical ground zero for me was the first Biblical pronouncement out of the gates: "In the beginning God created the heaven and the earth" (*Genesis* 1:1, King James translation). I couldn't believe this even at the crediting age of eight. It wasn't God's claimed capability of making something out of nothing that defied my belief, it was His ability to make matter by an act of thought and will ("God is not of this world"). This earth and water made by or out of thought? Sunk in my native, Cartesian dualism, of course it was hard for me to believe Genesis 1:1.

Only later did I learn that I need not feel an apostate's guilt for my failure to believe this basic Christian claim: It is impossible to believe an incoherent "claim." The only thing one can believe, correctly or mistakenly, is that a (coherent) statement is true or false; since you can't make a statement out of an incoherent set of concepts, there is no claim to believe. Anyone who claims to "believe" an incoherent congeries of concepts in grammatical sentence form is self-deceived.

It didn't occur to me, as it did to George Berkeley, that this incoherence obstacle to belief in creation could be circumvented by arguing that matter is mental and that the fault for this incoherence lies in thinking it's not mental. Thus, while religion's creation story aroused my cosmological interest, it also nourished philosophical doubts it couldn't settle, and fostered guilt because I didn't believe it.

During my eighth year, I had a set-to with the problem of evil, which aroused both ontological and moral doubts about God. I was lonely, the sole-surviving child living on a farm several miles from town. Yearning for companionship, I prayed that my parents would have another child. After several months there was still no sibling. I gave God a deadline, although I don't recall threatening Him if He failed to deliver on schedule.

The deadline passed without issue. It left a residue of doubt that would fester for years. I didn't doubt that God was all-powerful nor all-knowing, nor did I doubt that what I prayed for was good. Thus, I was left to doubt that God was all-good. Once again guilt was fostered by my inability to believe an unbelievable incoherence.

This moral doubt slowly transformed into a doubt about God's existence, made redoubtable when, as a naval aviator, I felt wholly secular during, and after, what I thought was to be a fatal flight error. I had blacked out when I pulled out too fast from an overhead gunnery run over Okefenokee Swamp. I came to consciousness over the swamp and under a sky covered alike with thin, milky clouds, preventing me from visually orienting my flight attitude. My altimeter showed I had lost 8,000 feet and the plane's high speed was intensifying. It appeared I didn't have enough time to orient myself before crashing. If I was right side up in relation to the earth, salvation lay in simply pulling back on the stick. If I was descending upside down, I *first* had to roll over, *then* pull back. By simply pulling back while in this flight attitude, I would fly myself right into the swamp. Prayer here was a waste of precious time; fortunately, it never occurred to me.

The cosmological, ontological, and moral doubts religion had nurtured were not purely intellectual. They were agonizing; they turned against me: I was obviously damned inadequate if all about me other Christians believed instead of harboring doubts. During church services I felt none of the certitude in salvation, no ecstasy in the "house of my Lord," no joy in "my Redeemer," nothing of the serenity I thought I saw on the faces and in the poses of my fellow "worshippers." They affirmed these inferred states; however, try as I might, each of them always eluded me.

Agony was escorted by mounting resentment.

Freedom from both arrived one Thursday, April morning in 1948 in Ann Arbor during a philosophy of religion class taught by Roy Wood Sellars, who played Michigan's realistic Sancho Panza to DeWitt H. Parker's idealistic Don Quixote. The reading discussed that day was an excerpt from Walter Lippman's Spinozistic book. I am sure that my freedom came as beguilingly, smoothly, and finally (no turning back since that April day) as it did because Professor Sellar's atheism was tranquil; his cherubic face bore testimony to the felicity of freedom from having to believe the unbelievable.

Walking out of class that day into the arbored quad freshly greening under a warming sun was a blissful philosophic state that forty-two years later remains almost as vivid in memory as the original.

Yes, philosophy does bake bread. It liberated my mind wonderfully, affirmed my normality, washed away the grime of guilt unnecessarily accrued.

How I Became Almost a Philosopher

LEWIS WHITE BECK
University of Rochester

Nietzsche draws a distinction between philosophers and philosophic work-men. I am among the latter.

In 1925, I was awakened from my dogmatic slumber by newspaper ac-counts of the "Monkey Trial." John T. Scopes was found guilty of breaking a law of the state of Tennessee prohibiting the teaching of the theory of evolution. Reading accounts of both sides of the trial made me admit that Mr. Scopes was indeed guilty—there was no question about that—but made me see that the law itself was foolish. I bought and read *The Origin of Species*, which confirmed what became a new dogmatism for me. An uncle—a businessman with the heart of a scholar—had told me that there was some hot stuff in the infamous fifteenth chapter of Gibbon, and reading that planted some new doubts and new convictions in me. By the age of twelve, my education as the village atheist was essentially complete.

Two years later my sister gave me a copy of Will Durant's *The Story of Philosophy*. I cannot say how much I learned from and how much I delighted in that book; sixty years later I still remember it with pleasure. What was most important to me was discovering that there had been others before me who had had the kind of thoughts and had asked the kind of questions that had bothered me during and since the Scopes trial. What I had thought an idiosyncrasy to be hidden from others turned out to be a healthy and traditional exercise of thought. I discovered that I was not alone, and not the first to ask questions most of my fellows thought silly. Even then, however, I did not know that there was still extant a craft of philosophers and philosophic workmen with living practitioners. I wrote a few articles for our high school newspaper on topics vaguely philosophical, with purple passages taken from Thomas Henry Huxley. But it was Huxley's science, not his philosophy, that I studied, for I had by that time made up my mind to become a scientist.

I worked summers at the Agricultural Experiment Station near our town.

At twelve-and-a-half cents an hour I was employed in the botany and entomology laboratories. This experience got me a very informal job during the school year as "lab assistant" in the high school chemistry and physics laboratories. For setting up demonstrations and helping my classmates with their laboratory exercises, I was allowed to play in the laboratories after school hours, without supervision. My passion was for doing organic syntheses, for which I used to bring buckets of tar from the gasworks. The messes I made in the laboratory were never cleaned up, but my teachers were so relieved that I had not blown up the building when synthesizing TNT that they did not loudly complain about the odor and smudges of tar.

When I went to college (Emory), I was permitted to skip the ordinary introductory chemistry courses and to begin with organic chemistry. This was a mistake. I did not know as much inorganic as the professor thought, and my grounding was not sufficient for more advanced organic. In addition, I was overshooting end points and getting grotesquely wrong results in the quantitative lab. Thus I discovered (but kept to myself) that I was color blind. In those days, before much laboratory work was electronically instrumented, this was like a sentence of professional death. By some fancy use of the slide rule, however, I kept my secret so successfully that at the end of my junior year I was elected to an honorary fraternity for chemists, an honor not previously given to an undergraduate. To me, though, it was an empty honor because I knew I would never become a chemist, and I had no idea what other career would be open to me.

The investiture, or whatever it might be called, fell on a day when my laboratory work had been unusually frustrating. I had never heard of *Gedankenexperimente*, of course, but I must have wished for some discipline in which experiments could be performed in the armchair instead of in a hood, and at 6:00 P.M. on that day I did not know such a discipline existed.

To initiate the new members, there was a dinner followed by a talk by the professor of philosophy entitled "The Limits of Scientific Concepts." He spoke to me directly and almost personally. He dealt with the values and disvalues of science that had underlain my awareness of the science–religion dispute. I remember the lecture well (for I gave much the same lecture innumerable times later on!) It was based on Heinrich Rickert's *Die Grenzen der naturwissenschaftlichen Begriffsbildungen* and Cassirer's *Substance and Function*. Here I listened to a *real, living* philosopher, and I instantly saw that this was what I wanted to become. After a night sleepless from intellectual excitement, I went to his office and asked if I could change my major from chemistry to philosophy. It took some hurried scurrying since I had only one year to complete my undergraduate work. But he did cut the red tape and take on the extra burden of tutoring me and of having me live in his house during the vacation so that I could use his library under his guidance. One year later I entered graduate school in philosophy.

The man who made this possible, whom I remember with gratitude, admiration, and love, was Leroy Loemker.

Not a Philosopher

PAUL FEYERABEND

University of California, Berkeley

I am not a philosopher. I am a professor of philosophy, which here in Berkeley means a civil servant. Why did I become a professor? Because I was broke. A British friend suggested that I apply for a job in Oxford that had just become available. To raise my chances I applied for three jobs; one in Oxford, one in Bristol, one in Australia. I got Bristol, mainly on the basis of a recommendation by Erwin Schroedinger, who seemed to like the way in which I, a mere student, dealt with bigshots in public debates. "Three years, not a day more," I said when I started. Now, after thirty-five years, I am still in the business.

Why? Because being a professor sure beats being a nine-to-five working stiff. And why philosophy? Because there are no restrictions on what you can do. A professor of mathematics who uses "Topology III" to talk about Liliana Cavani will soon get into trouble. I had no problems when I turned "Epistemology I" into a discussion of Ian Kott. Why did I write so much? That, too, was an accident. I liked to talk and to travel and I accepted many invitations. My talks were mostly unprepared—I made a few notes, memorized them, and then performed without a script. Most of the talks belonged to series that issued in publications, so I was eventually forced to write them down.

Do I believe in what I write, or say? Sometimes yes, sometimes no. An actor (and for me a professor is in many ways an actor—I would fall asleep on my job if I felt otherwise) should present his lines in an interesting way; he does not need to believe them. It is up to the audience to decide about truth, plausibility, or whatever else they think is important. What am I apart from being a professor? To that my answer is: "I am not a *what*, I am a *who*." If somebody put a pistol to my head, however, and said "confess, or die!," then I would exclaim: "I am a journalist!" I have opinions like everybody else, but I write about them and I try to make them colorful and attractive. I did not invent the opinions I have. I accidentally picked them up, from newspapers, plays, novels, political debates, and even from a philosophy book now and then. Some of these opinions, I thought, were excellent; since they were being maligned by ignoramuses (people who call themselves philosophers among them), they deserved a good defense, and I decided to defend them. I defended not only their content, but also the style of life they represented. The best content, the most liberating message, changes into its opposite when spread by people with "truth" or "a conscience" in their soul and a mean look on their faces.

Aristophanes, not Socrates; Nestroy, not Kant; Voltaire, not Rousseau; the Marx brothers, not Wittgenstein. These are my heroes. These people are not philosophers, and philosophers, though flirting with them in their pastime, would not accept them in their midst. This is why I, though of much smaller talent, have no interest in being found there either.

Just Lucky, I Guess!

HENRY E. KYBURG, JR.
University of Rochester

When I was very small—perhaps four?—I was fascinated by numbers. I wrote my first book (it was very short) at seven, but I really wanted to be a painter. I loved music, but recognized early on a monumental lack of talent. My parents very strongly encouraged in me a desire to be an engineer. True, I had a talent for, and took pleasure in, breaking things and fixing things. And inventing things—particularly if they involved gunpowder.

I not only knew nothing of philosophy, back then I knew nothing of scholarship and was an abysmal student, perpetually called on the carpet at school to account for my delinquencies.

Through a series of accidents, one of which was World War II, I went off to Yale at sixteen. The admissions office didn't have many applicants to choose from, and no doubt they hoped that the intellectual stimulation that their institution could provide would awaken my obviously dormant intellectual talents.

Alas.

I went through Yale as a chemical engineer and a decidedly second-rate student. Obedient and bored, I took all the prescribed courses (philosophy was not among them) until my senior year, when I revolted and took a course in drawing and rendering. No philosophy.

But perhaps the admissions office was right: I was touched by philosophy, in the persons of several of my more intellectual classmates. I had been introduced to the work of Russell and Whitehead, and to Sartre. I became interested in being a writer, but I had no ambition to become a philosopher. On the other hand, I had even less interest in becoming an engineer. I thought philosophy was rather fun, and I went on to spend a semester at a small college studying philosophy, and reading on my own. It really *was* fun. I took the G.R.E.s, did well, and entered Columbia. Note that I had graduated around the middle of my class from a rural high school, around the middle of my class (perhaps a bit lower) from college, and had spent one semester taking actual courses in philosophy. Columbia, perhaps suffering from the same ideals as Yale, nevertheless admitted me as a graduate student.

I still had no idea of "becoming a philosopher"—I just liked reading and writing philosophy, and saw no need to worry about where or how I was going to get a job. Something always turned up. Before and during my graduate education I held various jobs, including a job as a chemical engineer. I did not imagine becoming a professor (I was much too shy to consider standing in front of a class), but it did occur to me that getting a Ph.D. might be useful for something, although I really wasn't sure what. It just seemed a reasonable thing to do at the time.

The part of philosophy I liked best—in keeping with my insistent inconsistency—was not the literary philosophy that had interested me at Yale, but the mathematical philosophy that I discovered in the deeper Russell's *The Principles of Mathematics*. I studied logic, set theory, and probability theory. I got a Ph.D. And, I got married.

Still, I didn't get a job teaching for some time. I did carpentry, and wrote a book. When I finally began teaching, it was partly based on a misunderstanding: Warren McCulloch recommended me to Wesleyan under the mistaken belief that I was a mathematician. It turned out that I could do what they wanted, and I was hired as Visiting Assistant Professor of Mathematics for three successive years.

Eventually I ended up in a full-time position in a philosophy department, but was I a "philosopher?" I haven't felt more of a philosopher than I did when I first began trying to write philosophy before I'd studied it. I've identified with a group of people—people employed by universities to teach philosophy—but perhaps that identification has been on a relatively superficial level; it has been primarily at the level of day-to-day activities and obligations, rather than on a deep intellectual level. This is not to say that I don't learn a great deal from my friends in the philosophical profession, because I do. Still, I learn significantly more from their books than I do from them directly. And I learn significantly from books and articles by people in other professions as well. So I have felt uncomfortable about calling my colleagues and myself "philosophers." It smacks somehow of hubris.

In recent years a new factor has come to play a role in my professional life. I have become involved in Artificial Intelligence (AI)—an enterprise that seems to me to involve exactly the same kinds of inquiries and studies that I have been most concerned with in philosophy. AI is a bit more practically oriented: we want things to *work*. It would be easy to think that I am coming full circle—that through AI my childhood interests in engineering (*sans* explosives)—have re-emerged. Perhaps philosophy was just a detour?

I think not. I think what led me to philosophy in the first place was a combination of dissatisfaction with everything else, and a resistance to having boundaries dictated to me. Here we may be coming to a central feature of the intellectual character of many philosophers: a strong reluctance to be fenced in. "Don't tell me that what I am studying is not part of my field of study!"

If that is so, then we are faced with an anomaly: the very qualities that lead people like me toward philosophy lead also, centripetally, away from too focused a concentration on any particular area. If there is anything that I find shockingly unbecoming in a philosopher, it is the assertion (whether made of a colleague or of a student) that what X is doing "isn't really philosophy." Everything that is a source of wonder, or puzzlement, or practical challenge, is a fit subject for philosophical inquiry. Lacking focus, it seems to me that the only thing antithetical to philosophy is a narrow focus.

So I became a philosopher because none of the many things I have been lucky enough to enjoy doing and studying were sufficiently compelling to hold my exclusive attention. Lack of focus? Breadth of interest? Both together? No matter. I imagine being asked, "How did a healthy, ambitious, accomplished man like you, with all the advantages you have had, end up in such a useless dead end of a profession?" To which I would smugly answer, "Just lucky, I guess."

"V-Yooze"

DAVID LYNN HALL

University of Texas, El Paso

HOW I BECAME A PHILOSOPHER

There were eighteen hours traveling time left and I hadn't the slightest talent for sleeping on a bus. Granted a thirty-minute rest stop in Pecos, Texas, I went in search of a book. Inside a cafe I found a decrepit wire book-rack of the sort that mercifully occupies every bus-rider's oasis. Praying for "just anything interesting," I spun the wobbly roulette wheel that was to determine my fate for the next several hours. The motley hotchpotch of titles hanging from this leaning tower of Babel was almost completely unappealing, even to an indiscriminate adolescent.

The book that finally captured my attention had a colorful, rather exotic cover and a subtitle that promised "A Brilliant History of Mankind's Great Thoughts." (Its only serious rival had been *The Way of Life: The Tao Te Ching*). I paid fifty cents, boarded the Trailways bus, nestled into my narrow seat and into the vastness of the desert spaces—and soon into the yet vaster spaces of humanity's great thoughts. The adventure begun that day opened me to the "endless beginning of prodigies" which life affords the fortunate.

As I recall that first encounter with philosophic thinking, I seem to capture the exact emotion—a mixture of intrigue and perplexity, a congealed sense of awe—the apotheosis of which is the feeling philosophy now represents for me.

The Mentor paperback of Whitehead's *Adventures of Ideas* which introduced me to philosophic thinking is still on my shelf, held intact now by a rubber band. I cannot but think it to be an interesting comment on the present fate of the philosophic enterprise that upon last opening that book the pages fell piecemeal from the cover, landing in disparate array on desk and floor. Since its publication, "the history of mankind's great thoughts" has followed a course not unlike that of this particular copy of the founding document of my intellectual life.

HOW I BECAME THE SORT OF PHILOSOPHER I AM

I

"Well, I feel that Augustine . . . "

"*Mr.* Hall . . . " I realized my mistake too late. My fellow students sat frozen in various posture, fixing their eyes on ceiling, desk or wall while their colleague received The Message: " . . . in this class you are not asked to feel, but to *think*. And when you *do* think you are asked to think about the text. Your heart-felt opinions, however inspiring you may believe them to be, are of no interest to us here. Now, again . . . "

My tenure as a seminarian at the University of Chicago was filled with encounters of just this kind. I studied philosophical theology, which meant that I read the works of the great philosophers and theologians. These texts had meanings that, upon excruciatingly precise analysis, could be exposed. My professors were not interested in comments about the texts or their historical background. It was the text, and only the text, that was to be understood.

And always the great, *primary* text—whenever possible in the original language. No secondary sources. No surveys or commentaries were allowed. In the words of one of my visiting professors from Tübingen, a professor of New Testament theology: "Vell, gentlemen, *gut*. At Chicago, I understant zat you shtick to zeh texts."

II

After three years of "shticking to zeh texts," I completed my seminary degree and went off to Yale for a Ph.D. The scene again is a seminar room, this time in New Haven. The Professor is somewhat younger; I am slightly older.

"Yes, of course, Mr. Hall. But I should like to learn your *opinion* of that argument. How would you *e-val-u-ate* it? Do you, Mr. Hall, find it *per-sua-sive?*"

I, quite innocently, reiterated The Message: "I do my best to analyze textual meanings; I want to avoid as much as possible introducing my own opinions."

The Professor was unimpressed. "And where did you come by such a methodology, Mr. Hall?"

"At Chicago."

"Of course." The Professor rolled his eyes and wrinkled his nose just enough to make it clear how scornful he was of such an approach to philosophical education.

"Very well, Mr. Hall . . . " The Professor said this with a world-weary condescension that suggested he had given this lecture before. " . . . we now know what *had been* expected of you. May I inform you what *should have been and indeed will be* expected? At Yale, Mr. Hall . . . " The Professor straightened in his chair, apparently uplifted by the mere thought of Glorious Mother Yale. " . . . we are not required to hide ourselves in the interstices of the text. You see, at Yale, Mr. Hall, we are expected to have . . . " The Professor's upper teeth lightly touched his bottom lip. His chin raised slightly, then lowered, then raised again—higher this time—as he concluded his sentence, " . . . *views.*"

The word was sounded quite slowly, with two syllables, taking perhaps three or four seconds to pronounce. It sounded like, "*v-yooze.*" "At Yale, Mr. Hall, we are expected to have *v-yooze.*"

The word wasn't actually spoken; it was thrust from The Professor's mouth in the manner of a plush red carpet rolled forward to receive a guest who, though at present most undeserving, would nevertheless attain royal status once he had set foot upon it.

That metaphor may be too grand. To be more consonant with my ambiguous feeling I might rather say that The Professor's pronouncement ("At Yale, Mr. Hall, we are expected to have *v-yooze*") reminded me of a frog's slow-motion demonstration of the correct manner of catching a fly.

III

My education at two great universities taught me three fundamental truths:

The First Truth. By 323 B.C.E. (the year of Aristotle's exile from Athens), the definitive concepts, principles, and values defining our cultural tradition had already been developed. Thereafter, thought had taken on the character of variations played upon a small finite number of principal themes.

As a Chicago graduate, I was dutifully persuaded of this fact.

The Second Truth. If one is to be responsible as a scholar and a teacher, one cannot simply mimic the Great Voices of the Past. One must have (there is no choice) . . . *v-yooze.*

As a Yale Ph.D., I, reluctantly at first, but then most readily, yielded myself up to this credo.

These apparently contradictory pedagogical advices led me to:

The Third Truth. The truly important *v-yooze* having already been taken, there being nothing new under the sun, one's only choice is to chart galaxies whose worlds are warmed by other stars.

My attempt to weld the first and second truths into a viable tenet that could sustain both of my deeply felt loyalties accounts for the borderline, some might say bizarre, character of many of my *v-yooze.*

Seeking Sophia's Friendship

NATALIE DANDEKAR
University of Rhode Island

You ask me to share my private mythos of becoming a philosopher. What a compliment! Can it be you already perceive me as actually having become that which I aspire to be? Do you think it might be helpful to others if I reflect in print about the beginning of that aspiration, the stages of obsession, longing, voicelessness, and rage through which I've passed thus far? How do I account for the differentness that led me to what some have called the "philosophic discipline"?

Aristotle suggests that the best poets tell a story from the beginning. My story starts with an early obsessive love of reading. I still remember something of the original seductiveness all books presented to me. I loved the power of choosing just one from the many and by that act bringing into being the specialness of what seemed a book until with my collaboration it became enchantment itself. Did I love the book, or did I love the power it brought? Did I love the certainty of knowing that when I chose, I could enter small private worlds entirely built of words? I never stopped to analyze my dependency. I simply read voraciously. I walked, often daily, to a branch library so small that when I was very young I truly thought I could read every book there was. During that time, I never met a book I couldn't love more than, for example, my schoolmates, who were so much harder to grasp. Where children asked so many pledges of loyalty from those they would call friend, books made no demands beyond the reading itself.

I believe that if I am different, or simply perceive myself as different, this differentness has taken its rise in the easy amplitude books have given my life, and in the way recourse to books has led me to avoid so many of the interpersonal struggles of the schoolyard. This differentness, however, marked every one of the "brains" at my school. If there had been no second crisis, it would have led to intellectualism, but not perhaps to philosophy. I might have grown into an intellectual reader, but not necessarily one committed to dogged Socratic pursuit of philosophic truths.

Philosophy took hold of me by way of a humiliating first encounter with genuine philosophic depth. Secure in my belief that whatever was transmitted by writing was fairly easy to comprehend, I persuaded my college advisor to let me take an advanced philosophy course rather than the introductory level appropriate to my ignorance. How truly I did not know that I did not know. The very first assigned readings—Kant and Aristotle—shattered my self-confidence. At first, I read them in what was then my standard fashion, racing along from beginning to end. Utterly confused, I was obliged to stop looking for an overview and read more slowly. I took notes. I made charts. I struggled. Then one night, epiphany! I understood a whole (short) argument in Kant. Aristotle took longer, but I was beginning to understand the point of this struggle—to see arguments link up with each other, brave and vulnerable and going somewhere. Having had a high opinion of my intellect, I now found myself challenged and humbled. Others in the class could quite demonstrably already read philosophy more easily than I. But I kept trying.

By the time I approached my first dialogue by Plato, my conversion was complete. Philosophy seemed at once the most difficult and, in terms of my self-development, absolutely the most worthwhile of all my college courses. The satisfaction of eventually understanding a difficult text was beyond anything I had felt before. Only two questions remained: First, could I ever do philosophy well, myself? Second, given that I was embroiled in an obviously troubled world, was it unconscionably selfish to spend years in college and graduate school having this kind of "unproductive" fun? These were the years of civil rights marches and Vietnam. Male friends took shelter from the draft in college classrooms, or openly faced jail. One accused me outright of taking up graduate school space that could save a male life. In anti-war activities, I felt the injustice of being out of danger, while the men risked penalties that might cloud their futures. Guilt came to color my world as I hid out with Hegel and Plato and sought to understand transcendence. I felt small, overprivileged, and guilty.

A fellow graduate student, during my first year at Columbia, did a great deal to help me with this problem when he presented a paper on the limits of "helping" a country like South Vietnam resist communism. This was 1964 when I was actively working against continued U.S. involvement in unjust military adventures. His paper showed me that I could focus my own dissertation on the limits of political obligation. Surely my activity could be shown to derive moral force from the possibility that a conscientious individual could both decide to disregard specific obligations, and yet also act to support the political community.

But what of the subtle constraints of loyalty and emotional commitment? Surely, socialization itself works as a form of coercion, limiting autonomous choice. I wrote a dissertation, but felt so unsatisfied with its incompleteness that for some years I became philosophically voiceless. Personal emotional commitment, so necessary to meaningful human life, worked in my case to limit my capacity even to focus on philosophy and write in my own voice during the time I was in that classic middle position, between aging parents and a dependent child. I think the idiosyncracies of biography may work to interfere with other more clear patterns of philosophic commitment. Among women philosophers my age, however, it may be that many others share the same non-linear career pattern, the experience of split foci suddenly converging, and the threads of the years weaving together, to form a new level of clarity in one's midyears. Still, I don't know whether I've just described one female's encounter with philosophy under patriarchy, or one typical form of female encounter with philosophy under patriarchy. I only know that I've been very lucky.

I found a refuge that allowed me to stay in the field during the years when I was not publishing. As I began to regain focus, I found mentoring from a much younger woman working in the same department, and I found colleagues willing to support my re-entry into philosophical productivity. Of course, I also discovered that some philosophers (mostly male) in positions of power simply could not accept that, after years of non-productivity, I might find my own voice again. For them, only the standard career pattern could be valid. Since I had not followed that pattern, and since I had so clearly for some time put family first, I could not be accepted as a philosopher among them.

Color the world with bitter rage, something like an ochre wash.

But I found others (also, mostly men) at a different school more open to a nontraditional career track. To my eternal gratitude they, too, were willing to take up mentoring tasks with cheerfulness and candor. In collegiality, I do believe that I am finding my voice, and I may yet be able to say something philosophically worth hearing.

So, you ask me how I have become a philosopher. On reflection, I seem to have thus far passed through four stages of becoming. In the first, I fell arrogantly in love with reading. In the second, I found the first of a series of epiphanies—philosophy texts that I could not easily understand, but which clearly repaid persistent effort. In the third, I split myself in two, trying to live a domestic life, and also to be productive in philosophy, feeling as a result that my efforts were insufficient, and that my focus was lost. Now, in the fourth stage, re-mentored and reconnected, I think my split foci are merging. The threads of my thoughts, my reading, and all the years of discussions with students are finally reaching a point at which I feel capable of participating in the great discourse. Put another way, I see a peculiar dialectic that began with the illusion of collaborative power between me and every book I cared to read, until in a second moment the more stringent requirements of great philosophic arguments revealed the ignorance of my earlier arrogance. The epiphanies of recognizing philosophic arguments and finding myself able to grapple with them then reversed when I entered into the ultimate particular commitments of living my life as a human female, blending in the peculiarities of transformative power and voicelessness. Yet this situation, too, has become self-transformed as I rejoin the other participants in the voiced discourse seeking Sophia.

Youthful Reminiscence

JOEL FEINBERG
University of Arizona

I can trace my interest in philosophy back to a specific episode that occurred when I was fifteen or sixteen years old. I was to pick up Brenda, a classmate, and escort her to some routine high school function. Was it a club meeting? A dance? A basketball game? I cannot recall. Brenda lived directly across the street from me, and this made it convenient for us to attend school functions together at times when it would have been inconvenient for each of us to have a "date," with all the game-playing that dating involved. There was one thing about Brenda, however, that was inconvenient. She took an unconscionable amount of time dressing, and thus was always late. On the occasion in question she kept me waiting almost forty-five minutes, a delay that did not surprise me, but embarrassed her mother who invited me, warmly, to browse in the family library while waiting. Brenda's family was not particularly intellectual, and their library collection, fed mostly by their memberships in popular book clubs, was largely unread.

It was on a shelf in Brenda's family's library that I found a new copy of what had been a best seller in the 1920s and 1930s—Will Durant's *The Story of Philosophy*. I picked it up idly, and soon began to read. Forty-five minutes later Brenda had to pull me away. One week later, having borrowed and read Durant to the finish, I decided that I would major in philosophy when I enrolled, after the war, at our local college, the University of Michigan. Twenty years later, I returned the well-read volume to Brenda's mother.

Durant obviously had immense admiration for the great philosophers and a love for their works. His "gosh, gee" attitude was utterly contagious. I was not to lose it until I myself became a professional philosopher, sensitive to the presence of logical flaws and unsolved problems in any work. I had become a technical philosopher, and was soon to learn that nothing is more fatal to the spirit of romance than to convert it into a technique. Will Durant's romantic introduction to the subject matter of philosophy and to its most creative writers may not repay a return visit in middle age, but it set many a teenager, in the years before World War II, on the path toward further study, including two of my slightly older colleagues at Brown University, where I began my teaching career.

The Story of Philosophy, originally published in 1926, was part of an unorganized movement at the time to "humanize knowledge." Best-selling works had such titles as *The Story of Mankind* and *The Human Adventure*. Noting the popularity of the word "story" in "humanized" books of the period, Durant later wrote:

> As for the word *Story*, which has since been so abused with use, it was chosen partly to indicate that the record would concern itself chiefly with the more vital philosophers, partly to convey the sense that the development of thought was a romance as stirring as any in history. (preface to the second edition, 1933, p. x.)

Both of these purposes may properly be characterized as "romantic" in one or more senses of that confusing word, and both were amply fulfilled in Durant's book. As for the "stirring romance" in the development of thought, Durant must have meant to suggest some strong analogy between the story line in a work of romantic fiction, when it unfolds in an exciting or moving way, and the steps in an innovative philosophical argument as it unfolds to reveal some unsuspected conclusion.

It was Durant's first purpose, however—that requiring focus not just on the philosophic product but on the "vital" person who was its producer— that could catch the fancy of sixteen-year-old youths bent on having adventures in life, whether real-life adventures or intellectual ones. Even before I read Durant's book, I needed no persuading that adventures also came in intellectual form. I had no greater pleasure in those days than engaging in spirited speculations with one or more partners, on the meaning of life, love, sex, or the proper attitude toward death; on the quarrel between moral absolutism and moral relativism; on the limits of voluntary human motivation (are we all egoists or is genuine altruism possible?); the relative importance of environment and heredity in human development; the riddle of determinism and free will; the nature of aesthetic value; the best and worst forms of political governance; and so on. The discussions were so engaging that frequently some of us would spend the small hours of the night absorbed in them while walking the eight miles from our weekend place of employment, the downtown branch of the U.S. Post Office, to our suburban neighborhoods. The excitement of these discussions was equaled only by their naïveté. It was to become one of the disappointments of my later career that as naïveté diminished, the social excitement declined along with it.

Philosophy as presented by Durant invited the unlettered romantic youth not only to admire the imaginativeness, ingenuity, and subtlety of the classic philosophic positions he was encountering for the first time, but also to identify with the heros (Plato and Schopenhauer were my favorites) who were their authors. Socrates' teachings (or questionings) were presented right along with the story of his trial and the hemlock; Spinoza's doctrine was sketched against the background of his excommunication by the Jewish community of Amsterdam; Nietzsche's turbulent relationship with Wagner was integrated into the exposition of Nietzsche's thought.

Durant knew what he was doing in presenting philosophies to us through the mouths of the plausibly romantic heros of our philosophic tradition, for once we can admire and care about the author as a human being, our inevitable identification with him excites our vanity:

> And we may flatter ourselves with . . . a thought of Emerson's, that when genius speaks to us, we feel a ghostly reminiscence of having ourselves, in our distant youth, had vaguely this self-same thought which genius now speaks, but which we had not art or courage to clothe with form and utterance. And indeed, men speak to us only so far as we have ears and souls to hear them; only insofar as we have in us the roots at least, of that which flowers out in them.

There was in that sentiment, however just or unjust it might have been, an exaltation that survived even the onset of sophistication. Very often when we professional philosophers cite a corroborating passage in a great philosopher, we are not modestly sharing the credit, so much as pointing with pride to a genius on our side.

When I say that my high-school companions and I were, in a sense, "romantic" youths, I do not mean that we were partisans of some clearly articulated ideology or world view, or of some definite historical approach to art, literature, and music. We knew little of such things. Rather, our "romanticism" consisted in a dedication (at least in our imaginations) to adventure, risk, emotion, and living life to the hilt. Each of us might have said (in less grammatical Latin): *Homo sum; ergo nihil humani alienum a me puto.* ("I am a human being; therefore nothing pertaining to humanity do I deem foreign to me.") In my case that meant that I wanted to experience to the fullest all of the basic human experiences (I even claimed to anticipate with eagerness military combat), to travel everywhere and savor the full diversity of human cultures. Romanticism, however, also meant that I wanted to read all the great books, and to study avidly the writings of psychologists, anthropologists, sociologists, novelists, and all sensitive commentators on the human condition.

Still another strand of my adolescent romanticism was a determination to stay out of the economic "rat race," off the beaten track, and away from the humdrum life of the mainstream. Later, I could sympathize with Santayana's suggestion that the best job for a philosopher (and even philosophers need jobs) was not teaching in a university, but rather "tending the umbrellas in some unfrequented museum." The life of the philosophical umbrella-tender was surprisingly appealing to me even as an adolescent, since it was far from the rat race and left much time for the earnest assault on all human knowledge to which the intellectual side of my romanticism aspired. But there just aren't enough adventures to be had in dusty museums: no secret dangerous missions, no profound love affairs, no camping in wildernesses.

The time soon came when I had to choose between the bookish and the adventurous forms of romanticism. I had befriended a chap from Milwaukee when we were both in the army. He had been a pianist in the orchestra of an ocean liner before he was drafted into the service. He was much taken by my "philosophy of life" and suggested that we team up after our discharges. He told me exactly how to acquire seaman's papers from the Coast Guard and a union card from the appropriate labor union. I couldn't very well play in a ship's orchestra, but my friend was confident that he could arrange a soft job for me on the same ship. Then we would travel regularly around the world, saving immense sums of money with which to subsidize romantic adventures in all the major ports of the world. When our ship sailed off again, I could spend my nonworking hours producing stories and novels in a style at once reminiscent of Joseph Conrad and W. Somerset Maugham.

One month after my discharge, I received two interesting items in the mail. One was a letter from my friend announcing that he was a civilian again and all ready to begin the adventurous collaboration that we had planned. The other piece of mail contained one of the most exciting books I had ever received, a kind of outline of all human knowledge, with a *carte blanche* invitation to sample whatever parts of it I wished. It was the official catalogue of the University of Michigan, which I had ordered earlier.

I wrote my friend and asked for a three-year postponement of our joint adventure, so that I could use up my accumulated G.I. Bill credits in earning a degree. I assured him that my new plan was no betrayal of our earlier agreement, for I would eschew any course that had any practical value whatever in preparing a student for the rat race, and concentrate instead on philosophy (whose practical uselessness could not be denied), the social sciences, and literature. It seemed logical to pursue the bookish part of the Great Plan first and only then, well-armed with knowledge, to take to the high seas and the great ports of the world. I cited in my support Plato's scheme in *The Republic* (as described somewhat inaccurately by Durant) for the education of the guardians. My correspondent never replied.

I enrolled at the University of Michigan in February 1947, and have been, there and elsewhere, a student of philosophy ever since. The recognition, endorsed and enhanced by Durant, that philosophy can be adventurous, too, was no doubt essential to my getting into the field, but once I was in, it quickly became insufficient to keep me there, and even detrimental to my development. What I came eventually to expect from philosophy, and how I tried to make my own sober contributions to the discipline, however, are other stories, with no unusual features. My avenue into the subject through adolescent romanticism makes a better tale.

Starting with Nothing

WILLIAM F. VALLICELLA
Case Western Reserve University

I began with nothing and worked my way up. I must have been seven or eight years old when the following thought descended on me: Supposing God hadn't created anything, then nothing would exist, except God. But what if God hadn't existed? ("Necessary being" was not yet in my vocabulary.) Then there would have been just nothing, nothing at all. This fascinating thought of sheer nothingness that put the whole of existence into question induced a sort of giddiness that to this day I cannot quite recapture. I would now say that the giddiness was due to the thought's bringing me to the very limit of intelligibility, the boundary of the sayable. Philosophers like to hang around boundaries, marking them when not overstepping them. Thus I began at the beginning with Father Parmenides: Being is; nonbeing is not. Onto-genesis recapitulates phylogenesis.

From metaphysics we move to ethics. One day a few years later I was delivering newspapers and pondering the questions: Why is good good and evil evil? What makes the one preferable to the other? Why ought we do good rather than evil? Where does the oughtness come from? At the time the core questions were about as untransparent as they could possibly have been—but they were not artificially induced "puzzles" that I had received second-hand from a book or a conversation: I had stumbled upon them, and they struck me as important. Later on, when I read G. E. Moore's remark to the effect that he never would have done philosophy if it hadn't been for the puzzling things he found in books by men like Bradley, I took that as almost the definition of an inauthentic philosopher: one who gets his prob-lems, not from life, but from books. My reading of Schopenhauer reinforced this view in me. Now there was a philosopher; he knew how to write, he knew how to think, and he went for the throat of the fundamental issues. I should say, though, that I have come to appreciate Moore as a master of analysis. Where my adolescent mind saw pointless nit-picking far removed from the Big Questions, I now see essential distinctions the nonobservance of which renders futile any assault on the Big Questions. Unfortunately, some never mature. It is one of the many exasperations of teaching to find students semester after semester who write off careful thinking as "mental masturbation" and "logic-chopping." Even more depressing are the professors who embody this attitude.

One cannot be much of a philosopher without a good measure of detachment, even alienation. To see the Cave as Cave one must be in it, but not of it. One who dwells comfortably in the human-all-too-human may make brilliant contributions to logic and linguistics, say, but will never get the length of an Augustine or Spinoza. A philosopher is one who is haunted by Transcendence, whether in the form of the really real, authentic existence, or genuine knowledge. The other side of the coin is that one must submit to the discipline of the Cave before one can even think of the transcendence of the Cave. I here borrow titles from two fine books by John Niemeyer Findlay, that argonaut of the Absolute with whom I had the privilege and good fortune of studying.

Findlay was something else, one of those rare birds who unlike most "philosophers" today had a sense of the greatness of philosophy. His was no underlaborer conception of philosophy; he genuflected before the sciences as little as he did before ordinary language. He was properly derisive of the work of the later Wittgenstein, a "plumber's philosophy" he once remarked. Findlay amply, if partially, incarnated my philosophical ideal: the philosophical maverick, the amphibian of the concept. He expounded Gödel and fathered tense logic, but he also wrote the best book there is on Meinong, in a long labor of love translated Husserl's massive *Logische Untersuchungen*, and furthered axiological ethics with his *Values and Intentions*.

I am grateful for the contingencies of circumstances that helped me develop the requisite detachment from the conventional. One such was growing up in the 1960s, that time of questioning and ferment when the truth-seeker was less of an oddball than is the case now. Even so, it was extremely difficult for the practically-minded electrical engineering major that I was to give up security for the questionable embrace of fair Philosophia. But I felt I was being called. Who or what was calling? That is one of the questions philosophers are called upon to unravel. I am still working on it.

Of Butterflies and Frogs

SUSAN L. ANDERSON
University of Connecticut

My parents have told me that one summer when I was very young, about four years old, my favorite pastime was to walk up to people, not to start a conversation, but rather just to stare at them and listen to what they were saying. I was apparently just very curious about *people* and I would observe them as long as they would permit me to do so. Eventually I would make them nervous and they would either "shoo" me away or walk away themselves. I don't know whether there is any connection between this and the fact that much of my work in philosophy has been focused on the Self—on questions like: What exactly are persons? and How are they different from other entities?

A little later, I remember having loved to dance, read, and play games. My favorite reading material was the latest Nancy Drew mystery. My favorite game was the still popular "Clue." (I remember playing it so often that I wore out the board and had to draw it again on my younger sister's discarded crib headboard.) I loved "deducing" who committed the murder, in which room, and with what weapon. Much later I found the same kind of enjoyment doing natural deductions in logic.

I also organized games of "good guys versus bad guys"—in our case Butterfly people versus Martians—which were elaborate play sessions, complete with costumes, involving my brother and other neighborhood children. I, of course, was always one of the "good guys," a Butterfly person. The Martians were evil, stupid, and slow moving. They were no match for the heroic Butterfly People who could fly and become invisible whenever they wanted, so it was easy for them to escape whenever they were attacked. Wouldn't it be wonderful if, as I could so easily legislate it in my *imaginary* world, goodness and power in the *actual* world went hand-in-hand? In any case, the "good guys" always won in *my* dramas, even if they didn't necessarily in real life.

I remember having had strong ethical sentiments from childhood on. I see this not only in my early play sessions, but also in my reaction to something that happened to me in my first year of college. I was taking a year-long course in biology to satisfy a science requirement, and my lab instructor insisted that each one of us pith a frog and then dissect it. I was horrified by the thought that we were being asked to *murder* dozens of innocent animals. When I protested, saying that I couldn't bring myself to kill the frog and I didn't see why it was necessary in any event that *all* those animals be killed, the instructor replied that it was an important part of the training of scientists to "harden oneself" to such things. I then pointed out that few of us were going to become scientists—I knew *I* certainly wasn't if "hardening oneself" in this way was a necessary requirement. But my protestation did no good. I was given an ultimatum: either do what I was told, or flunk the course. I'm ashamed to confess that the issue was resolved when one of my classmates pithed my frog for me, behind the instructor's back. Even now strong feelings of moral indignation are aroused by recollecting that incident, and I deeply regret that I did not object more strenuously to a practice that I believed to be morally wrong.

Eventually I discovered philosophy as a discipline. I had entered college with the intention of majoring in mathematics, which had been my best subject in high school, though I was also very interested in music and psychology. I didn't happen to take a philosophy course until my sophomore year, but I loved it immediately. I was losing interest in my math courses, and I discovered all that I had liked about mathematics, and much more, in the field of philosophy. Philosophy had the rigor of mathematics, but it was applied to things that really mattered to me: people, moral choices, and rational inference. I decided to switch my major to philosophy, which I discovered was not going to be easy. The head of the philosophy department insisted, in a half-hour interview with me, that I "convince" him that I should major in philosophy before I would be allowed to do so. He was of the opinion that everybody ought to take many philosophy courses, but he thought very few people should major in such an impractical subject. I apparently argued well enough that I should be one of the few.

From then on, I traveled a fairly straight path toward becoming a philosopher or teacher of philosophy. Since my sophomore year in college, thinking about philosophical issues has been the most interesting and challenging way I can imagine occupying my time. It has also been as natural and essential to my life as breathing. It would be impossible for me *not* to think about philosophical issues.

In Defense of
Philosophical Intemperance

ROGER T. AMES

University of Hawaii

I watch my back. I am persuaded that one day soon someone in authority will come up behind me, tap me on the shoulder, and say, "You didn't think you would get away with this, did you?" And the jig will be up. In anticipation of such a day, I offer here the briefest confession of how I stumbled into this self-indulgence called "comparative philosophy," and how I have arrived at my present state.

I should begin by abandoning all excuses: "My name is Roger Ames. And I am a comparative philosopher." I am by habit, intoxicated.

My entrance into the world of philosophy began on a high note; in fact, it is poetic. As a young man growing up in Vancouver at the tail-end of the beatnik era, I would spend long melancholy evenings at the "Black Swan," a coffee house on Robson Street taken over by amateur artists as a forum to publish themselves. In spite of the rich dollop of passion I invested in every line, I was keenly aware that as a person, behind the obligatory moroseness demanded by my coffee-house persona, I was thin and vacuous. I had no stuff, no content, no depth—I suffered like a west coast Woody Allen.

I began my university career by going to Redlands as a deliberate attempt to leave the familiar soil of western Canada behind and to seek out "content" in the very residence of meaning, southern California. In spite of exploratory Tijuana runs, all night truck stops, and whatever other self-articulating products were fashionably available at the time, my personal content quotient and my poetry marked only the most marginal growth. Life was mid-range; no highs, no spikes, no free falls.

By some fortunate accident (and there is so much accident in a life), Redlands in the mid-sixties had an exchange program with the Chinese University of Hong Kong. With visions of neon and unholy sultry nights, gins-and-tonic under the ceiling fans at the Peninsula Hotel, typhoons and tiger balm and leggy *cheung-sams,* and the full splash-in-the-face of a truly exotic culture, I climbed the steps of a DC-10 and never again touched the ground. Like one lost in the innocence of first love, I discovered in Hong Kong that welter of stimulation which could cram one's lifetime with wonder. China was a civilization which had matured almost entirely beyond the influence of Indo-European cultures and languages and was as different a world as could be imagined. I was totally intoxicated by it, and in love. It was the radicalness and complexity of cultural difference that got me, and I have never recovered.

The dozen years that followed were spent mainly at institutions in China, Japan, and Europe, in an attempt to acquire the philological skills necessary to explore what I came to recognize as not only a different way of living together, but as a profoundly different way of thinking.

But there was a major problem in trying to find an education in classical Chinese philosophy. At this juncture, Western philosophy was not sympathetic. In fact, as a discipline, professional philosophy was almost entirely persuaded there was no such thing as Chinese philosophy. I found this incredible. If we as a culture were to claim that only Western civilizations had history or literature, an economy or a society, such assertions would be dismissed as condescension. And yet the discipline of philosophy seemed to operate on the assumption that Chinese thinkers did not think philosophically.

The reluctance of the discipline to legitimize it as an area of philosophical inquiry is at least in part traceable to the translator's impoverishment of the Chinese lexicon. Interpreters of this exotic tradition have not served it well. Simply put, our existing formula of terms for translating the core vocabulary and problems of Chinese philosophy has been freighted with a cosmology not its own and thus has perpetuated a pernicious cultural reductionism. The Chinese texts can be neither interesting nor philosophically important when reduced to the cultural importances of our own tradition. An alternative inventory of presuppositions has been at work in the growth and elaboration of Chinese civilization, and the failure on our part to excavate and acknowledge this difference in our translations and interpretations has rendered the Chinese worldview deceptively familiar. When a philosophic tradition other than our own is thus made familiar, and at the same time is adjudicated on standards of rigor and clarity foreign to it, it can never be more than an inferior variation on a Western theme.

On the other hand, uncritical presuppositions about "humanity" as a category, and the fear in some quarters that too much difference led to incommensurability, disguised and obscured the radical degree of difference I thought we owed the Chinese in observance of their distance from us as an exotic and radically different order of humankind.

It gradually became clear to me that to *begin* translating and interpreting Chinese philosophy into Western languages, we must recognize the problem of cultural reductionism and formulate a strategy for avoiding it. This strategy would require the combination of both philosophic and philological sophistication and a resolutely suspicious attitude to universal claims. It is comparative philosophy.

While I am persuaded my direction has been the right one, I can claim only marginal success in an impossibly ambitious project. Over the years, beginning with successive degrees in philosophy and the Chinese language, I have gradually been able to piece together a foundation in comparative philosophy which works both sides of the street. I translate and write commentaries on classical texts to recommend myself to the Asianists, and wax speculative to try to impress the philosophers. Most importantly, recognizing the near impossibility of any one person assembling the expertise necessary to do comparative philosophy, I quickly became persuaded of the virtue of the "correlative" model of philosophizing, where collaboration becomes the most effective method for collecting and applying the relevant skills. Thus, I determined early to take collaborative projects as my professional signature, choosing to work with established scholars who have talents different from my own.

Besides, it keeps me intoxicated, and hopefully postpones that killer hangover I'll have when the inevitable tap on my shoulder finally comes.

Smiling

JOHN MURUNGI
Towson State University

There is a man whom I have known for some years who has laid a heavy burden on me. He has insisted that I put into writing the manner in which I came to embrace philosophy. Up to this time I have managed to put him off. I have done this not because I have been too busy, nor because I am too lazy to meet his request. Rather, it is because the request perplexes me.

The African roots of my being reveal that in the true African spirit the initiate cannot be the master of his own initiation. Initiation is a birthing event and one cannot witness one's birth. In the matter at hand, philosophy is the master and I am one of its many initiates. It gave birth to me. The event of birthing me is beyond my comprehension. This is a predicament understandable to those who have a sense of what is at stake.

The question—"How did I become a philosopher?"—is posed in such a way that I am called upon to account for my being both a "philosopher" and a human. Herein lies a part of the predicament. I have no knowledge of the origin of the time that is decisive in determining what I am, and I have no knowledge of the end of the time that is equally decisive in determining what I am. I am a creature of a time that is beyond my comprehension, which is another way of saying that what I am is beyond my comprehension.

The question touches my innermost being. That is, the question regarding my becoming a philosopher is a question regarding my becoming what I am, and since the question addresses the innermost aspect of my being, the answer, accordingly, can only be given in a manner that illuminates what I am.

This is why it is unsatisfactory to claim that I became a philosopher because I read philosophical writings. As many philosophy professors will attest, there are many students who read philosophical writings, and do not, thereby, become philosophers. The fact that many individuals who pass as professors, or students of philosophy, read texts that are widely considered to be philo-

sophical tempts one to accept the assumption that one becomes philosophical on account of others. To say, however, that one is what one is because of others suggests parasitism. On the other hand, surely one is what one is because of others in at least the sense that it is only in the context of other human beings that one is human. This does not render individuals parasitic to each other. It is simply a recognition of the common humanity that makes each human being a human being. It is in the task of doing the archaeology of this relationship that one embraces philosophy. My friend has pushed me onto this path. From many of the messages he has sent me it appears that embracing this task and making it a part of my being is the just cost for philosophical friendship.

I recall once being in a hospital in which an attendant needed information in order to fill out the forms. She asked me for my religious affiliation. I was tongue-tied. In the West, the conventional view regarding the religious landscape in Africa allows for only three religions: Christianity, Islam, and animism. I am not a Christian and I am not a Muslim. Animism conjures to my mind non-religion or anti-religion. This is, precisely, the view of the Christian missionaries; otherwise, they would not be so anxious to evangelize among those they regard as animists. Regardless of what the word *animism* may mean to others, it reminds me of a beastly quality—which is, precisely, how Europeans thought of Africans during the colonial days. I do not believe that there is a sensible human being who thinks of himself as such. At least, it is not the way I think about myself, nor the way the people I grew up with think of themselves.

The hospital attendant put me in a conceptual and perceptual bind. My cultural background does not permit me to think of myself as a theist, an atheist, or as an agnostic. Perhaps the easiest thing for me to do was to tell the lady that I have no religious affiliation. The lady might have assumed that between her and myself there was a common understanding of the meaning of what it means to be religiously affiliated. Under the circumstances I could not make this assumption. I asked her to skip the line she wanted to fill. I appreciated the fact that she did not pursue the issue.

I cite my encounter with the hospital attendant to illustrate the predicament in which an African philosopher finds himself or herself in his or her encounter with those that are regarded as philosophers in the West. Western philosophers are likely to regard an African philosopher as a philosopher if he or she is a convert to Western philosophy. I do not believe that there is any place for conversion in philosophy.

Consequently, in the realm of philosophy, those who think of themselves as converts or converters are unphilosophical. The question that my friend asks me—how I became a philosopher—is a question that calls for an answer that has nothing to do with conversion. Being philosophical is not derived

*from without. This does not mean that to find out how one becomes philo-
sophical one has to turn inward, if, by "inward," one means turning away
from other human beings. "Without" and "inwardness" understood in their
oppositional sense are inadequate terms for expressing the spatiality of being
philosophical. No human being is a human being in isolation from other
human beings and, as a human being, a philosopher is not an exception to
this fact. He or she is what he or she is by being in communion with other
philosophers. This communion is integral to what it is to be philosophical.*

My friend believes that I have the key to how I became a philosopher.
He is right. But he, too, has the key, as do all those who are philosophical.
What is within reach is usually out of reach, and what is out of reach is
usually within reach. My friend understands this. In part, this is why we are
friends. We became friends the way we became philosophical. Next time I
see him I will ask him how we became friends. I will read his face for an
answer, and, as I read it, he will be reading mine. Out of the facial dialogue
will emerge the answer to my question and the answer to his question. The
visual has a place in philosophy, too, for, contrary to the protestation of
some of those who pass as philosophers, every philosopher is an incarnate
being. Every discourse on philosophy both radiates from the body and is also
of the body. My friend understands that philosophy, as an intellectual interrogation, is deeply rooted in what is corporeal. This is why he appears to
be so taken by the view that a smile has inestimable philosophical significance. I concur. To smile is to be released from oneself and to experience
oneself as a breeze blowing toward . . . It is to undergo an experience of being
open to oneself in such a way that this openness invites the openness of the
smiling others. When reciprocated, a smile becomes a wedding of lived
openness. In such a moment, the experience of oneself as a subject gives
way to that elemental experience where one is distinguishable by being
indistinguishable from others. Nothing about a smile makes elemental sense
except to the smiling ones. The event is analogous to being philosophical.
Philosophy evidences itself in the process of ingathering those who are philosophical, and in preserving those who are so gathered in the openness that
they share with one another.

*Any attempt to use this evidence to persuade non-philosophers of the
philosophical mode of coming-into-being is of no avail, for the evidence is
accessible only to those who are philosophical. Moreover, it is senseless to
persuade those who are already philosophical of the evidence of becoming or
of being philosophical for, being already philosophical, they need no evidence.
However, this is the first half of the truth of what it is to be philosophical.
The other half appears to be contradictory to the first for it demands that the
philosophical life provide evidence for itself. This appearance should not nec-*

essarily be confused with reality, for what is at stake in philosophical life may be beyond the dictates of logic.

Since it appears important to philosophy to seek evidence in support of its own being, a philosopher recognizes intrinsic limitations to this search. The search simply witnesses the absence of opacity in philosophy that is philosophy's intrinsic openness onto itself. Since I have already conceded that I have been initiated into philosophy, let me also concede that this initiation as well as what I have been initiated into still remain an enigma.

Of Mentors and Family

"At every moment of history there exists not one generation but three: the young, the mature, the old."
ORTEGA Y GASSET, *What Is Philosophy?*

Radical Journeys*

ANGELA DAVIS
San Francisco State University

Although I was on the verge of receiving a degree in French literature, what I really wanted to study was philosophy. I was interested in Marx, his predecessors, and his successors. Whenever I could find the time, I read philosophy on the side. I didn't really know what I was doing, except that it gave me a feeling of security and comfort to read what people had to say about such formidable things as the universe, history, human beings, knowledge.

During my second year at Brandeis, I had picked up *Eros and Civilization* by Herbert Marcuse and had struggled with it from beginning to end. That year he was teaching at the Sorbonne. When I arrived in Paris the following year, he was already back at Brandeis, but people were still raving about his fantastic courses. When I returned to Brandeis, the first semester of my senior year was so crowded with required French courses that I could not officially enroll in Marcuse's lecture series on European political thought since the French Revolution. Nevertheless, I attended each session, rushing in to capture a seat in the front of the hall. Arranged around the room on progressively higher levels, the desks were in the style of the UN General Assembly room. When Marcuse walked onto the platform, situated at the lowest level of the hall, his presence dominated everything. There was something imposing about him which evoked total silence and attention when he appeared, without his having to pronounce a single word. The students had a rare respect for him. Their concentration was not only total during the entire hour as he paced back and forth while he lectured, but if at the sound of the bell Marcuse had not finished, the rattling of papers would not begin until he had formally closed the lecture.

One day, shortly after the semester began, I mustered up enough courage

*Excerpted from *An Autobiography*, Random House (New York, 1975), pp. 133–35; 135–36; 142; 143–44.

to put in a request for an interview with Marcuse. I had decided to ask him to help me draw up a bibliography on basic works in philosophy. Having assumed I would have to wait for weeks to see him, I was surprised when I was told he would be free that very afternoon.

From afar, Marcuse seemed unapproachable. I imagine the combination of his stature, his white hair, the heavy accent, his extraordinary air of confidence, and his wealth of knowledge made him seem ageless and the epitome of a philosopher. Up close, he was a man with inquisitive sparkling eyes and a fresh, very down-to-earth smile.

Trying to explain my reasons for the appointment, I told him that I intended to study philosophy in graduate school, perhaps at the university in Frankfurt, but that my independent reading in philosophy had been unsystematic—without regard for any national or historical relations. What I wanted from him—if it was not too much an imposition—was a list of works in the sequence in which I ought to read them. And if he gave me permission, I wanted to enroll in his graduate seminar on Kant's *Critique of Pure Reason*.

"Do you really want to study philosophy?" Professor Marcuse asked, slowly and placing emphasis on each word. He made it sound so serious and so profound—like an initiation into some secret society which, once you join, you can never leave. I was afraid that a mere "yes" would ring hollow and inane.

"At least, I want to see if I am able," was about the only thing I could think of to answer.

"Then you should begin with the Pre-Socratics, then Plato and Aristotle. Come back again next week and we will discuss the Pre-Socratics."

I had no idea that my little request would develop into stimulating, weekly discussions on the philosophers he suggested, discussions which gave me a far more exciting and vivid picture of the history of philosophy than would have emerged from a dry introduction-to-philosophy course.

. . . During that last year at Brandeis, I made up my mind to apply for a scholarship to study philosophy at the university in Frankfurt. Marcuse confirmed my conviction that this was the best place to study, given my interest in Kant, Hegel, and Marx. The remaining months of the school year were consumed by intensive preparation in philosophy, German language, and the final requirements for my BA degree, including a year-long honors project on the Phenomenological Attitude, which I thought I had discovered in the works of the contemporary French novelist Robbe-Grillet. The most challenging and fulfilling course was the graduate seminar that Marcuse conducted on the *Critique of Pure Reason*. Poring over a seemingly incomprehensible passage for hours, then suddenly grasping its meaning gave me a sense of satisfaction I had never experienced before.

. . . Frankfurt was a very intensive learning experience. Stimulating lectures and seminars conducted by Theodor Adorno, Jurgen Habermas, Professor Haag, Alfred Schmidt, Oscar Negt. Tackling formidable works, such as all three of Kant's Critiques and the works of Hegel and Marx as well (in one seminar, we spent an entire semester analyzing about twenty pages of Hegel's *Logic*).

. . . My decision to study in Frankfurt had been made in 1964, against the backdrop of relative political tranquility. But by the time I left in the summer of 1965, thousands of sisters and brothers were screaming in the streets of Los Angeles that they had observed the rules of the game long enough, too long.

Watts was exploding; furiously burning. And out of the ashes of Watts, Phoenix-like, a new Black militancy was being born.

While I was hidden away in West Germany the Black Liberation Movement was undergoing decisive metamorphoses. The slogan "Black Power" sprang out of a march in Mississippi. Organizations were being transfigured— The Student Non-Violent Coordinating Committee, a leading civil rights organization, was becoming the foremost advocate of "Black Power." The Congress on Racial Equality was undergoing similar transformations. In Newark, a national Black Power Conference had been organized. In political groups, labor unions, churches, and other organizations, Black caucuses were being formed to defend the special interests of Black people. Everywhere there were upheavals.

. . . The more the struggles at home accelerated, the more frustrated I felt at being forced to experience it all vicariously. I was advancing my studies, deepening my understanding of philosophy, but I felt more and more isolated. I was so far away from the terrain of the fight that I could not even analyze the episodes of the struggles. I did not even have the knowledge or understanding to judge which currents of the movement were progressive and genuine and which were not. It was a difficult balance I was trying to maintain, and it was increasingly hard to feel a part of the collective coming to consciousness of my people.

I am certain that what I was feeling was a variation and reflection of the same feelings that were overwhelming larger and larger numbers of Black people abroad. Many others of us must have felt pained, when reading about some new crisis in the struggle at home, to be hearing about it secondhand.

I had thought mine was the perfect dilemma: the struggle at home versus the need to remain in Frankfurt until the completion of my doctorate, for I was certain that Frankfurt was far more conducive to philosophical studies than any other place. But each day it was becoming clearer to me that my ability to accomplish anything was directly dependent on my ability to contribute something concrete to the struggle.

Adorno had readily agreed to direct my work on a doctoral dissertation. But now I felt it would be impossible for me to stay in Germany any longer. Two years was enough. I arranged for an appointment with Adorno at the Institute and explained to him that I had to go home. In my correspondence with Marcuse, he had already agreed to work with me at the University of California in San Diego, where he had accepted a position after having been practically pushed out of Brandeis for political reasons. I wanted to continue my academic work, but I knew I could not do it unless I was politically involved. The struggle was a life-nerve; our only hope for survival. I made up my mind. The journey was on.

A Little Dab Would Have Done It

WALLACE I. MATSON
University of California, Berkeley

There ought to have been a reason why I decided to become a professor of philosophy. If there was, it may have been admiration for Bertrand Russell and a desire to emulate him. I think, however, it was more a matter of causes than of reasons, chief among which was panic at not being able to make the apparatus gas-tight.

But let's start nearer the beginning. I was an only child, brought up by my mother (who was widowed when I was three) and her mother. They sent me off to school in knickers, which were correct according to the Eastern magazines, but not in fact worn by kids in Fresno. That bad start was compounded by my early ability to read and cipher, on account of which I skipped a grade and a half; nearsighted and unathletic to begin with, I had to compete on the playground with boys a year or two ahead of me in physical development. I gave up, and from the bottom of the pecking order endured the jeers as best I could. To this day I cannot throw or catch a ball properly, and have to lie low when it's softball time at the department picnic.

Thus as a child I was a loner, and bookish, of course. My inheritance from my father consisted of $500 and the works of Mark Twain, which I devoured as soon as I had progressed past *The Motor Boys, Tom Swift*, and *Bomba the Jungle Boy*. Fresno had no orchestra, no theater, no museum; but it did have a Carnegie Library. On Saturday mornings I was condemned to demonstrate my ineptitude at swimming and gymnastics at the YMCA; but when that was over I could go next door to the library and revel in *Collier's Encyclopedia*, H. L. Mencken, Voltaire, H. G. Wells, George Bernard Shaw (I liked the prefaces better than the plays), and Edgar Rice Burroughs (I liked the Mars books better than Tarzan, and after reading Percival Lowell, I became for a long time a true believer in the canals).

At ten years of age I was already philosophizing, though I didn't know it. All children argue, but I argued more than the others. In particular, I argued with the Sunday school teacher. Since my mother and grandmother were Christian Scientists, more or less, I was put into a class conducted seminar-style by a professor of physics at Fresno State College. I came at once to the conclusion that Mary Baker Eddy's stuff was nonsense, and the Bible not much better. The professor, a kind, humorous, and rational man—whatever was he doing there?—amiably disputed with me, treating me as an equal. One Sunday, however, the class was taken over by a substitute, a thin-lipped elderly woman who was not amused by my precocious blasphemy. Not only did she shut me up, she called my mother and told on me. Mom was devastated. "If you don't believe in God," she wailed, "you can never be elected to public office!" But I had already learned from Mencken that the presidency was not for the likes of me.

I first heard of Bertrand Russell around that time, the early 1930s, when one Sunday the San Francisco *Examiner* ran the famous portrait of him wreathed in pipe smoke, illustrating an article that vituperated him as an enemy of the people, an atheist, and immoralist. He was quoted as having described his outlook as like that of Lucretius—an admission which the author exploited: "All we know of Lucretius comes from Bishop Eusebius, who in his *Chronology* notes for the year 55 B.C.: 'T. Lucretius Caro died. Having been driven mad by a love potion in intervals of sanity he wrote some poems which were edited by Quintus Cicero.' " "That's the kind of man Russell is," the indignant scholar continued: "an admirer of sexual psychopaths"!

Next day I ran to the library to find out more about Russell—and Lucretius, too, whose poem, I discovered, was still extant. So I took up the study of philosophy because William Randolph Hearst disapproved of Bertie. There must be many of my generation who got their first enthusiasm for philosophy from an encounter with Russell's work. Not his epistemology or logic, but his popular books. What shocked Hearst opened a new world to us—those cooly sensible, humorous, and humane disquisitions on what kind of life is worth living for a human being. (Not until his autobiography appeared in 1967 did I learn that his lordship had managed to "conquer happiness" little better than most ordinary people do.)

Still, I formed no intention of making a career of philosophy. I entered the Big U (of California, Berkeley) in 1938 as a chemistry major. Five of my teachers subsequently had buildings named after them; three, including two who were hands-on teaching assistants in the lab classes, got the Nobel. Notwithstanding these advantages, I switched to philosophy in my sophomore year. The way was prepared by a friend, an economics major, who spoke with awe of Philosophical Naturalism, purveyed by Professor Dennes. There was room in my program for an elective; I took Dennes' survey course in Greek philosophy and was captivated. For the first time in my experience,

I met (not just read about) a respected adult who thought the same thoughts that I had all along, all alone in Fresno. It was euphoric.

What directly precipitated my hegira, though, was the debacle of Chem 8: Organic Chemistry Laboratory, "Cooking School." Measured amounts of chemicals were doled out to us from which we were to concoct various compounds. Our grades depended on the quantity of our "yields." There was no intellectual challenge; it was an exercise in setting up apparatus, particularly in making gas-tight junctions of glass tubing with rubber hoses and stoppers. I did this very badly; my yields mostly vanished into laboratory stink, and I nearly flunked. So I panicked and switched my major to philosophy. Who knows? If only I had thought (or if someone had told me) to dab a bit of Vaseline here and there, I might now be about ready for a gold watch from DuPont or Dow.

The Value of Bad Grades

WALTER SINNOTT-ARMSTRONG
Dartmouth College

I wanted to be a chemical engineer. DuPont was my dream, Delaware was my goal. In high school, chemistry seemed fun and easy, and I would even get to play with computers. I couldn't imagine anything better.

My college guidance counselor, however, suggested that I sample a few more fields before I decided what to do with the next fifty years of my life. I couldn't disagree, since my senior year so far was filled with math, physics, and chemistry. I did take a Shakespeare course taught by a strange little man who had us call him "Uncle Roy." Uncle Roy told me that I had no aptitude for the humanities, but he added that I should try them out anyway. Not knowing any better, I decided on a liberal arts college.

My first term at Amherst College was erratic. I recall writing one paper in a scant two-hour period before I donned my cheerleading outfit and went to a football game. I got a good grade, but I was bored. Another paper took weeks of work, but my grade was not so good, and I didn't understand why. One English teacher almost made me give up on the humanities when he said my interpretation of Hamlet was obviously wrong, but he could not cite a single line or scene that supported his views over mine.

Luckily, I heard intriguing rumors about a Professor Kennick. Everyone said that his courses were very hard, but they were always filled with students. I figured that he must be something special. Why else would so many students ruin their social lives and grade averages?

Kennick's course the next term was even harder than I had been told. It covered philosophy from Descartes to Kant. Yes! The readings for a single term included Descartes, Hobbes, Spinoza, Leibniz, Locke, Berkeley, Hume (The Treatise!), and Kant (The First Critique!!). Almost 200 pages of reading a week, and I already knew that philosophy was not a quick read. There were also five papers and a final exam. When I saw the workload, I almost dropped the course.

But something grabbed my attention. The first lecture was on Descartes, and he seemed to raise some of the very questions that had bothered me about the science I had studied. Not that I stayed up nights worrying about evil demons, but I did wonder what was common to the methods of the various sciences and why everyone thought experiments were so conclusive. These questions had never been raised in my science courses. We were just told to learn theories and do experiments in a particular area. We never compared the different sciences or asked fundamental questions about scientific method in general, much less about knowledge in general. So I decided to stick with the course.

The first paper almost changed my mind. I chose to write on Hobbes' theory of free will because I thought that I had something wonderfully new to say. I don't remember exactly what it was, but I do remember that I was very proud. I thought that I had refuted one of the great thinkers of our tradition. What a rush! Then I got back my paper. Kennick had given me a *D*. A *D!* What a letdown! I had never received a grade that low since my first term in prep school.

My earlier *D* was in a history course, and when I complained to the teacher, he simply told me that I had included only 60 percent of the information that he had wanted. He completely failed to see that I had carefully chosen my information so as to construct a new interpretation of something in early modern Europe. I didn't simply want to include as much information as possible, I wanted to organize that information in a new way. He didn't seem to care about this, so I never took another history course.

I expected the same kind of reaction from Professor Kennick when I went to his office hours. Why was I going to see him anyway? I was sure he'd just put me down. But I had four more papers to go, so I'd better find out what he wanted. I had plenty of time to get nervous as I waited in the hall before my turn came. By the time I entered his office, I was also mad. I controlled myself and simply said, "This grade is ridiculous. What's wrong with what I said here?" So he told me. The answer was so clear that I saw immediately why that sentence was wrong. "But what about this?" He told me again. "But surely there is something redeeming in my conclusion." He showed me that all of my mistakes culminated in my conclusion.

What was unusual was that he listened to me and showed me why I was wrong. He didn't just say that I had left out 40 percent of what he wanted. He tried to understand my position, and he gave me arguments to the contrary. He treated me like a real philosopher. I felt honored to receive his criticisms.

Well, almost. My pride was still wounded, but at least I understood what I needed to do in the next paper. I also understood why it was needed. I needed to define terms, spell out assumptions, and so on, because where I ended up depended on where I started. This method seemed important, so

I was willing to give it a try. The next paper was a little better (C +), the next even better, and so on. My last paper was an A. I thought I had finally figured him out, so I took it easy when I studied for the final exam. I got a B. You could never take it easy with Professor Kennick, and I never took it easy again, even though I took six more courses from him—I even wrote my thesis with him.

Why did he turn me on? The first answer is that he had standards. My other professors rewarded me for ideas that even I knew were simplistic. He made me dive deeply into complex issues. This was a person from whom I could learn, both because he had a lot to teach, and because he made me learn.

The main reason that he turned me on was that he gave arguments. While I was growing up every adult claimed the right to tell me what to do, but nobody bothered to give arguments or to listen to contrary arguments. They assumed authority. I wanted reason. I found it in philosophy.

I remember this experience every time I give a bad grade to a student. Maybe this student will also go on to become a philosopher. It doesn't happen often, but the lesson is still important. We should not be afraid to give bad grades or to criticize other people as long as we are ready to listen to them and show them why they are wrong. Sometimes the most constructive event in a person's life can be a bad grade.

Philosophers Make Philosophers

JAMES WADDELL
University of Redlands

My father was planning a drunk that day thirty-five years ago when he was driving me to my grandmother's home. He was an alcoholic who went on a binge about once every three or four years. The binges were legendary in my family. Binges of straight bourbon without branch water (my alcoholic uncle preferred Dixie Bell gin); days without sleep; trips all over West Virginia, Ohio, and Virginia; a week of blackouts—were all common feats of my dad.

As he drove through the West Virginia valleys with their hair of slag heap fire, I told him I wanted to be a minister and needed to go to college for seven years. Years later he told me he decided to put off his drunk to figure out how to help pay for the schooling. As a hardshell Baptist he wasn't convinced that the learning was necessary, but he would go along with my newly found Methodist learning. I suspect that my adolescent decision had something to do with a religious awareness that sociologists tell us is typical in people of this age. It also has something to do with my anger about unfairness.

I had decided to go to Duke University. My father decided we should go look at the school before I set off in the fall. We got two of my high school buddies and drove eleven hours to Durham. Dad decided he didn't want to sleep in the car with us on the Duke East Campus and found himself a motel room. We woke up on the property of Duke Women's College and were impressed with the Georgian buildings surrounding three old horse racing tracks. The gothic loftiness of the West Campus moved my friends, Don and Rhenus, to bet that inside a year I'd be back in West Virginia.

Duke chewed me up in my freshman year, but didn't spit me out. The University taught me to appreciate the many sides of most matters and to reflect about life in general. It also exposed me modestly to high Southern culture. This was important to a boy whose great-great-grandfather had been a private in Stonewall Jackson's army. While answering a call of nature, my ancestor had been shot in the head by a Yankee sniper. He lived, and a smart aleck member of my family has observed that that shot in the head was probably the first event that led to my becoming a philosopher.

By my senior year I knew that the ministry would not be enhanced by my presence. I took courses in philosophy, and they were awful. Dry, boring, touching on nothing important to young adults; they were simply hours accumulated toward graduation.

My mother and father enjoyed the commencement service. Dad again had postponed his binge to come. He even brought one of his A.A. friends to help him stay on the wagon.

But what to do now? I could go to West Virginia University Law School, or I could go to Duke Divinity School and buy time to figure out where my life should go. The rumor was that there was a guy at the Divinity School who took nothing off nobody and, if you weren't afraid of having everything you believed challenged, he could teach you something.

W. H. (Bill) Poteat was the first existentialist I had ever met. His intensity about the importance of this moment, every moment, stopped time for me. His notion of place, of presence, helped me appreciate my land of West Virginia, my family, and my self. I couldn't have talked about it in these words then, but he was one of the few philosophers trying to rescue the body, my starting place, from idealism. He turned me back to Hume, the "dead, old man" of the boring days of undergraduate philosophy. I was hooked intellectually, and, more importantly, personally. Philosophy was the way I could forge some sense out of what seemed ridiculous.

One day Bill asked if I would like to have lunch with a visiting professor from Oxford. He thought we might have some common interest in religious language. We did, and the next year I found myself in Oxford, reading with Ian Ramsey. Eighteen months later, with a D.Phil., I started my career as a philosopher-interested-in-religion at Princeton University. Today I serve at the University of Redlands as a dean of an adult learning program in business and education.

The last time I saw Bill was five years ago at Duke. He had just helped rescue my daughter academically. I couldn't say to him all that needed to be said. So I am saying part of it now.

What am I to conclude? Perhaps it is that philosophers make philosophers. My encounter with Bill Poteat certainly made me into one.

Any regrets? One. My father never had his binge. He kept putting it off, because I needed something. I think he owed himself one, he did enjoy them so much. He died ten years ago. So I think I'll have a drink for him now—one drink. And make it in appreciation of Bill Poteat.

Philosophy on a Clear Day

DIANE P. MICHELFELDER

California Polytechnic State University

I could say I became a philosopher because of the weather. It wouldn't be true, of course, but then again I do think of the weather whenever I think back to my first encounter with philosophy. Or, to be more accurate, to my first would-be encounter.

It was a spring day in Eastern Pennsylvania, one of the first days of spring. I was a freshman in college, and a friend of mine had asked me if I wanted to go with him for a ride in the country. We went out driving along the Schuylkill River. Greenery was beginning to overwhelm the bareness of the branches and the forsythia—that staple of an East Coast spring—was flourishing. All of a sudden, without any warning, he turned around the car. "Gotta go back," he said, "I want to be on time for my philosophy class." I felt deflated, gypped. For months one had been unable to drive along with the windows down. Why turn back now when everything was so pleasant? "Look," he said, "why don't you come with me? You'll enjoy the class, too."

It was very hard for me to imagine how that could be anywhere close to the truth. I had never attended a philosophy class before and I had no plans ever to go to one. The only person I knew at college from my high school had proudly showed me, some months before, her copy of the Bollingen edition of Plato's dialogues. I was put off by its material presence: so many thin pages, so many lines to a page. Instead, I intended to become an English major, and later a poet. The books I had to buy for my freshman composition course seemed handier, more accommodating to the body, more open. I felt any book too heavy to be easily carried would contain only the most general insights and say nothing to me personally. Without knowing it at the time, I was much like Glaucon and Adeimantus, the young participants in Plato's most famous dialogue, the *Republic*, who preferred images and stories to arguments and proofs. I could not imagine spending the rest of that spring day inside, with such uncompromising volumes. So I said I wasn't interested. He dropped me off, back at Bryn Mawr, and went on to class.

A few years later, I told this story to the very professor who had taught that class that spring afternoon. By this time I was a graduate student in philosophy, I was about to begin writing a dissertation on Heidegger, and he was to become my dissertation advisor. I don't quite know what happened in the years following that springtime drive that led me to this point. It could be, I sometimes think, that one becomes a philosopher the same way one becomes many others things: a lover, a neighbor, a friend, an adult. You wake up one morning to discover that is what you have become; more, so it seems, as the result of a natural rhythm of growth than a series of conscious choices. How did I get to be a philosopher? No particular event is so transparent in its meaning that it stands out as an answer to this question.

What I do come up with, rather than events, are some traits of temperament and some accidents of upbringing that made me, in retrospect, predisposed to philosophy. As far back as I can remember, I have relished a challenge. I enjoy finding myself in a situation where the odds are against me. I usually credit this to something that happened when I was three years old. That was the age when I began to read, and what I had immediately at hand was the daily newspaper. Unwilling to worry me with crises and crimes at such a young age, my parents gave me only the sports section. I had books to look at, too, but it was the sports section that for the next two years—after which I was finally permitted to read the whole paper—exercised on me a special pull. It opened up a new world for me, a world full of challenges, and, like the baseball season, of time set apart. It was a serious world, but also a world of fun—more fun, I suspected, than the world I could catch a glimpse of before the front-page headlines were whisked out of my sight.

Philosophical questions, as I found out when I finally signed up for a philosophy class, were very challenging, and very serious, and, yes, a lot of fun. I remember one question in particular, from one of the first philosophy classes I ever took—an upper-division course on Heidegger's *Being and Time*. Considering my lack of background, I had no business being there. I think I signed up for it because I was interested in one of the guys in the class. I tried my best to look inconspicuous, not an easy matter, since we all had to sit around a large table. The question came up early on in the semester: "How is your Being-in-the-world different from the way this pen is in my pocket?" I had never heard a question like that before. I thought it was just terrific, and I fell for it immediately. Later on, I would come to understand how the pen rests in my pocket, one thing in another, taking up space, while the way I am "in" a space cannot be separated from the meaningful involvement I have with things—so that what is physically nearest to me can be more remote than things actually lying "over there." Even now, the pen I hold in my hand does not seem as close to me as the mountains a few miles away, distracting me as I write. At that earlier moment, though, I didn't have the slightest clue as to what the answer might be or even where to start to look for one. Still, I wanted to stick with the question. It looked like fun to pursue, even though I was sure the pursuit would be no easy matter and I wasn't certain where it would lead me.

No doubt I wouldn't have been so excited by this question had I not been already accustomed to sitting for long stretches of time, thinking one or two thoughts, while believing I was having a good time. I had the good fortune, growing up as an only child, never to have experienced the frustration of having to compete for time. I had lots of it: time to be alone, time to invent games and put on plays, time to think. Time accompanied me in my childhood like a good friend. Along the way I attended a Quaker school. Once a week with my classmates, for seven years, I would leave the routine of classes behind to go into a room to sit in silence for a while under the assumption that, through sitting and listening, I could come out with more understanding than when I went in.

With this background, I could never have become like the philosopher Kant, whose daily walks were supposedly so punctual that people would set their clocks by them. For me, walks are strolls and meanderings. Whenever I go on a walk with another person, I always feel like I am struggling to keep up. The philosopher Wittgenstein once said that when two philosophers meet they should greet one another by saying: Take your time. To me, this has always seemed like sound advice.

I live now very close to the campus where I have taught for the past ten years. Here, where a short drive brings one to the Pacific Ocean, it is almost always a clear day. I walk to work. Slowly. I think and write about philosophers, such as Heidegger, who stressed the importance of listening, of dialogue, of experiencing time in a different way than as a succession of present moments. And I am still having fun.

Big Questions and an Answer

RICHARD SCHACHT
*The University of Illinois,
Urbana-Champaign*

Long before I went to college and took my first philosophy course, or ever dreamed of making a career of philosophy, I somehow developed a relish for the Big Questions (e.g., God, the soul and immortality, right and wrong, "the nature of man," and, of course, the meaning of life). I later discovered that they were not very original; however, to me and a few like-minded others, they were rivals in their fascination with the other more typical preoccupations of youth in the Midwest in the 1950s.

The fact that I did my growing up in Madison, in the shadow of that oasis of enlightenment, the University of Wisconsin, may have had something to do with it also. A few of my splendid teachers at the university high school gave me some positive reinforcement. But it probably all began around our family dinner table. There my father used to liven things up with a nightly barrage of talk spiced with words of wisdom and challenges to our wits, that expanded our horizons and made us think. As the oldest of five children (and therefore more able to keep up with him) I enjoyed this rather more than my younger siblings, and acquired an enduring taste for inquiry and argument.

My father, a former high school history teacher who moved into adult education programs at Wisconsin after World War II, had found his calling as an apostle and practitioner of liberal education and life-long learning—a natural educator, loving wisdom and debate, and going about seeking to plant the seeds of that love in others. They seem to have taken root in me. He was also probably responsible, as my first "model," for my coming to take it for granted early on that I would have an academic career of some sort. He liked to think of himself as a kind of layman philosopher. It did not occur to me at that time that I might actually wind up choosing philosophy as the discipline I would pursue. Yet the stimulus he gave to my appetite for "ideas that matter" may well have set me on the road to it.

Still, it was the sciences that first attracted me. They were the hot subjects in those days, in the aftermath of Sputnik, and I found I had a flair for them. It seemed clear to me that they were the path to true knowledge, and the obvious choice for the best and brightest of my generation. All through high school I saw myself as headed for a scientific career, and aspired to theoretical physics in particular as I progressed through the scientific curriculum. Einstein was my hero.

All the while, however, my love of the Big Questions was finding another outlet and expression, outside of school—in the youth group of the church in which my family was very actively involved. It was a liberal protestant congregation with a youth group in which what you believed mattered less than that you really "cared." This enabled those of us in the younger set who were closer in spirit to the even more liberal Unitarians in town (believing in "one God at most") to feel quite comfortable there. Endless discussion was standard fare among us, much to my delight.

Skeptic though I was, I became an officer of the group, and even more amazingly was elected president of its statewide organization in my senior year. With missionary zeal I went around the state trying rather quixotically to spread the "debating society" character of my local chapter. The next year I even became involved on a national level in the collegiate Student Christian Movement; but the paradox of being at once an increasingly convinced unbeliever and a budding "organization Christian" soon became intolerable for me. I needed some other venue in which to pursue my love of inquiry with greater consistency and a clearer conscience.

My enthusiasm for theoretical physics meanwhile had waned as I realized that I did not have it in me to be another Einstein. It also dawned on me that I was much more interested in the Big Questions than I was in subatomic particles anyhow. Until then, philosophy had only been a word for me. But some of my parents' university friends had suggested that I give it a try, since my interests seemed to them actually to be neither scientific nor religious. I quickly found that they were right. By the end of the year I was sure that I had found "my thing."

I had two professors in these early courses who helped to convince me of this. They could not have been more different; but both had a passion for philosophy that was contagious, and were figures that made a deep impression on my impressionable young mind and soul. One was Raphael Demos—the grand old man of the department, with whom I took both a Presocratics-to-Pragmatism survey course and a year-long freshman seminar. The other was John Wild, who introduced me to existentialism, and who deserved his name in every way.

Demos seemed the very embodiment of the Platonic sage (complete with Greek accent and lofty bearing), and became my temporary new father-figure, picking up where my father left off. He made the great philosophers come alive for me, as a company I longed to join. I was thrilled beyond words when, at the year's end, he inscribed my copy of his edition of the Jowett translation of Plato's dialogues (which my parents had given me at my request for my eighteenth birthday), "To Dick, who is on the way to becoming Plato's philosopher: 'spectator of all time and existence.'" It was an inspiration to sit at his feet with others of his following at Sunday afternoon teas in his home as he held forth in response to our questions. That was the life for me!

Wild, on the other hand, met the need I felt to rebel as well as to revere. He seemed to embody the spirit of the existentialism that he made so appealing to me—youthful romantic that I was—as perfectly as Demos embodied that of the sage. Ranting and raving polemically throughout the semester, he made the philosophical wars seem as exciting and important as anything could be. That he and Demos were poles apart somehow didn't seem to matter. I thought it ought to be possible somehow to combine the Olympian wisdom of the one with the existential concerns and passion of the other. Then Paul Tillich arrived on the scene and seemed to be heavensent proof that their synthesis was an actual philosophical and human possibility. His magnificent courses seemed to show the way.

As I began taking other philosophy courses along with them, I discovered that the Big Questions which Tillich took up in grand style were utterly out of favor in academic philosophy proper. The philosophy department barely tolerated his courses, and took a very dim view indeed of those of us who were drawn to his flame. The Day of Analytic Philosophy had reached its high noon. One had no business and no future in the discipline (I was informed in no uncertain terms) if one was unwilling to go with the flow of the triumphant "analytic mainstream." The department chairman himself told me so quite bluntly one day in his office, in response to my expressed wish for more courses on Continental philosophers after Kant. I found myself alienated from the discipline to which I aspired. It was not a happy time. What to do?

I spent some time shopping for an alternative discipline that would be more congenial to my interests. I considered English. Intellectual history. Psychology. I even tried sociology! In the end, however, finding myself more dissatisfied with what I found in other pastures than I was with what philosophy had become, I decided to bite the bullet. I would do what I *had* to do to earn my union card, playing the game by the rules set by the "analytic establishment," in order to attain the right and the freedom one day to do the kind of philosophy I *wanted* to do. This was the path I resolutely followed, as I finished up at Harvard—with an honors thesis on "The Feeling of Guilt"(!)—and went on to do my graduate work at Princeton.

Early on, however, these experiences led me to form another resolution which has affected virtually everything I have done in my now quarter-century in the profession. I resolved to do all I could, working from within the discipline and its institutions, to contribute to the building of bridges over the gaps that made things so difficult for me. (Perhaps not so coincidentally, the topic of my dissertation and first book was "alienation"—how to think about it and what to do about it.) I took it to be my "mission impossible" to try to make the profession more hospitable to students and future philosophers drawn to philosophy as I was, without sacrificing the benefits to be gained by learning to think clearly and rigorously. It is deeply gratifying to me that this is the direction in which we appear to be heading today.

But *Freunde, nicht diese Tone.* I will conclude on a different note, revealing how I discovered the key to being a successful lecturer. I was in awe of the superb lecturers I encountered at Harvard; I longed to learn the secret of their success in order to be able to follow in their footsteps. Among them none surpassed Paul Tillich in that respect. One fine day toward the end of his four-semester masterpiece on "The Self-Interpretation of Man in Western Thought," I discovered the answer.

As one of the most devoted of his disciples, I had been honored with the assignment of tape-recording his lectures that semester. This task required and permitted me to sit on the floor behind him, on the platform in a crowded lecture hall, to run the tape recorder. I observed that each day he would remove the paper clip from his lecture notes, put his hands behind him, commence lecturing, and fiddle ceaselessly with that clip while his lecture flowed majestically on.

One day, in midstream, the paper clip slipped from his fingers and fell to the floor. Suddenly the majestic flow became halting. The fingers groped helplessly, and so did he. After a moment of shock, I realized what the problem was, picked up the paper clip, and returned it to the helplessly groping hands, which were still held behind him. As if by magic, the majestic flow immediately resumed! Tillich neither looked around nor said anything afterward, but that was of no consequence to me. I had saved the day, and that was reward enough.

Thus I learned the trick of successful lecturing. When I began teaching some years later, I recalled the incident, and, feeling in need of all the help I could get, on my first day in front of a class I tried Tillich's method. To my infinite relief, it worked! I have employed it ever since, and would not think of giving a lecture without my trusty paper clip in hand. I am indebted to Tillich for many things, but the secret of the paper clip is at the top of the list. And so, to all who would be successful lecturers, I say: Don't leave home without it!

Approaching from Above

SAMUEL GOROVITZ

Syracuse University

I write these words aloft, returning from a meeting in Geneva of the International Medical Benefit/Risk Foundation, on whose Board of Overseers I sit. That is as peculiar for a philosopher to be doing as it is to have become a philosopher in the first place.

No one is seated beside me on this airplane. That's just as well; I can work, or loaf, in peace. Often, there is someone next to me, often someone quite sociable. Not always. One large, ruddy, thoroughly nineteenth-century Englishman sat beside me from Hamburg to London one day, and was anything but sociable. He did not speak to me, and when spoken to replied with a peremptory grunt. Only when our imminent landing was announced did he become verbal. "I say," he harumphed, "Do you happen to know, when we approach Heathrow Airport, from which direction will we approach it?"

"Yes, I know," I replied as he leaned forward eagerly. "We will approach it from above."

"*That*," I thought as he withdrew in dismay, "will teach you to fly unsociably next to a philosopher."

Typically, however, in-flight conversations turn to the question, "What do you do?" If I reply that I am a philosopher, reactions range from the rare glimmer of recognition, through the usual puzzlement, to occasional stark terror. I explain as well as I can, and sometimes am rewarded by signs of comprehension. Yet I cannot avoid concluding that the level of public understanding of what we philosophers do—even among the college educated, which most of these travelers are—is subterranean.

The contrast could not be more vivid when I talk about administrative work. They all understand that; that's real, almost like business. They also understand, always, if I talk about issues in clinical medicine or health policy. But I am getting ahead of the story.

Asked to write about becoming a philosopher, I take the question to be

"How did I get like this?" As "this" is constantly evolving, I cannot answer in terms of any single event or consideration. I can only tell a story about a process, and I have a fair degree of skepticism about the accuracy of the tale. The etiology of our attitudes and choices is not always what we take it to be. I have heard stories about me that I like better than what I think is true; but can I—can any of us—be sure that what we think is true is unaffected by what kinds of stories we like?

My interest in philosophy was helped along, if not fully started, when I read a bit of Plato in high school. My college experience was chaotic; starting with mechanical engineering, I lurched from one discipline to another, my interests apparently changing as a function of what I seemed to be good or bad at, and of what influence my teachers had.

I cannot overemphasize the influence of those teachers. Most were adequate or good, a very few were deeply awful, two or three were simply irritating, and remarkably many were powerfully inspiring. I note with interest that nearly all these sources of inspiration were non-philosophers; they taught history, literature, classics, linguistics, mathematics, physics, and even mechanical engineering. Some were figures of great renown; others were little known beyond the campus.

Each, in some way—and their ways were very different—injected some distinctive excitement into my undergraduate days. Some were brilliant lecturers, others impressed with an unremitting kindness and concern. One invited his class home to dinner—and how we loved being in that gracious house, eating good food, engaging in mature conversation, and acting uncharacteristically refined! Another, in a Western Civilization class of thirty sophomores, brought a guest one day and said, "We have a visitor. We won't follow the syllabus. He won't give a lecture, but he'll be happy to talk with you and answer any questions you'd like to ask. This is Niels Bohr." The excitement of that magical hour lasted visibly for weeks; some of it lingers still.

And two lecturers—as different as could be—taught a class together; one, an irreverent, iconoclastic cynic, and the other a meticulously traditional, classical scholar. "You may, of course, Ladies and Gentlemen, disagree with Aristotle in various places, where you feel that you must. But always, always, with the utmost respect," he admonished. He later explained, "Plotinus puzzled about whether the forms were instantiated in, as it were, an indifferentiated substratum of existence, or whether, instead, a rather more specifically defined substratum, so to speak, were required, as in the case of, for example, say, a horse, which, ah, could only be instantiated in, in, as it were, in, ah . . . "

And the other interrupted, "In horsemeat, Harold. In horsemeat!"

The net impact of all this was to convince me that a university environment was simply more fun than I could imagine any other to be. I think I wanted first to be a professor, and only later, secondarily, to be a professor in philosophy.

I enjoyed writing, and wasn't bad at it—better at least than at technical material. In physics, for example, even when I got the right answer, I didn't do it as those destined to be physicists did. *Which* of these mathematically correct solutions to this equation is of significance to the problem of physics represented by the equation? Some people just *knew*, apparently intuitively; I just ground out solutions.

Years later I saw a parallel phenomenon in the Berner Oberland, and remembered some of my classmates in physics. I had expected the Swiss ski instructors to ski better than I, but how I resented the fact that they could even stand around better than I! It was a matter of grace, of being completely natural and at ease in the context—of having been good at it as long as they could remember. That's how it was with the naturally gifted physicists and mathematicians. I was no more one of them than I was a potential ski instructor.

Philosophy offered the appeal of the big question. So did literature, of course. Still, I liked the rigor of philosophy, which I saw as a somewhat less radical abandonment of the technical path on which I had embarked. Best of all, the philosopher's agenda seemed unconstrained, since *whatever* one was interested in, one apparently could inquire into the philosophy of *that*. The various styles and ways of knowing in the different disciplines provided me with an intriguing juxtaposition of intellectual differences, about which I wanted to learn more.

I wrote a senior thesis on the role of intuition in mathematics and in ethics. I doubt that it amounted to much, but the painful experience of writing it, under stringent tutelage, taught a lesson that has served me well ever since: a good fourth draft, much improved over the third draft, is simply not good enough if there are ways to make a fifth draft even better. There was no possibility of majoring in philosophy, but in the end, my academic accumulations entitled me to a degree in humanities and science.

Armed with that, and with the advantage of having survived eight semesters of mathematics, I went to graduate school in philosophy, interested from the outset in its application to other realms of thought. Once again, as is expected, I was profoundly influenced by my teachers in various ways. In many cases, the influence was substantive; their philosophical views and modes of thought made their mark. But there were other, equally powerful kinds of influence.

It is a challenge for any thoughtful writer to know how long to struggle with or polish a work, and when to send it forth with all the prospects for praise and perils of denigration that attend public exposure. How risk-averse a philosopher is as a writer is partly a question of the height of his or her standards, and partly of the confidence, or insecurity, or thin-skinnedness, or objectives of that writer. I watched the full range. One withheld stunningly good pieces from public view for years on end. Another, whose assistant I was for a time, had a style more suggestive of the corporate executive than of Mr. Chips. He actually once strode into his office in my presence one day, turned to his secretary, and began a prolonged dictation with "Louise, take an article." (And his articles were *good!*)

It was years before I felt comfortable about my own approach to calling a piece of work finished. I prefer to think that the way I have chosen to do it is based on a decision that advancing the debate is more important than insisting on getting everything exactly right. I suspect, however, that I have been greatly influenced by the fact the former is much easier for me to do than the latter.

Again, I saw a great variety of approaches to teaching. Some provided models of what to avoid; others are probably discernible in every presentation I make, if not in every conversation I have with a student.

My peers, too, were important teachers. We considered the role of teaching assistant to be a high office, and spent serious and structured time trying to learn both how to teach well and what to teach in order to have a lastingly beneficial impact on our introductory level students. Since our professors did not devote visible attention to such matters, we took them into our own hands. One result was a little text that a group of us prepared, which was subsequently published and (to my astonishment) is still in use here and there, more than twenty-five years later.

I have remembered that project in recent years expecially when the use of teaching assistants has been under strong attack from many critics of higher education in the research univeristies. We took our teaching extremely seriously. We were apprentices, not serfs or exploited employees. We had a sense of a calling, and we served our students well. I am certain that many teaching assistants today are just the same, and their instructional role is more properly extolled than defended. (Of course, I also have strong views about the obligations of mentoring that any professor has who is provided with teaching assistants, and there I fear there may be rather more that calls for apology.)

There wasn't much about graduate school that I didn't like, and the rigors of my undergraduate education helped me get through it quickly. I had the good luck to enter the market at a favorable time, so I was soon making my living teaching philosophy. It would be hard to claim that I had yet become a philosopher, however.

At first my courses were largely reflections of what I found best in the courses I had taken, and my writing was more the work of someone wanting to join the club than of one with fresh ideas about what sort of club it should be. I suppose I had some independence of mind early on; probably we all did. Graduate school, however, has only limited tolerance for deviant interests; a few of my colleagues had even thought it a bit strange that I took one course in literature!

I had learned to write philosophy as the philosophers did, and what the respectable questions and prestigious journals were, and I relished the chance to use what I had learned in the classroom and at my desk. The standards by which I measured what I did were largely those of the core of the profession.

Five years later, my relationship to the discipline was very different. What made the difference was my emerging interest in decision-making in medicine—an interest that some within the profession considered "rather journalistic," to use what was uttered as a philosopher's term of denigration. Getting a grant to support that work at once gave it an aura of respectability in certain philosophical eyes and a faint odor of pandering to the market in certain philosophical noses. But the old idea of philosophy as an approach to understanding other domains had survived my transition into the profession, and provided a bonus at that. In turning to the world of medicine and health care as a philosopher, I was brought back to some of those big questions that motivate so much earlier philosophical interest, and which are understandably forced into the background in any graduate program (or early career) that gives pride of place to the development of rigor and to a mastery of the current literature in pure philosophy.

In thinking about medical care, one thinks about human frailty and mortality, about what in life is of most value, about relationships of trust and caring. In asking how decisions in health policy should be made, one asks traditional questions of political philosophy about the fabric of social organization—about such matters as collective responsibility and individual liberty, but one asks them in a context of heightened intensity, since the health and even lives of one's fellow humans may be influenced by how one answers.

Here, once again, a tension emerges, between the temptation to be of use—to bring one's philosophical (and perhaps even rhetorical) skills to bear on specific, pending questions—and the imperative one was to have internalized as a student of philosophy to follow one's question tenaciously, wherever it leads, with regard neither to practical matters nor to how much time the pursuit requires.

As I grapple still with this one, I am aware that some of what I have done invites the observation that I have gone into philosophy and out the other side. Perhaps that is true, at least from time to time, but I am no longer much concerned with what the boundaries of the discipline are; at times I fancy that such insouciance is itself a mark of philosophical progress. I know, at least, that everything I do bears the stamp, if not the standards, of my philosophical mentors—that how I approach administrative questions, as well as intellectual ones, is as it is because my field is philosophy.

If the flight is long enough to allow for a real conversation, I'm likely now to say that what I do is consider problems of decision-making in medicine. An example or two will get almost anyone talking, sometimes autobiographically, often reflectively, about the pain and uncertainty that such problems portend. Soon we're a level or two beneath the surface of the issue (having approached it from above), and some question of basic values or underlying assumptions is raised by my neighbor. "Yes, that's it. That's the sort of thing I work on," I explain. "I'm a philosopher."

Living and Ideas

LAWRENCE K. SCHMIDT
Hendrix College

Experiencing and thinking. Living in the concrete, bustling world. Questioning and critically examining. With others in conversation and alone contemplating. Trying not to extrapolate too much in organizing my thoughts. How did I become a thinker? Many paths, some taken deliberately, but mostly finding myself already wandering along. Born on October 2, 1949, in Rochester, New York, I am told I lived in several places those first years as my father, Paul Schmidt, completed his studies at Yale and began his career as a philosopher. As a child I did not receive any special philosophical tutoring, as J. S. Mill received from his philosopher father. I did not know then that I was going to become a philosopher. Philosophy and philosophical thinking were simply in the air.

Books were everywhere, and I enjoyed being read to and looking at the pictures. I remember Homer's *Iliad* and *Odyssey* retold for children and illustrated with large pictures from Greek vases. There was no TV, no newspaper, and I do not even remember a radio. There were records: bird songs, jazz, and classical. Sundays we would go for a picnic, or I'd play in the sandbox. I escaped any particular religious indoctrination as a child and thereby avoided those conflicts, which others speak of, between their early, almost subconscious beliefs and what they were thinking and feeling as adults. I received another perspective that included many of the same human values, but without transcendent guarantees, threats, or promises. So I did not inherit a ready-made absolute world picture that I could continue to think about and support. Nor would I require a dramatic experience to destroy the absolute and open space for philosophic thought. I began, rather, within this relatively open and uncertain world of experience.

As children we were encouraged to speak up and give reasons; force was hardly ever used. I remember once arguing that my parents had said only that they *rather* I did not, and not that I *could* not, ride my bicycle across town to a friend's house. My mother related recently that I had complained at the library's story hour, which I loved, that it lasted only a half-hour and not an hour; so why was it called story *hour*, I had asked.

When I was eight our family of six piled into an old station wagon and drove from Oberlin, Ohio, to the West Coast. We spent the whole summer camping in various national parks. I remember the great mountains, wild woods, glaciers, geysers, and bears in the Glacier. I fell in love with the high clear alpine landscape—its openness, its vistas. The next summer we returned through the Southwest, the desert, and canyonlands. I have arranged to spend blocks of time in the mountains or canyons ever since. The natural environment continues to be my refuge, a place for contemplation and learning. Nature is not a deity, as it was for Emerson. Nature is the place where I (like Thoreau and John Muir) experience the interrelationship and dependence of human being upon the environment—our small place within the whole where an unconsidered act may precipitate a confrontation with one's mortality, as when I put an ice axe through the snow and peered down into the crevasse below.

When I was thirteen, my parents divorced. I lived with my mother and three brothers. My mother soon remarried and I went to a private high school in Vermont. It was 1965. The political–social world appeared in its coarse reality. I began reading *The New York Times*. The war escalated; we fasted. I concentrated on mathematics and science, where there appeared to be structure. The clarity and conclusiveness of mathematics enticed me. I was able to grasp the theoretical perspective; deriving formulas came without problems—it was logical. In my senior year I participated in a small, socially acknowledged study group. We read Campbell's *A Hero with a Thousand Faces* and, I believe, parts of Kaufmann's *Existentialism from Dostoevsky to Sartre*. Campbell's thesis that there was an underlying structure to all myths presented me with a way of thinking about society that was comprehensible. I was able to speak to the point, to this conceptual structure. The existential ideas appeared so obvious. Did I not attempt to live without absolute guarantees, facing a world without promised ends? Was I not in an existential state myself, socially on the edge, half there and half not: half in the natural world of hiking and skiing, and half in the political–social turmoil? I chose Reed College over MIT. Both were strong in mathematics and philosophy, but the West, the wild mountains, drew irresistibly.

During my first year at Reed I became relatively certain that I was going to be doing philosophy for some time. I felt the need to work hard to meet the challenge; I read slowly and there was a lot to read. The required Humanities course was exactly right. We began with classical Greek culture and continued reading the classical works of Western civilization. I probably complained and yet have always been thankful for being exposed to so much that I know I never would have otherwise received. I also studied calculus and argued my way into the introductory philosophy class, although it was usually reserved for sophomores. The direction appeared. Calculus went slowly, in spite of an excellent teacher and a theoretical approach. I did well, but the excitement of viewing new mathematical problems faded, the sparkle of mathematical structures dimmed.

The search began for a more encompassing theoretical structure through which to understand my lived experiences. In philosophy I discovered a new puzzle, a new challenge, a new perspective, and new enthusiasm. My first teacher may well have smiled. I could hardly keep quiet. Plato, I naïvely thought, just could not really be serious about those forms—ideal, eternal, and other-worldly. The argument from degrees did not convince me. I thought I could judge better and worse, more or less beautiful, or just and unjust without knowing the perfect, ideal forms. It was a matter of degrees and extrapolation of what appeared to be similarities and differences within *lived* experience. That year I also turned eighteen and had to register for the draft. The war continued, and continued to be morally wrong in my opinion. Something needed to be done. I refused to apply for a student deferment and stated that my conscience was against this war. A practical test of my values. The next three years involved appeals and protests. I burned my draft card during a Joan Baez concert and joined the resistance. I was involved in draft counseling, civil disobedience, and the increasing outcry against the war. I was drafted. Armed with literature, I refused to step forward. The FBI watched the house where we lived. Finally it was agreed that I could do two years of community service or go to jail. I did not want to go to jail.

The late 1960s were also a time of personal rebellion, a search for alternative ways of living, an examination of cultural values, and an exploration of other ideals and ideas. I lived in various student communes, participated in alternative theater, ran lights in light shows and open-air concerts—all the while studying the classics of Western civilization and philosophy. There was even time for contemplation, hiking alone under the great fir trees in the Columbia River Gorge or watching the sun rise from the snow fields of Mt. Hood, the Three Sisters, or Mt. St. Helens.

I discovered my philosophic mentor in the late Edwin Garlan, most of whose classes I attended. We studied the great metaphysical systems, often meeting at his home in the evenings for several hours, conversing and drinking coffee. I began to see in him a vision of what I might become: his obvious joy in teaching us, his depth of perception, equipoise in the often-heated debates that were carefully guided to the main issue and which he was able to conclude in such a way as to give order and insight into what had been for me often a wild discussion. We had occasion to discuss matters other than those directly related to my studies. His manner of living with ideas inspired me. He had a serious, quiet satisfaction in life and an excitement in discovering a new work or an old one in a fresh perspective. One sunny afternoon close to graduation I remember a brief conversation with Ed Garlan in his garden. He spoke of the life of a philosophy teacher and some of its limitations. Had I considered law? I had not. I felt I would enjoy the time to think and the freedom to choose what I thought about. The life of a philosophy teacher beckoned in spite of the financial limitations. But first I felt the need to experience other parts of the world.

The Wanderjahr turned into three. I went to Freiburg, Germany, to learn German and study contemporary German philosophy—primarily Heidegger's quest for the meaning of Being. Heidegger seemed correct: that one was thrown into the world, that thinking began long after a perspective had already developed, and that all understanding was an interpretation. This appeared to me to be what I was experiencing. Yet, the crucial question had not been answered, as Habermas noted. How is the critique of tradition, of one's inherited perspective, accomplished? Where are the criteria? Do we need criteria? I had compared and chosen different perspectives, had criticized and continued to criticize my own inherited perspective. Could this be without justification, without reason, a mere play, or a play of unconscious forces?

Of many conversations, one stands out: the visit by Hans-Georg Gadamer to Werner Marx's seminar on hermeneutics in summer semester of 1974. We had collected questions for Gadamer. I had formulated one concerning the problems of discovering truth within the hermeneutic situation. We gathered in one of the beautiful *Weinstuben* in Freiburg. The course of the conversation did not resolve the question as much as develop the perspective from which an answer might arise. I was drawn to a closer study of Gadamer, for this question is one I have asked and still contemplate: How does one justify one's choices from the finite human situation where there are no transcendent ideas, no absolutes, and no firm foundations?

The Alexander Tradition in Philosophy
(1873–1992)

One branch of the family name of Alexander uniquely spans three generations of philosophers in America. Hartley Burr Alexander, Hubert G. Alexander, and Thomas M. Alexander comprise an unbroken chain of father–son influences that in the least attests to a very special kind of relationship hearkening to the discipline of philosophy. The following is a composite account tendered by Hubert and Tom Alexander reflecting upon their participation in that unfolding event.

[EDS.]

HUBERT G. ALEXANDER
University of New Mexico

I

My father, Hartley Burr Alexander, was an important contributor to American philosophy during his lifetime (1873–1939). Among other things, he was president of each of the three divisions of the American Philosophical Association: of the Western Association in 1918, of the Eastern Division in 1919, and of the Pacific Division in 1929.

He was born in 1873 into the family of a devout Methodist preacher who had moved west from Rhode Island after the Civil War and had settled in Nebraska (the end of the railroad in those days) with his wife and three children. His father eventually took over the local newspaper where the young Hartley worked as a typesetter and writer. About the age of thirteen, in accordance with the evangelical tradition of the Methodist Church, my father was expected to feel the full effect of a conversion experience, a "warming of the heart," on the occasion of inspiration by a visiting revivalist. In his book, *Nature and Human Nature*, he recounts how this did *not* happen.

At about that time he was interested in the scientific developments of the day. Hartley, like many thoughtful people of that period, was torn between religion and science, and was deeply worried about truth. He was also deeply interested in people, especially in the ethnic differences found in a country where American Indians and new migrants of many varieties lived in close proximity. A missionary once had left a copy of *Uncivilized Races of the World* with his father. This work, denied him at first, became a source of extreme fascination later when he was finally permitted to read it. Hartley's benevolence and aggressive human loyalty could be exemplified in a number of ways, but, as Professor Cailliet writes in a biography I recently translated from the French, one instance that stands out is his unselfish defense of a favorite professor at the University of Nebraska. At the risk of his own degree, Hartley castigated the administration, in print, for its dismissal of the philosopher.

Hartley Alexander graduated from the University of Nebraska in 1897, and received his doctorate from Columbia University in 1901. What focused Hartley Alexander's interest on philosophy must have happened during his stay at the University of Nebraska and must have stemmed from his early dissatisfaction with and puzzlement over the conflict between religious teachings and science, from his curiosity about the diverse mores and beliefs of different ethnic groups, and finally from a dissatisfaction with the current philosophical systems at the turn of the century, which varied from grandiose idealisms (*à la* Bradley) to oversimplified naturalisms (*à la* Spencer). Later, his own philosophy as developed in numerous essays and books would focus upon the neglected importance of the human-based metaphors we use to understand our world—metaphors that he called our "vital symbols," and which orient our major cognitions, both scientific and religious. Thus, he tells us:

> For myself, from early childhood and from out the oblivions which lie beyond memory, I have been beset with the consciousness that things and moments are but the hieroglyphs of reality, that physical nature is tell-tale with scars (geology became my passion), and that metaphysical nature, if it be not void, must be spiritual in the one sense in which spirit for me, from the first, included horrors along with beatitudes. For all this I needed no teaching; indeed, it could not be taught. The solitudes of childhood are incommunicably remote—tears and laughters alike incalculable—but this, at least, is their commonplace, that every unsayable perception is a message-bringer and a banner militant with meaning: the *heres* are portals and all the *nows* dramatic vistas. This is the particularism of "just this world," which is the only world that childhood knows and the only world that can ever be real; it is a particularism in which all objects are symbols, "play-things" in a literal sense, not dead counters of abstractive commodities, but personal opportunities, magical with promise. In so far as I have been able to penetrate the mind called

primitive I find that there also this same symbolic particularism is the commonplace of life; nature for the fresh intelligence is wit-challenging heraldry, blazoned with local bearings, not some vast fortification to be breached and mined by the slow campaigns of theory. And if we ourselves will but lay aside the garment of our sophistication, we shall perceive that within our own lives the sense of symbolism is the nude actuality. As to myself, certainly, I cannot find that conviction of the symbolic character of the perceptual or of the vital moment has any origin or source; it is, and has been, omnipresent in the occurrence of such moments. Therefore, for me, no set of mechanic points can combine into the metaphysical image.   (ADAMS AND MONTAGUE, EDS., *CONTEMPORARY AMERICAN PHILOSOPHY*, LONDON; NY, 1930, PP. 99–100.)

II

As for myself, from my earliest recollection I came under the influence of my father, whose life and work were for me the ideal. I remember thinking that "philosophy" must be the highest profession, but one far above my intellect. Then one time in my teens during a family lunch I was bold enough to question the interpretation of a certain word my father had used. He looked squarely at me, and said that I could be a philosopher. For the first time in my life such a goal seemed a real possibility for me.

Later, I went to college and majored in classical languages with a minor in philosophy. My father sent me to France to study for a year at the Sorbonne, after which I went to Yale and completed a philosophy doctorate in 1934. But my interest had always been in languages, and while at Yale I audited a seminar of Professor Edward Sapir, the famous linguist, who had a special interest in American Indian languages. Ever since, I have been interested in how our linguistic customs influence our modes of thought. In line with my father's own great interest in the field, I was given the opportunity to inaugurate such a course at the University of New Mexico, done on public educational television from 1959 to 1969 over our local educational station, KNME-TV. In fact, I was able to use much of the visual material that my father had collected during the development of a similar course at Scripps College. Although I retain audio tapes of the telecast lectures, it is a matter of deep regret for me that a video record (videotape had not yet been developed) does not exist.

Now, I am delighted and grateful that my son, Thomas, has followed in this philosophical interest and tradition.

THOMAS M. ALEXANDER
Southern Illinois University, Carbondale

When it is discovered that I am the third generation in my family to teach philosophy, comments range from those preferring a genetic explanation to others, more classically oriented, that recall the curse of the House of Atreus. I have never seen this happen when someone admits to being a third-generation lawyer, and the life of teaching and inquiry seems quite natural to me. I am the youngest of three sons, and my brothers, at least, seem to have escaped philosophy.

My story cannot be the typical one most philosophers have of living with an inarticulate sense of something unasked and unanswered, and then suddenly reading a book or attending a class enigmatically called "Philosophy 100" and having the heavens open. My heavens were, in a sense, always open and I often have a hard time understanding how they might be closed. However, I can point quite definitely to several experiences that contributed toward my choice of career. Growing up in an academic household meant that education was always accepted as a primary value. My mother taught piano at home, so teaching was a common topic of family discussion. In fact, my mother is probably most responsible for my subsequent development. I recall that my mother encouraged me from a very early age to ask any questions I could, mainly by offering me a morning of "school" when all my friends had gone on to the first grade, leaving me behind. I'm sure they were the typical questions any four-year-old child would ask, but we would try to answer them, which often meant my mother pulling out volumes of the family encyclopedia and trying to explain the articles in some way intelligible to me. I can't imagine any more positive influence on a child than to encourage this natural curiosity, and I imagine it was this experience that eventually made me recognize in Dewey my strongest philosophical inspiration.

My mother's piano teaching also affected me a great deal, though I never acquired any skill at music beyond listening. Her teaching was one-on-one, and each pupil presented a different set of needs and problems, from the very gifted to those who could never expect to be very skilled. Yet for these latter, my mother constantly tried to make music a meaningful experience. For her, teaching was itself an art, each lesson a performance demanding great inventiveness and sensitivity on her part. Watching her teach and listening to her discussions with my father impressed me deeply and gave me a sense of how good teachers approached their students. Thus my first experience of the "Socratic method" was in the context of teacher and pupil exploring the meaning of simple but beautiful pieces of music, like those in Bartok's "Microcosmos." To the extent that my mother used language to help teach, it was a poetic and emotional language designed to help the student quit simply playing mere notes and achieve a musical expression.

I grew up in a large rambling adobe house in New Mexico that was filled with books and strange artifacts, many inherited from my grandfather Hartley Alexander. I recall spending hours under one of my mother's two baby grand pianos with enormous, old volumes filled with Gustave Dore's illustrations of Dante, Milton, or the Crusades. On the wall of my father's study hung a Shoshone deerskin depicting a buffalo hunt. Wild warriors on pink, purple, green, and blue horses flew around the edges while at the center a stately buffalo dance was performed. Old painted Pueblo bowls, Paleolithic fist axes, Great Uncle Simeon's old seaman's chest, a Greek rhyton: Each object evoked a vanished world that could be touched at the end of my fingers. To feel one's boyish hand close around a flaked stone that a human being held over 30,000 years ago to skin some prehistoric animal takes one to the threshold of our human mystery. This, and the trips to the nearby Pueblos for the ceremonials, visiting the ruins standing out of the stunning silence of the desert under the light pouring from the New Mexican sky—all these experiences made it impossible for me to be a dogmatist, especially of my own culture's values. The plurality of human worlds of meaning, directly and concretely experienced, is for me the possibility of philosophy itself.

I grew up knowing that my father taught at the University, but I always understood him as a teacher without any handle as to what "philosophy" was. He never tried to engage me in philosophical questions; indeed, his major concern seemed to me that I start learning foreign languages as soon as I could. His love of language was very evident—one of my earliest memories is of the beautiful lullabies he would sing in French or German. Even today I wish I knew half the languages he does half as well, languages that include Navajo as well as Greek. For one week at the beginning of June, however, he conducted an aesthetics workshop in Taos, and my mother and I went along. The University of New Mexico had acquired the property and large ranch house of Frieda Lawrence, widow of D. H. Lawrence. The speakers (who included artists as well as philosophers) stayed up at the ranch with the students in the various accommodations the superintendent, Al Bearce (related, they say, to Ambrose Bierce), assembled over the years. Here I saw teachers and students in an ideal environment, the artificial constraints and anonymity of the classroom gone and a truly friendly, democratic dialogue of fellowship and intelligence amid a wild natural beauty. The more formal talks didn't mean much to me, of course, but the artists spoke intensely and were able to use their works as illustrations. Perhaps here is the source of my belief that aesthetics, not epistemology, gives philosophy access to what is of real importance for reflection. The centrality of myth, art, and imagination is common to my grandfather's, my father's, and my thought.

My introduction to philosophy really began in the control room of the University television station, KNME-TV (this was back when PBS was National Education Television). Instead of luxurious programs in color professionally shot and assembled with world-renowned figures speaking to you from the Acropolis, or from beneath the sea, educational television was a decidedly local affair. While it was very homemade, it was also very human and contributed to the sense of the university being an active part of the community. My father conducted a year-long course simply called "Humanities." It began with the emergence of civilization in the Near East, progressed through Hebrew, Greek, and Roman culture, and so on to the twentieth century, ending with a look at East Indian and Chinese culture. Not only did this program provide the fundamentals of "cultural literacy" indispensable for the humanistic outlook that should be the primary aim of all higher education, it also contextualized philosophical developments within other artistic and cultural achievements. Furthermore, though my father was host and often the only speaker, colleagues from the university were often invited to present some topic or other, and my father would then engage them in conversation. Being allowed to sit in the dark control room, wearing a pair of enormous earphones and smelling that peculiar smell of vacuum tubes, rubber, and electrical equipment, listening to the banter of the cameramen as well as the higher-level dialogue from the little set presented me with a powerful sense of the university as a community of dialogue and shared wisdom. On numerous occasions people would stop my father in a grocery store and express how much they enjoyed his show; it established a personal bond with the community.

My interests, however, did not quickly settle on philosophy as a pursuit. My first hero when young, after Hopalong Cassidy, was the former head of the American Museum of Natural History, Roy Chapman Andrews, who probably did invaluable service to science by writing books for young children. His story of going to Outer Mongolia to excavate dinosaur bones and discovering the eggs of Protoceratops made me want to be a naturalist. I read *Natural History* avidly and thought that a life spent understanding some aspect of nature from the ecological perspective would be immensely desirable and blessed. A strong competitor was Egyptology, and, as the momentum of the 1960s picked up, the ancient Egyptians, with their peaceful, stable world seemed very impressive.

The 1960s made everybody think, sooner or later. It was a very formative period in my own life. Like everyone else, I had grown up with the awareness of the imminent possibility of total nuclear annihilation, vividly presented by episodes of "Twilight Zone" and by the Cuban Missile Crisis. The civil rights movement affected me deeply and gave rise to the first strong ethical beliefs I consciously held. Later, the war and the changing youth culture could not be evaded. It is hard to imagine such a time of intense hope and rage. As Linda Ellerby once said, "In the '60s there were no time-outs." My older brother spent a year in Vietnam, getting out just before Tet; I spent every night that year intensely watching the news trying to grasp what was going on there.

It sank in the night Walter Cronkite warned those of us who were squeamish not to look. We all looked, of course. What we saw was the disemboweling of a suspected Viet Cong irregular. The famous footage of a man being executed by a pistol shot to the head came later. Every week we got *Life* magazine, whose title, as the war entered into its pages, became more and more ironic. There was the famous issue with the photographs of the My Lai massacre and then the one that simply printed the photographs of all the American soldiers, 221 of them, who had died that week.

Everyone argued: parents and children, friends, strangers. I had two close friends then, one a theist and adept mathematician, the other a musician and budding conservative, and we stayed up late debating everything. I found myself in between the old argument of a Platonist and a Nietzschean and could agree with neither. Every day the country seemed just a little crazier. The rhetoric from the radicals and from the government seemed to vie in hysteric irrationality. Coming of age then was a very hard experience. But there was also a sense of the questioning of the middle class values of American society *in contrast to* more "spiritual" ones. Like many others, I explored Eastern philosophy, probably because I was mainly impressed by its support for pacifism. I read widely, and finally one day while still in high school I went to my father's study and asked him what would be a good philosophy book for a beginner. I thought perhaps he might hand me a college textbook, but he simply turned around and handed me a very old, yellowed paperback, which contained Jowett's rendition of the *Apology*, the *Crito*, and the first book of the *Republic*. I poured over these books during study periods the following weeks. In the context of those days, I was overwhelmed by the very idea people could discuss important issues calmly. Gradually it dawned on me, however, how relevant each of these documents was to my own time. My father's moderation, basic common sense, and calm reasonableness, his reassurance of sanity in an insane time and gentleness in a violent one, were invaluable to me as well. One of his most timely gifts to me then was a volume of Montaigne, in whose humanistic skepticism I found a ballast in the storm.

The year I graduated from high school America turned its guns on its children. The student demonstrations that followed led to a military sweep and occupation of the University of New Mexico, half a block from my house. Having grown up believing in the sanctity of a university as a place of free inquiry, to see masked soldiers with fixed bayonets wounding students shocked and enraged me. This radicalized my views, and I still think that philosophy is a political activity.

I entered college without any idea of becoming a philosophy major, though it was likely I would choose the life of a teacher. But the need to raise philosophical questions in my other classes gradually made me realize the significance of the philosophical enterprise. My other teachers, especially my science teachers, were, it seemed to me, completely unable to deal Socratically with their subjects. I remember in particular an astronomy professor who told me that anyone who asked such questions did not belong in science. The same experience forced itself upon me in literature, where highly complex theories abounded to justify amazingly bad writing and make some amazingly good writing appear impenetrable. At this point I also read some of my grandfather's philosophy, which presents philosophy as "the great art" concerned with the range and depth of human culture. Since then the tragic and comic dimensions of the human condition have been touchstones for my evaluation of any philosophy.

I found an excellent graduate program at Emory, which managed to have the pluralistic and historical orientation I find congenial. I also got married, and in the process further complicated my philosophical genealogy! My wife, Jill Adams, whom I met in New Mexico, is the daughter of the philosopher E. M. Adams. (See elsewhere in this volume—Eds.) Professor Adams had delivered a stirring talk to the graduate students at Emory, particularly exciting to those of us who thought that philosophy had a humanistic mission in modern society. I returned to New Mexico to write my dissertation and met Jill, although it was a while before it sank in that her father was *that* Dr. Adams. Getting to know him personally has impressed me deeply. While I don't have the temperament to hold to his strong value realism, his urgent demand that philosophy undertake a critique and exploration of humanistic, democratic civilization as its central task immediately attracted me and has helped me continue to focus on this topic. As anyone who has known Maynard can attest, the intensity and sheer human dignity with which he pursues philosophy is a powerful experience. He has taught me a lot about what it means to be a human being, and that is what a philosophical life should do.

If there is any common thread which runs through this story, it is that my grandfather, father, and I have all taken imagination and culture as central themes of philosophical reflection. While Hartley Burr Alexander tended to frame these interests in a form of idealistic humanism, my father has been more at home with empiricism and I with cultural naturalism. I will conclude simply by adding that the philosophical life is upheld by innumerable bonds of love and sheer human need: It is our peril and our hubris if we forget them.

The Rose Tradition

Those who fall in love with wisdom do so for a variety of reasons. The friendships formed with the bond of philosophy are also varied and strangely cast. The mantic Diotima was a friend to Socrates, as well as being his procreator and initiator into the rites of philosophy. In turn, Socrates was a friend and teacher to both Alcibiades the tyrant and Plato the pacifist. In Ancient Greece these lovers of wisdom often wined, dined, and talked together about their differences as well as their agreements. In the Middle Ages philosophy was called the Queen of the Sciences and all who were interested in the pursuit of knowledge were members of her court. Where those who are friends of philosophy are friends with each other, a special relationship is formed; where those friends are also family the relationship is doubly special. Occasionally, a philosopher, who is also a mother, finds that she has given birth, through some cosmic fortune yet to be understood, to a son who is also a philosopher. In the words of the latter, "The gods must have been either very happy or very angry with the Rose family to visit philosophers on them in two successive generations. Might we suggest that there is a philosophy gene . . . that sometimes, though rarely, afflicts even the best of families?"

[EDS.]

MARY CARMAN ROSE
Goucher College

Among my childhood experiences those that throughout my life have been by far the most vivid and rewarding to recall had to do with my love of nature. I believe that *love* is the appropriate word to use here. In fact, my spiritual and intellectual development has been fundamentally a matter of my finding new loves (e.g., the study, teaching, and investigation of philosophical issues). Of course, I have always been very much aware of pervasive tragedy and ugliness in the physical world. Nonetheless, it was in my relation to nature that I first discovered true wonder and the inevitable presence of the unknown surrounding all that we believe we know, and the intellectual and spiritual importance of mystery. I found my truest peace and delight in the experience of stars at night, the familiar patterns of leaves and blossoms, and the songs and feathered coats of birds. These experiences nourished my spirit, and, as I gradually came to understand, in them were the seeds of what for me has come to be the meaning of the love of contemplation of truth, the search for truth, and the possession and the use of truth.

There was no one whom I could tell of my love for these features of nature, but this preoccupation did not pass with childhood. On the contrary, by the time I was in junior high school this interest had developed to include what I saw as the mystery of the multiple relations between the human mind and the physical world. I had developed a great interest in the cosmos and had begun to wonder what else the structure of reality might include. One day in early adolescence there came to my mind the strong conviction that I would do well to seek a career in the mathematical sciences, particularly astronomy. There was no one to suggest to me that perhaps my interests would be satisfied only by philosophical inquiry.

Upon graduation from high school I enrolled in the liberal arts college of a state university, intending to major in astronomy. As far as the liberal arts curriculum was concerned, this meant an emphasis on astronomy, mathematics, and physics. I quickly discovered, however, that the physics and mathematics courses, which were offered only in the liberal arts college but which were also required courses for students in the School of Engineering and the School of Education, circumvented altogether the questions that had increasingly been my major preoccupation for over a decade: What was the status in nature of mathematical structure, time and space, and the conclusions of the really precise natural sciences? How were we to understand the complexities of the relation of the human mind to the external world?

I do not doubt that some of the science faculty privately considered these issues, but the courses were implicitly taught from the point of view that science is technology. Certainly there was only enough attention to theory in mathematics and to the nature of inquiry in physics to permit us to work out textbook problems. Where science is confused with technology, however, there is no place for wonder.

During these undergraduate years I began to discover that some serious spiritual and intellectual problems were inherent in my single-minded interest in the mathematical sciences and in my preoccupation with the epistemological and metaphysical issues implicit in these sciences. At this time my unrest over these problems had two dimensions. First, I was becoming increasingly aware of and uncomfortable with my inability to find value anywhere but in the sciences. Second, I was aware, albeit at first only dimly, that the love of science alone was far too limited an expression of the human capacities and needs to love.

It was in this mood that I elected to take courses with David F. Swenson, one of the foremost American discoverers and translators of the works of Søren Kierkegaard, and who as it turned out, was in his last year of teaching at the University of Minnesota. The effect of Swenson's teachings on me was immediate and profound; although it never occurred to me to discuss any of my spiritual and intellectual perplexities with him.

Swenson emphasized the shared human need to find what I have come to call "fundamental values," which in individual lives should not be analyzed as ends-in-view, but which ideally constitute the very bases of our lives. They are the source of our goals, and are found to be (as Swenson put it) "commensurate with the demands that life makes on us." These values included the integrity, faithfulness, commitment, sincerity, and clarity of thought that Socrates and Kierkegaard have called to our attention. I also came to understand that I was troubled spiritually because I tried to make my elitist, idiosyncratic desire for a career in the mathematical sciences do the work that only these fundamental values could do.

I have spoken previously of *finding* these values. Obviously I did not create them. The following anecdotes concerning Swenson have been, and to this day continue to be, inextricably bound with my personal as well as my professional development and commitment. Swenson liked to tell about his discovery of the work of Søren Kierkegaard and of how this discovery led to his making the important decision to enter philosophy as his life work. This is the story that many of his students heard several times.

On the eve of his graduation from the University of Minnesota (the school where he spent his entire professional life), Swenson was still undecided as to whether he would proceed to do graduate work at Minnesota in mathematics or philosophy. During this period he found a copy of the original Danish edition of Kierkegaard's *Concluding Unscientific Postscript* at the Minneapolis public library. Checking the book out of the library, he took it home, discerned at once its tremendous philosophical and theological import, and spent the entire night reading it. He decided immediately that he would choose a career in philosophy and translate Kierkegaard's works into English. Swenson was faithful to that decision. When I was his student at the very end of his teaching career at Minnesota, we all knew that he was working on the translation of Kierkegaard's writings and that, being a perfectionist in this task, he was very slow to finish.

A second anecdote recalls an event that has grown steadily in importance for me during my career in philosophy. On a day soon after he discovered that I was planning to work for the Ph.D. in philosophy, with the idea of having a career in philosophy, Swenson told his Plato class the previously mentioned story of his choice of philosophical inquiry for his profession. Having finished the story, Swenson looked fixedly at me, and with kindness, challenge, and query in his voice, added a more private reminiscence. He told us that upon making this decision he had wondered whether he would be able to meet the demands of a field that he saw as being uniquely difficult and as requiring spiritual as well as intellectual preparation. I had no doubt then, and I still believe now, that he was indirectly suggesting that I ask myself the same question. Of course, if he was indeed asking *me* this question, he was putting the question to a young woman whose background had been entirely different from his and who was ignorant of the challenges which at that time the philosophical communities were presenting to those who wished to continue their commitment to philosophy as the love of wisdom.

I vividly remember my unspoken response to the question I believed he posed to me. First, would I try to discern the nature of philosophy and of its vital roles in human concerns? Or would I endeavor to impose my preferences on it, thereby reducing it to something that spiritually and intellectually I found easily manageable and perhaps professionally advantageous to me? With no need for explicit reflection, I knew that I was ready because I had the capacity for love and the willingness to serve truth. Second, could I find my professional and intellectual peace and contentment in philosophy? I did not know yet, and I decided that for the time being I would leave the question unanswered.

What I learned from Swenson, his perspectives, and spirit have guided me to my own professional and intellectual peace. Swenson never explicitly articulated an answer to my second question, but by living his own answer, he "pointed the way." I have learned to try to serve truth. And *truth* is the word I must use here, because I have counted on the truth as being present to me ever since Swenson first taught me how Kierkegaard and the Kierkegaardian Socrates found intrinsic meaning in their lives. Further, my glimpsing and desiring to appropriate Swenson's answer has meant that I have continued to this day to ask myself what Swenson's view of commitment to philosophy means to me.

The answer is that I must be caring of my deepest emotional, intellectual, and spiritual needs and desires and also of the meaning I am able to find in my responses to my life's experiences. In making these intentions fundamental in my concerns, I gradually found that it was a way to grow out of self-centeredness in my personal life and out of egocentricity in my professional work. From this point of view there is nothing "trite" about the admonition to find my fulfillment in service to others, beginning with those closest to me and also in service to my work. I must also humbly note and learn from the aspirations, ideals, and commitment of others, whether these are persons I know or authors whose books I read.

I have come a long way on this path since those days, but what I learned from Swenson is that the health of the spirit and of the mind require a commitment to what he called "the true democracy of human beings." Further, this commitment requires my not forgetting my early experiences of wonder and mystery in the presence of nature. What has nourished my spirit since childhood I cannot reject, especially since, now, I find that these experiences have long been the preoccupation of many thinkers.

JOHN MARCUS ROSE
Goucher College

When I first heard about philosophy, I was a child, and did not understand what it was. Now that I am an adult, I still do not know exactly what philosophy is or how one becomes a philosopher. The difference between my childhood and now is that my not-knowing has come to be more sophisticated, better formulated, and in some ways more beautiful. My not-knowing has extended, is of a wider scope, and has grown deeper. When I was a child I was confused about everything, but I hardly noticed this confusion. Now, I am still confused, and, though I notice it more, I enjoy it more. Somewhere between the child's wonder at the world and the adult's attempt to cope, it is possible for the Socratic delight and joy in the question to intervene. When the joy in the question does intervene, then, I think, you have a philosopher. This intervention redeemed the process of education for me, and consequently philosophy and real learning—the love of inquiry and investigation in all disciplines—will forever be the same.

When I was young, I knew that there was philosophy because I knew that there was a philosopher: my mother. She is a philosopher—a professional philosopher—and philosophy is what philosophers study. Thus, philosophy exists. I would like to say that this was my first syllogism, but it wasn't. Despite being raised by a philosopher—and a professor of English literature as well—I remained fairly oblivious to it.

I first had a conscious experience of my mother *qua* philosopher (as opposed to *qua* mother) through the agency of another person, my seventh grade homeroom teacher. One day, one of my classmates asked him what a philosopher was. My teacher already knew my mother was one. I had gotten into a lot of trouble that year, and he had occasion to talk to her frequently. He gave the following illustration of the nature of a philosopher.

"Let's say 'so and so' "—he named a boy in the class—"wore an ugly tie to school, and someone else"—he named another boy—"said, 'I don't like your tie' and pushed him out the window. Now most people would just say that was wrong and punish the boy for pushing his friend out of the window for no reason, but a philosopher would ask, 'Why did you push that boy out the window?' And when he said, 'Because I didn't like his tie,' the philosopher would again ask 'why.' "

This simplistic contrast of the arbitrary moral judge and the philosophical investigator still strikes me with its irony. I wanted to tell my homeroom teacher that my mother had been known to punish behavior without asking "why?" That more usually I asked *her* "why?" I could not avoid noticing that in his eyes what a philosopher did was at least stupid, somehow in error, and perhaps even bad. I did not, however, stop him to question the claim that philosophers inquire into the fundamental causes of defenestration. I spent most of my time waiting for the last bell to ring, and I feared that causing him to pause in his explanations might slow down time's movement toward the end of the day. Despite his explanation, I remained vague about philosophy and rested in a subtle, private knowledge that school was not interesting to me and that someday, in the distant future of adulthood, I would not have to sit there anymore.

School seemed essentially arbitrary. We were told what was so; we were expected to remember "it"; and, if we remembered a lot of "it," then we were rewarded with good grades and stayed out of trouble. I hardly remembered any of what I was taught, and the disapprobation rained down. I forgot to do the homework assignment in first grade in which we were supposed to print our names five times on a piece of paper. Because I got caught trying to get it done while the rest of the class turned in their pieces of paper with their names printed five times on them, I got an *F* and got punished. Twelve years later, I forgot about the calculus test on arcane formulae and esoteric symbols, and didn't fare much better than I had in first grade. I forgot on a regular basis. None of it seemed to connect with anything I had or would experience. I was confident no one would ever ask me to identify the principal export of Brazil or to measure the height of a flag pole from its shadow.

Still I was expected to attend college. My father had implied some dark future awaited me—checking Hershey's Kisses to make sure they were each appropriately foiled—if I didn't start paying attention in class and actually reading those books he paid for at the beginning of the year. My mother hinted I would eventually find myself, but suggested I might start looking soon. I realized the last bell would not ring for a while, and I started thinking about college.

I went to an "Open Campus Day for High School Seniors" at Loyola College in Baltimore the day before Thanksgiving. Department chairs, I know now, had been made to sit in classrooms and wait for seventeen year olds to come to them and discuss the possibility of a college career. As a college professor who has done this too many times, I now realize the indescribable difference between a high school senior and a college freshman and the incredible patience of this faculty. The demeanor of the students present indicated that we were expected to pick a major and a career that day, and the faculty seemed quite determined that we would. A heavy snowfall was forecast.

I first went to the classroom that harbored the professor of history. The room was crowded, and the professor was telling the assembled seniors that there were no jobs in history but they should still major in it; and if they didn't, they would realize years from now that they had made a mistake. I then went to the English department's classroom.

I had enjoyed English; my father being one of its professors, my grades had been better in this than in anything else. I thought this might be a possibility. This room was very crowded too. The professor had written all the courses ever taught in the history of the English department on the blackboard and was expansively describing them to rapt students seated in school desks. But the bell had already rung, so I left.

Next, I went to the room whose sign on the door read "Philosophy." It was the smallest classroom in the building. This professor was a slight man, alone in the room, reading, smoking a cigarette, and drinking coffee out of a paper cup. I felt I was disturbing him, but he noticed me immediately and said to come and sit down. This man, who turned out to be a Hegelian, inquired if I was interested in a major in philosophy. I told him that though my mother was a philosopher—in fact the chair of the philosophy department at a nearby liberal arts college for women—I really did not have the slightest idea what a philosopher was. Then he started to talk to me.

He told me that philosophy was different from other disciplines. That it didn't really have answers that its students were supposed to memorize, but that it asked questions that people found in their own experience. He said one should not go to college to prepare for a career, but to learn. That I should pursue my own interests, whatever they might be. He then went on to explain that part of studying philosophy involved defining the activity itself, and that it was thus hard to say exactly what it was. Each philosopher defines philosophy anew. "Philosophy has a relationship to its own history," he said, "that is different from any other discipline." He explained why philosophers still read Plato and Aristotle. "Though philosophers' fundamental questions have not changed over 2,800 years, these questions have developed in many ways." What else was a Hegelian going to say?

He spoke quietly the whole time, with a British accent, and said a good many other things whose meaning I could only guess about then. He had offered me a cigarette and apologized for not having another cup of coffee to share with me. He then invited me back to his office to make some coffee and give me some literature on the department to read. It began to snow.

If I had an epiphany about becoming a philosopher, it occurred in that afternoon's conversation. This professor spoke softly yet so passionately about something he loved very much, and I noticed that I was actually listening, that I remembered what he said. I decided that day I would become a philosopher, even though I had no clear idea what it was. That was all the more reason to study it.

I still think the state of not-knowing is important. This professor, and his colleagues in the philosophy department, were the first teachers in my educational career to admit that the answers they were teaching came from questions that actual people had asked. In grade school and high school, I had never asked any questions about the principal exports of Brazil or the problem that the quadratic equation was intended to solve. I was made responsible for the answer, but I had never asked the question.

Without the question mark, there is no education, no real learning. Philosophy allowed me to ask my questions and to really start to learn. I became participant in my own education and began to earnestly read, write, and think—about everything. I even learned that calculus was *invented* (rather than dug out of the ground) to solve problems in the analysis of motion that had been spawned by Aristotle's definition of space as place. There really were questions behind all these answers. I stopped waiting for the bell to ring, and in college there were no bells.

The epiphany that day before Thanksgiving continued throughout college, into graduate school, to this day. In my sophomore year of college, I would occasionally ask myself, "When will I become a philosopher?" When I read Plato I thought, still to myself, that perhaps I was a fledgling philosopher, and that later, when the wings of my soul were fully grown, I would be full-fledged. In my junior year, I posited that the question, "When will I become a philosopher?" was already a philosophical question. If I could ask a philosophical question, didn't that make me a philosopher?

I soon realized that becoming a philosopher was not a state to be achieved but a process of questioning and thinking to participate in and maintain. This prolonged questioning meant that I had to reflect upon the different definitions that I was going to discover and invent. I have defined philosophy over and over again, redefining it long into graduate school and long into many nights.

When I began teaching Required Introductions to Philosophy at Enormous State Universities and Small Liberal Arts Colleges, I felt compelled, as I still do, to tell these conscripted students what was about to happen to them. I developed a shibboleth that I still repeat in all my classes: "Philosophy is an attitude of mind which seeks not to know all the answers, but first to understand the questions." This orientation seems to help my students, as well as myself, understand what we are doing in school. For most, the capacity to wonder, to tolerate not knowing, and to be amazed gets shunted to the side by various of life's pressures. The philosopher, to some extent at least, somehow escapes these pressures and at the same time tolerates the ambiguity of being uncertain. There is a positive side to uncertainty that philosophy both reveals and empowers. Beliefs that appear to be answers sometimes aren't answers at all but standpoints from which one is able to ask particular questions.

Some years ago, one of those students in the required introduction to philosophy was the daughter of my seventh grade homeroom teacher. I do not know if she went home and told her father what philosophy really was, but she said she enjoyed the class. She got a B. The second note is that the small liberal arts college at which my mother taught for twenty-eight years hired me four years after her retirement. And now, instead of checking Hershey's Kisses to make sure they are individually wrapped, I have succeeded to my mother's post as chair of the philosophy department. You never know.

Primal Scenes

The following essays were written by two brothers (literally)-in-philosophy. Both resound from different hills the ancient tune of Confucian philosophy, "Is it not indeed a source of enjoyment to practice at the appropriate time what one learns?" (Analects 1:1)

[EDS.]

LARRY R. CHURCHILL
*The University of North Carolina
at Chapel Hill*

In the last section of *The Examined Life,* Robert Nozick recounts how as a youth in Brooklyn he carried around a paperback copy of *The Republic,* "front cover facing outward," hoping to be recognized, acknowledged, or confirmed by some older person (303). Nozick wonders whether that older person whose recognition he then sought might not be the person he has become. Probably all philosophers have a similar scene from their youth to recount. For me the primal scene for philosophical aspirations is set in Mena, Arkansas, where while working on the construction of an earthen dam I toted around for an entire summer a copy of Bertrand Russell's *History of Western Philosophy.*

To recount scenes from my past, however, does not necessarily describe how I became interested in philosophy, or interested enough to call myself a "philosopher," not just once, or occasionally and off-handedly, but consistently, seriously, and over several decades. A fuller accounting of the "how" I became interested verges into and zigzags across the "why," the "where," and the various "who's" of my experience.

Part of philosophy's appeal was, frankly, the elitism of college upperclassmen (all male) who were declared majors. There was an appealing (and in retrospect, appalling) arrogance about them, an air of intellectual virtuosity and snobbery I found attractive. It seemed that while anyone might major in English, chemistry, or psychology, only the nervy and intellectually ambitious would tackle philosophy. I liked the feel of saying I was a philosophy major, and (hopefully in a less smug way) I still do.

Part of the appeal of philosophy was rooted in late adolescent rebellious ness. What better way to show disdain for the establishment (this is the mid-1960s) than to study philosophy, a subject (or so I thought) astoundingly irrelevant to the conventions and customs of ordinary life. Philosophy was liberation, a ticket out of social expectations, an exhilarating freedom from the track of "success." As a philosopher, preoccupied with the transcendental unity of apperception, the problem of evil, or how to deduce an "ought" from an "is," I could be excused from knowing how to fix the car or behave in accordance with social graces. Philosophers were, everybody knew, absent-minded odd-balls, social misfits. Thales, out walking and talking philosophy one night, fell into a well. Adam Smith, in a similarly distracted and absent-minded fit of philosophical conversation, fell into a tanning vat. Hence, even minor philosophical lights can be excused from falling into fits of abstract thinking and talking, and so be released from the expectation placed on more ordinary people. If Socrates stood dazed and distracted for hours in the midst of the Peloponnesian War, I could at least occasionally be dazed and distracted from the great maw of custom and decorum for which I already had disdain. In less intense ways, I still resonate to the luxury of being "spacey" because I am preoccupied by some philosophical problem. Being a philosopher has a social style that seems to agree with me.

The course of a life begins in some actual course that "took hold," solidified a possible choice for a major and eventually a career. Courses are embodied experiences, understood and remembered in terms of instructors, texts, and fellow students, and not primarily as a subject matter. A course that "took hold" for me, and in retrospect shaped a career, was an under-graduate soup-to-nuts ethics course, Plato to Prichard. The primary text was Melden's *Ethical Theories*, and it remains among the most prized of my books because it was the occasion for so much learning. Perhaps it is the desire to replicate the excitement of such courses that leads to academic careers in general.

Books must also be mentioned in the story of my succumbing to philosophy. Though this element might not figure into seduction to various other occupations, for me they figure into philosophy and are an essential part of the narrative. It began, as Nozick recounts, with the pretense, and then the habit, of carrying around books—everywhere. Many of us carry books to bed, to the toilet, to the beach, or onto planes. For others the relationship is more intense, and we feel naked or unbefriended without several volumes ready at hand. (The prehensile hand seems designed with a book in mind.) Returning to Chapel Hill on a plane from Boston in 1978 I was uncharacteristically caught without a volume. Luckily a UNC colleague (historian) occupied the adjoining seat and, seeing my predicament, opened his briefcase to reveal not one but a panoply of choices—novels, texts, commentaries, books in English, Latin, French, even a philosophical monograph. My relief was palpable. Most vacations are planned with equal weight given to two questions: Where to go? and Which books to take? As a philosophy undergraduate I came to see books as friends and companions. Being a philosopher is one of the ways I satisfy my addiction for books; it is one of the excuses I have for being around books, carrying books everywhere, spending hours in bookstores and libraries, building bookcases all around the house, and spending money on books that would more prudently be used elsewhere. Every philosopher, perhaps every academic, has probably had the experience of carrying hundreds of dollars in books to the cash register, only to realize in a wave of guilt that one cannot buy all of them, then paring the stack down to a modest sum, and finally reshelving everything and leaving the bookstore in a depression. Being a philosopher means that, once in a while, you can justify buying everything you can carry out of the store. Philosophers love books like Army generals love tanks and Air Force colonels love fighter-planes: The passion for them is irrational, one can't have enough to feel secure, and the latest version must be possessed and personally tested.

And then there is the Calvinist factor. My family of origin was Presbyterian and I learned early, and in a variety of ways, that an essential part of a full life was loving God with the mind. Just as the Calvinist God declares depravity to be total, s/he also requires the devotion of all one's faculties, not just the volitional and affective ones, but the cognitive ones as well. In a family of teachers, loving God with the mind meant sharpening one's mental faculties and using them to maximum potential. Undeveloped gray cells were flaws in stewardship and affronts to the Creator. This, of course, was never actually said, but it was practiced in a hundred ways, through encouragement, in terms of academic marks, or in dinner-table conversation. Though it never occurred to me at the time, I have no doubt now that I was impelled into intellectual pursuits by the Calvinism of my youth, which required mental agility and intellectual fulfillment as a part of religious piety. It is an acknowledgment I now make with enormous gratitude to my parents. With some theological emendations this still seems to me as sensible a perspective on a fulfilling and purposeful life as any other.

Getting interested in philosophy is one thing. Staying interested is another. Twenty-six years after the initial attraction, the allure is still strong. The reasons are many, but beyond the ones already discussed, I should mention the fun of teaching (mostly medical students), and the pleasure of conversation with colleagues and with my spouse and my brother (both of whom lay claims to philosophy as well). Perhaps there is also something in a naïve remark I made to my father about twenty years ago. Philosophers, I said, have very long periods of productivity. Mathematicians frequently hit their creative peaks in their late twenties; dancers and athletes rarely survive professionally beyond their mid-thirties; neurosurgeons—after decades of training—enjoy a few frantic years and get shaky in their forties or fifties. In philosophy, however, one can always realistically hope that one's best years are still in the future, and this hope can persist well into retirement. There are at least enough instances of late-flourishing philosophical virtuosity to counter-balance the examples of senile self-indulgence and keep us hopeful.

Philosophy, Football, and the Westminster Confession

JOHN CHURCHILL
Hendrix College

Two very different professional communities share the designation "philosopher." One community is comprised of aficionados of mathematics and physics. These admirers of clarity and precision are careful men and women whose greatest fear is that they might assert something false. They have a crazy passion for argument. Two of my friends, philosophers of this ilk, once got in a car and argued for 200 miles without a break. They stopped for the night, and when one of them awoke the next morning, he found that the other was already up and had been arguing with him as he had slept. These philosophers cultivate positions with astonishing attention to detail, working out rebuttals of responses to objections as military engineers once designed elaborate mazes of fortified trenches. Legend has it that a member of this clan once rose at a conference and challenged the speaker: "I have fourteen objections to your thesis."

The other community harbors refugees from theology and literature, seekers of insight or meaning, yearning men and women whose greatest fear is that they might miss the sense of things. These philosophers are continually wandering off into discursive musings, searching after some similarity of pattern, some parallelism of form between something in one field and something else in another, a link that will somehow make sense in both fields and fit them into a larger picture. These philosophers comb through massive bodies of literature and fields of learning in search of resonance. They are the reason no one is surprised when philosophers turn out to be full of stray tidbits about the Oglalla aquifer or Scythian cavalry tactics. So these philosophers read history, fiction, and theology; they accumulate masses of information. And they—unlike their science-loving colleagues—pay attention to the outmoded, all-forsaken ideas and systems that no one believes anymore. A mentor of mine, years ago, a polymath philosopher of this sort, chided me: "You know, John, you can learn a great deal from people who are quite wrong." And so many people are so wrong that there is much to be learned wherever you turn. I recently gave a paper on Wittgenstein's *Tractatus*, and heard the question "Why would anyone study a system you know is *wrong?*" The query came, of course, from a philosopher of the first sort.

The distinction between these sorts of philosophers is not the same as Isaiah Berlin's differentiation between hedgehogs and foxes, or between philosophical lumpers and splitters. Nor is it Rorty's distinction between the metadisciplinary professionals and the amateurish polypragmatic Socratic philosophers. And it is certainly not the line of demarcation between Anglo-American and continental philosophers. It may sometimes produce the same isobars as one or another of these distinctions, but none corresponds entirely. Rather, this distinction refers to the root interests that impel one group or the other into the practice of philosophy.

In my case, the root interest was first recognizable when I was thirteen and they tried to teach me the Westminster Confession of Faith. Man's chief end seemed splendid, if wonderfully obscure: what could it mean to *enjoy* God? But I became snared in the hackneyed conflict of freedom and foreknowledge. Of course, I had no idea that the problem was hackneyed. It seemed very immediate and fresh to me. I did not so much wrestle with the problem as thrash in it. One day on the sidewalk I tried to demonstrate my freedom to myself by committing a perfectly senseless, trivial, spontaneous, and unpredictable act: I jumped sideways a foot. Of course I immediately realized that God must have foreknown from all eternity . . . and so on. So when I discovered the rantings of Dostoyevsky's underground man, his gyrations looked familiar.

Nobody works out a course of study and reflection alone. To the extent that I have developed any virtues of philosophical practice, they have been built, as Aristotle knew they must be—on upbringing—early shaping of feeling and habit. If the confession of faith wasn't clear, it was made clear to me that the mind's play in language was both eminently worthwhile and great fun. I grew up in a family that valued talk—not chatter, but good talk about what's so and what isn't, how things add up, what is worthwhile. I developed a sense of the enormous power of language and its incredible intrinsic delight. I know that my affinity for the work of Wittgenstein is rooted in a childhood full of linguistic inquiry, supposing, explaining, describing, and playing in language with parents and siblings who implicitly valued talking as among the most humane ways to spend time.

This family emphasis on the life of the mind and education went back a couple of generations. Both my grandfathers gave up cotton farming, moved into town, took up storekeeping, and became teetotaling Presbyterian elders.

I knew them both in my childhood, and while both were full of twinkling good humor, each was, in his own way, a serious man. Both were readers, mostly of magazines and newspapers. Hearing them talk, even a child could sense that the world had in it things to be reckoned with. One of my earliest memories is of my father and his brothers squatting on one knee in the shade of a mimosa tree, talking about politics and baseball. Both my parents and both my siblings were or are teachers. My sister is in literature and my brother is a philosopher. I remember the pride I felt, then sixteen, telling my high school friends that my college-aged brother was majoring in *philosophy*: the ultimate intellectual pursuit. It seemed that the direction begun by my grandfathers was continuing. So it seemed natural to follow in that direction.

The confidence that knowing was good permeated my early life. Family dinners would be punctuated by trips to the bookshelves. How *do* you spell Katmandu? Are Bosnia and Herzegovina one place or two? What year did Ted Williams bat .406? My unquestioned conviction that knowing things is good was like all really deep beliefs, implicit. When I saw *Animal House* I noticed the college's motto and burst into laughter: "Knowledge is Good." I was the only person in the theater laughing; was I the only one for whom this slogan expressed a conviction so deep that its explicit statement was funny?

Throughout my childhood I heard the doctrines of Presbyterianism preached and discussed on a regular basis. Calvinism is a fertile matrix for nurturing philosophical inclinations. From the premise that God's justice is inscrutable and His mercy arbitrary, it is a short step to the conclusion that there simply is no practical moral algorithm defining a relationship between goodness and happiness. And from the doctrine that every human endeavor is tainted with the worm of depravity it is easy to move to the view that theological argumentation itself may well be unusually easy to prostitute to self-interest. These ideas, with a background of metaphysical doubts, took me at various times in various directions. For the past few years I have been trying to work out hints about religion manifesting deep and sometimes sinister aspects of human beings. The exploration of that idea now consumes my attention, and I regard this activity as continuous in descent from the sideways jumping of my early adolescence.

Unquestionably, the impetus for my entry into philosophy came from religious issues. But like my friend whose initial acquaintance with scripture was Chapter 9 of *Ecclesiastes*, I always found more nourishment in the tradition's minority reports than in its orthodoxy. Between the broad brush-strokes of confident assertion, I always attended more to the background of unanswered questions, the ignored or marginalized issues, the dissonances, and the abyss of inexplicable surds. At the same time, like hundreds of thousands of people educated into the culture of literature, I came to draw my master images from novels, poetry, and films, instead of exclusively from the Biblical texts that supplied generations in the West with their paradigmatic stories and pictures of life. This makes for enormous differences. Most people who heard or read the parable of the prodigal son did so dozens, even hundreds, of times. On the other hand most people whose culture demands familiarity with *Moby Dick* or *Absalom, Absalom* have read them at most once. So while the traditional pattern was repetition and reinforcement, the pattern of literature entailed multiplicity and continual novelty. The canon of literature is both large beyond numbering and open on any number of fronts.

Beyond my family, I owe my entry into philosophy to another nurturing mother—my undergraduate college, Southwestern at Memphis (now Rhodes College). Dividing my time between philosophy and football, I was particularly grateful that at Southwestern one could be a serious student and at the same time an athlete. One fall, three members of the defensive backfield were in a Plato seminar. On a road trip we were discussing the *Theaetetus*, citing passages, mounting arguments. The head coach, who had just come to Southwestern from a very different situation, listened in for a while. As he stepped away we heard him muse: "I just can't get over you guys. The last place I was, when we went on road trips, the team picked sides and counted cattle."

Only once did my combination of philosophy and football cause trouble. My senior year, I roomed during two-a-days with our most promising freshman recruit, a linebacker like myself. I was to encourage him, mentor him, and solidify his commitment to the college and to football. Unfortunately, I was reading Lao-tse at the time, and talking to whoever would listen about inaction, emptiness, being like water, avoiding conflict, and seeking the lowly. These are not the virtues of a linebacker; I should have been reading Nietzsche. As it was I had soon accidently converted my charge to Taoism, and one day I found him packing for home. He was longing for his pacific backwater home in the Tennessee hills, looking forward to a life of obscurity and calm. I was deeply alarmed at my inadvertent success. Thinking of my own skin, I quickly offered an argumentative antidote, and saved the freshman from joining that unknown number who have been lost to football because of Lao-tse. I still don't know whether my mistake was in the conversion or the reversal.

It seems clear that the origins of philosophy lie in the attempt, among other things, to get critical distance on the intense and powerful mass emotional experiences that supply the ritual bonding of communities. A consideration of Socrates or of the Hebrew prophets will illustrate this point. That is why philosophers, in continuing that effort, need to conceive themselves as standing apart from their communities, and are, I believe, so conceived by the communities that tolerate them. I mean, tolerate *us*. The communities need us: "The unexamined life . . . " and so forth. But we also need them. Philosophy may or may not be a discipline, but it certainly isn't a field of study. Its fields of study are elsewhere, and philosophy exists as dialogue with and about people who play football, confess the faith of Westminster, and who do and say all those things that cause us to ask: What is that *about?* What does it *mean?* Is it *right?*

III

From Catechisms to Missions

"The way up and the way down is one and the same."
HERACLITUS (60 DK)

Autocollage

JERE P. SURBER
University of Denver

The first occasion in my life where I can remember encountering at least the basic elements necessary for something like "philosophy"—a text, a question, a situation where each must take the other seriously with myself as their field of encounter—had to do with my initiation into something called *The Baltimore Catechism*. Presented in the form of questions and answers, it was the backbone of the sort of Irish Catholic education that, I was always told at home, I was "damn lucky" to receive.

QUESTION: "Who made you?"

ANSWER: "God made me."

QUESTION: "Why did God make you?"

ANSWER: "God made me to know his goodness and to make me happy with Him in heaven."

So far, so good. However, a couple of chapters into the text (which we "learned" by memorizing both questions and answers and reciting them, when called upon, at the risk of no "recess" or "lunch period" if memory should lapse), I began having problems with the idea that this one "God that made me" somehow included three "persons." Though I could not have put it this way then, I was troubled by the idea that, in the end, "God was a committee," having always before been assured that "He" was most definitely "One." About the same time, of course, we were learning arithmetic, where it was totally unacceptable to appeal, if you had made a mistake, that you had learned from "catechism" that 3 could equal 1. When I finally asked, in "catechism class," how this could be true, having been firmly told in "arithmetic class" that this was impossible, Sister Ciaran replied, "This, my boy, is a great mystery, and you must pray that God will give you the faith to understand it." (That the answer was as "heretical" as the question still amuses me.)

When I was a graduate student I was passionately involved in my study of Hegel. (In a very different sense, I still am.) Of all the "philosophers," Hegel seemed to me, at that time, to provide the "answer" to that "old" question that I had asked. Actually, reading Hegel made me aware that both the "question" and the "answer" were misstated. Reading Hegel, I learned that "one," "three," and "God" were terms no less problematic than invocations of "mysteries" and "prayer." Yet, Hegel's ability to see the mystery in what initially seemed commonplace, and the comprehensible in what at first appeared mysterious, had a strong appeal for me at that time. Since then, I've come to think that the one "philosophical position" in the entire history of philosophy that can in no way be maintained is that of Hegel. As some of my earlier pieces suggested in various ways, even Hegel could not have been an "Hegelian." I gradually came to realize both to what a great extent Hegel succeeded in his project of attempting finally to fulfill and bring to "closure" the "philosophical tradition," but also how radical and far-reaching were the implications of his "success." For what Hegel and his Romantic and Idealist cohorts accomplished was nothing less than throwing into radical question the most fundamental processes of reading, writing, thinking, and experiencing. In the face of this, I gradually came to think that "philosophy," as our tradition has understood it, presents only a weak and, frankly, "mystified" response to such a challenge.

A few years after I had reached this point, aided and abetted by a few other so-called philosophers who had found their own way to the same place, I was living in Denver and could not resist the temptation presented by "mountain living." Having built a modest but comfortable home on several acres in the mountains, I couldn't wait to show it off to my Irish-Texan grandfather who had raised me. R. H. O'Neal was one of those "grand Hibernians" who had a story or saying for every occasion, who rather literally invented his life as he went along, who prided himself on never having read a book "all the way through," and, yet, who could recite long stretches of verse verbatim (and in several languages to boot). The pride of my mountain home was my study, the walls of which I had lined myself with fine wooden bookshelves. Of course, directly behind my antique claw-footed desk I had placed the books to which I most often referred at that time, books with titles like *Being and Time, Time and Being, Being and Nothingness, Being and Essence.* When R. H. finally came to visit, I conducted him, with tremendous pride, into my study, whereupon he went instinctively to the shelves of books closest to my desk. He spent a few minutes reading the titles, bending over or squatting as he looked them over. Finally, he stood up, turned to me, and very casually observed, "Well, I'd always thought that anyone who had the cheek to get themselves a book with real covers published must be pretty smart. But it seems like they've all kept writing books about the same thing. If they were s' damned smart, you'd think one of them could'a written a book on the topic, done it up right t' begin with, and then they could'a all moved on to something else instead of wasting their time ploughin' over the same sod."

At the time, I at least had sense enough to realize that judgment had been pronounced and further discussion would be pointless; what I did not know then was that I would, much later, come to appreciate both the humor and sound judgment of his response. I am certain, however, that, were he alive today, he would be no less critical of the titles of the books now on my desk, even though they are certainly more diverse and inventive. They might, however, lead to some interesting discussion between us, which "Being" or "Time" did not.

Philosophical Sacraments

GARY BACKHAUS
Morgan State University

Two "omen-ous" sorts of events from my youth have perhaps preeminently shaped a mental predisposition for philosophical problematics. As a young schoolboy I attended a parochial school. In the early hours of the morning, like all the others, I was required to be at Mass. The lighting was always very dim and the smell of incense permeated the pews. The priest routinely performed his ceremonial gestures and his familiar but exotic incantations in Latin. During the long periods of arduous kneeling, I darted my eyes around the morbid sculptures of the Stations of the Cross. This devotion, or should I admit, distraction, satisfied my need for mutual commiseration.

When school finally began, often after the confessional, I, like the others, wrestled with perfecting the memorization of the catechism. I was eight years old when a burning theological question entered my thinking. I finally screwed up enough courage to ask: How do we *really* know Jesus Christ is God? By asking such a question as this, I immediately found out how great a sinner I had become. Deep consternation turned into outright mockery of me. The good Sister saw to it that strong peer pressure would squelch such outbreaks of sinful insolence. Instead of responding to the cure, however, I found similar forbidden questions haunting my prayer.

The following year, another good Sister explained that only Catholics could go to Heaven and that all others would be destined to Hell, or in special cases, Limbo. I informed the Sister that my own father was not a Catholic and asked if his destiny would be to burn in the eternal fires. Upon grasping how this ordinance upset me, she responded with the explanation that if this man lived a good life, perhaps God would allow him entrance to the Kingdom of Heaven. I believe something snapped in me at that moment. Somehow, in a child's way, I had penetrated indoctrination and felt the barbs of deceit in this reprehensible brainwashing. I railed at her defiantly, "Well, if he only has to be a good man to get to Heaven and I have to worry about not eating meat or missing church before I die, then I would do better following him." I must have outsmarted this Bride of Christ, because she said nothing. From then on, I made it a point to miserably fail all religious examinations. Through this insistent courage, a "Hobbesian" reaction was set in motion. By way of mutual consent, my formal religious education reached its conclusion. Although I would carry along the emotional scars contracted through committing this "original sin," I came to realize later that I had portentously promoted my authentic baptism—philosophical thinking.

The second wrenching of consciousness happened to me as a high school student. I had been practicing the art of underachievement assiduously, when I somehow came across a copy of Sartre's *Existentialism and Human Emotions*. I became enraptured by the seriousness of Sartre's problematics. Next, when I immersed myself in Dostoyevsky, a feverish passion overtook me. With another "snap," the familiar world appeared radically trite, superficial, and empty. Enveloped in contemplation, I became absorbed with Dostoyevsky's *The Possessed*. I disregarded the ding-dong school bells, and spent many hours searching out study halls in order to read. When I was not reading, I walked about awestruck, suffering a radical transformation under the weight of profundity. Ever since this confirmational experience, initiated through the inspiration of Dostoyevsky's genius, I have not been well-suited for much else besides philosophy.

What all this has to do with the academic game of philosophy, your guess is as good as mine. For me, genuine philosophical experiences are magically birthed and rebirthed in these irruptive sacraments. Filled with meaning, these omens are nevertheless ominous in the sense of foreboding calamity. The philosopher's task is to live dangerously enough; that is, a philosopher must sacrifice his/her own being for the sake of something greater. Such a sacrifice is either a philosophical sacrament or . . . well, ask Socrates, ask Bruno, ask Nietzsche.

Philosophy, a Bus Ride, and Dumb Luck

ALFRED MELE
Davidson College

It is easy enough for philosophers to find signs of a philosophical disposition in their childhood. However, if, as I suspect, most children entertain philosophical questions and thoughts, these signs probably count for little. Children strike me as being by nature small athletes, scientists, and artists as well. Perhaps some of us, for some reason or other, never shed our childlike curiosity about things philosophical and our associated appetite for explanation.

I remember pondering as a child questions that I now know to be philosophical: when I was eight or nine, for example, my catechism teacher told the class that we must love God more than we love our parents. I worried about that all day. I knew that I loved my parents most, and I didn't see any way to change that. Furthermore, I did not understand how children *could* love God more than their parents, since we knew our parents but didn't know God. I decided that the catechism teacher had to be wrong, that God could not make impossible demands on people; and I felt OK. The next day, after church, I asked my brother Ron whom he loved more. He said "God," and I started to worry again. But I suspect that many of the kids in my catechism class had similar worries—or worse ones: the venial/mortal sin distinction was a real puzzler, for example; and if one couldn't get straight on that, how was one to avoid hell? In any case, I (and they) thought just as hard about issues that we later learned fell under the heading "physics," or "biology." Once, at about the same time, after learning that the earth rotates, I tried to figure out how anything on the earth could move in the direction of the earth's rotation unless it moved faster than the earth rotates. I spun my globe and raced one of my toy cars along its surface, over and over again, but I don't recall coming to a conclusion.

So much for my childhood. It was intellectually uninspiring, as you can see. Besides, I spent most of my free time playing baseball and football.

I first heard of philosophy, I think, in high school—a Catholic high school in Detroit. I was doing some research for an essay on religion when I came across Tolstoy's *My Religion*. That was my first encounter with what I regarded as rational reflection on religion. It struck me as brilliant, and when I finished it I wanted to read more. A search of the card catalogue, however, turned up only Tolstoy's fiction; so, I decided that I would just wait for college and take a philosophy course there. (We did read Paul Tillich in high school, but I recall thinking that Tillich sounded a lot like the nuns, and I was already fed up with them. Understandably, the feeling was mutual. I was expelled a month or so before graduation in 1969 for radical behavior— refusing to cut my collar-length hair, as I recall. My mother tried to persuade the good sisters to let me back in, using a dozen homemade pizzas to soften them up. That failed, and so did I.)

Eventually, I got to college by being recruited by the football coach of the Kalamazoo College Fighting Hornets: The conjunction of my SAT scores and All-State football honors outweighed all those Fs in my final term of high school. I took a class in philosophy of religion in my first term. The reading material (which undoubtedly was first-rate) seemed to me to pale by comparison with Tolstoy. So I turned to mathematics for a time before transferring, at the end of my freshman year, to Wayne State University— back in Detroit. In the meantime, I married Connie, who transformed me into a serious student.

At Wayne State, I gave philosophy another try. At the same time, how- ever, I re-discovered literature. After a year or so, I had to make a choice between English and philosophy. Surprisingly, in retrospect, it wasn't an easy choice to make. I stayed up all night—first trying to decide on a decision procedure, and then, after I settled that issue, making the actual decision. What it came down to, as I recall, was this: Both philosophy and literature were enormously enjoyable (this was in the pre-deconstruction days, of course), but philosophy, in addition, was challenging; and, I thought, en- joyment plus challenge defeats mere enjoyment.

I had no thought at the time of actually becoming a philosopher myself, which wasn't surprising, since I rarely thought more than a month ahead back then. In fact, I'm not sure that I would even have gone to graduate school if I hadn't run into Robert Baker (another teacher of mine) on the bus one day on my way home from school. He asked what I was planning to do after graduation. I replied that I hadn't given it much thought. He mentioned graduate school as a possibility, which struck me as interesting, so I asked him where I might apply. He recommended the University of

Michigan, which was pretty much in the neighborhood, and after a thoroughly enjoyable year laying bricks and painting HUD houses, I went there.

That is where I fell in love with philosophy, though it took several years. It was twelve to fifteen hours a day in the company of absolute brilliance that did it—Aristotle, that is, whose theory of motivation was my dissertation topic. Prior to that time, my main philosophical interest was in solving philosophical puzzles. That is how I approached interpreting Aristotle as well. How can virtuous actions uniformly be products of choice, and therefore of deliberation, if, as Aristotle also said, there are instances of "sudden" virtuous action, as on the battlefield? How can it be true that virtuous agents uniformly perform virtuous actions for the sake of the actions themselves, or as ends, if virtuous actions issue from deliberation, and the function of deliberation is to identify means to ends? And so on. To feel confident that one understands Aristotle well enough to see how textual tensions are to be resolved, one needs to read a lot of Aristotle, which I did. That was my first real exposure to systematic philosophy. Everything in Aristotle, I came to believe, was importantly related to everything else—metaphysics, ethics, philosophy of mind, physics, logic, political theory, epistemology, philosophy of biology, and so on. I finally had a glimpse of philosophy writ large, and I was hooked.

Only when my dissertation was nearly complete—by then I was thinking about two months ahead—did it become clear to me that I wanted to stay in this line of work. Fortunately, I found a teaching job that year—at Davidson College. I enjoyed teaching and had ample time to continue exploring Aristotle and some of the philosophical issues that he addressed. I could think of no better way to spend my remaining years.

Like most philosophers, I now find it hard to imagine myself doing anything else for a living. If catechism and high school religion classes made a contribution to my now being a philosopher, I am grateful for them. It is a good thing, too, that I ran into Robert Baker on the bus.

Why Be Moral?

BART GRUZALSKI
Northeastern University

My philosophical journey began early in adolescence. Raised a Roman Catholic, I took very seriously the "should's" and "shouldn't's" of the Ten Commandments. The burden of keeping these commandments led me to question the basis of morality. I may have been drawn to this question because of hormonal activity: sexual fantasies were my constant companions at early adolescence. But I never posed the question in terms of forbidden thoughts. Instead, I wondered why people should not just rob gas stations for money. What was wrong with robbing gas stations? Why be moral?

The more I considered these questions, the more I became puzzled. What was wrong with robbing gas stations, so far as I could tell, had to do with the existence of God. Thus, at the beginning of my adolescence, I began worrying about the existence of God. Despite hormones bombarding my intellect, I turned to metaphysics.

That was the main reason why, at age thirteen, I went to a Catholic seminary. I understood that I would eventually get a chance to study philosophy and the proofs for God's existence. After six years in the seminary I was still unable to prove that God existed.

I completed an undergraduate degree in mathematics, and began a Ph.D. in philosophy. Throughout my graduate training, however, I discovered few attempts to answer the big questions that had propelled me into philosophy. For example, when professional philosophers of that era wrote about "Why Be Moral," they tended to decide that the question had no good answer if one were asking for prudential reasons, and was senseless if one were asking for moral reasons. At moments like these I felt a bit like the hero in Antoine de Saint-Éxupery's *The Little Prince*:

In the course of this life I have had a great many encounters with a great many people who have been concerned with matters of consequence. I have lived a great deal among grown-ups. . . .

Whenever, I met one of them who seemed to me at all clear-sighted, I tried the experiment of showing him my Drawing Number One [of a boa constrictor, from the outside, digesting an elephant], which I have always kept. I would try to find out, so, if this was a person of true understanding. But, whoever it was, he, or she, would always say:

"That is a hat."

Then I would never talk to that person about boa constrictors, or primeval forests, or stars. I would bring myself down to his level. I would talk to him about bridge, and golf, and politics, and neckties. And the grown-up would be greatly pleased to have met such a sensible man.

I read popular philosophical writers, including Carlos Casteñada and Alan Watts. A good friend, fresh from a three-year stay in an Indian ashram, tried to show me that the world was other than I conceived of it in my one-dimensional way. It was during this period that I made my first contacts with Hindu gurus and Buddhist monks, people who exemplified philosophy as a living tradition.

The Vietnamese War also stretched my horizons, for to me it was an unjust war grounded on my government's hypocrisy. I had to confront the fact that ethical principles are not worth much if they only remain intellectual doodads. Although at the time I felt I was jeopardizing my completion of the Ph.D., I decided to protest the war and, when armed troops invaded our campus, to protest that violation of our university.

Although I did complete my doctorate, almost immediately I began thinking that a more useful path might be that of a physician. I took my MCATs and began the application process for medical schools. But before I completed any applications, I reflected on what I was and what skills I had acquired. I was a fully trained academic philosopher in a profession that seemed to have lost contact with the fundamental issues concerning how to live one's life. I decided that I was better able to do some good as a professional philosopher in re-enlivening what people take philosophy to be, rather than entering a new profession in my thirties.

One summer I went to India for a month. I stayed in ashrams in Kashmir, in Rishikesh, and in New Dehli. I had a personal interview with the Dalai Lama in Dharmsala. The trip was more than I could have ever planned, even now. The idea of trusting in the way things unfold, an idea completely foreign to me before the trip, gained purchase in my consciousness.

My interests continued to develop along the lines that first propelled me into philosophy. The study and practice of Buddhism proved helpful in illuminating a content to classical Western philosophy that seems closed to contemporary Western philosophers. Epictetus was a case in point. I recall finding an old text of his that I had read in graduate school. I had underlined all the wrong sections and had criticized his "arguments" in the margins. I had completely missed his warning to professional philosophers:

> The first and most necessary department of philosophy deals with the application of principles; for instance, "not to lie." The second deals with demonstrations; for instance, "How comes it that one ought not to lie?" The third is concerned with establishing and analyzing these processes; for instance, "How comes it that this is a demonstration? What is demonstration, what is consequence, what is contradiction . . . ?" It follows then that the third department is necessary because of the second, and the second because of the first. The first is the most necessary part. . . . But we reverse the order. . . . Wherefore we lie, but are ready enough with the demonstration that lying is wrong.

I had also missed his advice about how a philosopher should live life:

> The ignorant man's position and character is this: he never looks to himself for benefit or harm, but to the world outside him. The philosopher's position and character is that he always looks to himself for benefit and harm. The signs of one who is making progress are: he blames none, praises none, complains of none, accuses none, never speaks of himself as if he were somebody, or as if he knew anything. And if any one compliment him he laughs in himself at his compliment; and if one blames him, he makes no defense. He goes about like a convalescent, careful not to disturb his constitution on its road to recovery, until it has got firm hold. He has got rid of the will to get, and his will to avoid is directed no longer to what is beyond our power but only to what is in our power and contrary to nature. In all things he exercises his will without strain. If men regard him as foolish or ignorant he pays no heed. In one word, he keeps watch and guard on himself as his own enemy, lying in wait for him.

If I had missed all of this in Epictetus, plus his wit and humor, what else had I missed? I soon found that I had missed important gems in Plato. My schooled assessment of the classical philosophers was unreliable.

I have since made a fresh acquaintance with Plato. I have found fully satisfactory answers to the "why be moral" question in classical Western philosophy and in the living traditions of Buddhism and Vedanta. And I have become involved with ecological issues, for they have deep spiritual and philosophical dimensions, as well as urgent implications.

I am no longer an adolescent driven by newly activated hormones. I am, instead, an academic philosopher who takes philosophy to be a study that can touch the inner and outer life of everyone. It is, I believe, a practical path that can lead to a grounding within one's own life, as well as a clear foundation for activism when that is necessary. Both aspects of philosophy make it an eminently practical, worthwhile, and satisfying discipline.

From Street Corner to Classroom

RICHARD L. PURTILL
Western Washington University

In the early 1950s I was coming out of Foyle's bookstore on Charing Cross in London when I saw a rather surprising sight. In a blind alley between two parts of Foyle's was a small folding platform, rather like a stepstool with a tall railing on one side. On the railing was a crucifix and a rectangular sign on which was painted in rather faded gold letters, "Catholic Evidence Guild." Standing on the platform, leaning on the railing, was a young man who was speaking with an Australian accent about the Catholic faith. He was surrounded by a small crowd whose members frequently interrupted him with questions and objections.

As I walked over to the platform the young man was arguing about free will with an older man in the crowd. In light of later knowledge, I imagine that they had gotten onto the topic by way of the problem of evil and the argument that a good deal of the evil in the world is due to human misuses of free will. The man in the crowd was defending determinism, denying that we *have* free will, and I was not entirely satisfied with the young man's reply. I don't remember if I intervened in the argument, but after the young man finished speaking and came down from the platform, I buttonholed him and said something like this: "Why didn't you refute what he was saying by telling him that if determinism were true, he was determined by causes beyond his control to believe in determinism and you were determined by causes beyond your control not to believe in it, so there would be no use arguing."

I think my thought was something along the lines of C. S. Lewis's argument against naturalism in *Miracles*: since the man did seem to think there was some use in arguing, this in itself might be an argument against determinism. The young man with the Australian accent, whose name turned out to be Tony Coburn, replied amicably that he was trying to convince the man, not just refute him, and we got into an interesting dision.

Tony said, "Some of us are planning to have some tea at a shop near here. Why don't you join us?" I then saw that some of the crowd were still waiting nearby and were evidently friends or associates of Tony's. We went to the tea shop, and over tea and cakes I discovered that my companions were all speakers or prospective speakers for the Catholic Evidence Guild, a group mostly composed of Catholic laypeople who explained and defended Catholic doctrine at street-corner meetings like the one I had just observed.

I told them in turn that I was a recent convert to Catholicism, currently serving in the U.S. Army in England, and on weekend leave in London. My own conversion had been due in great part to reading the work of G. K. Chesterton. I had encountered him first through a Father Brown story in a collection of detective stories for children, which I had found in the children's room of the local library. Afterwards I had read the rest of the Father Brown stories, much of the rest of Chesterton's fiction, and then gone on to his essays. By absorbing G. K. Chesterton's intellectual progress into the church, I explained, I had become convinced to follow in his footsteps.

Somewhere in the midst of this explanation, a rather dowdy, older lady in the group said, "Oh, I see you have my book." The book in question was Maisie Ward's *Return to Chesterton*, a supplement to her major biography of Chesterton. Wondering if the lady was a trifle dotty because she thought that my book belonged to her for some reason, I said that I had just bought the book at Foyle's.

Someone in the group laughed and said, "She means that she wrote the book. This is Maisie Ward." I think I was a little suspicious at first that my leg was being pulled, as the English say. But my conversation with the lady soon convinced me that she was indeed Maisie Ward, and I tried to convey some of my appreciation for her biography of Chesterton, which had helped me to see his life and thought in perspective.

Toward the end of this conversation Maisie said, "You know, with your interests, you should really join the CEG." Not making the connection with the sign I had seen on the platform I said, "Oh, is there a Chesterton society in London?" thinking vaguely that the "C" stood for Chesterton. I soon learned that the CEG was the way most of its members referred to the Catholic Evidence Guild, that there was a training program for speakers on Saturday nights, and that I was more than welcome to attend and see if it might be my cup of tea.

Although Maisie wrote under her maiden name, she was Mrs. Frank Sheed, co-owner with her husband of the Anglo-American publishing firm of Sheed and Ward. St. Paul said you can have many teachers, but only one father in the faith; Chesterton was my father in the faith, but Frank and Maisie were certainly my godparents. I owe a very great deal of my happiness, my sanity, and such sanctity as I have managed to Gilbert, Maisie, and Frank; my life has been immeasurably richer because of them. The only comparable influence on me has been that of my older brother in Christianity, C. S. Lewis. The meeting with Maisie was tremendously influential on my own life; without it and the meetings that followed, I might not be a philosopher, a teacher, and a writer today.

After my first meeting with Guild members I did become a regular speaker for the Guild, both at their "pitch" among other speakers of Hyde Park Corner and in lonelier "pitches" in remote parts of London. There were regular training sessions in Catholicism for Guild speakers and one of these sessions was a course on Thomistic philosophy taught by Frank Sheed. I had my first introduction to metaphysics, to such distinctions as matter and form, act and potency, and metaphysics has fascinated me ever since.

My early Anglophilia has been replaced by Hellenophilia and now I visit England only on my way to, or from, Greece.

Huston Smith's Story*

HUSTON SMITH
University of California, Berkeley

I was born of missionary parents, in China, and spent my formative years there. I don't suppose one ever gets over that.

Because we were the only Americans in our small town, my parents were my only role models, so I grew up assuming that missionaries were what Westerners grew up to be. When I left for college in America, therefore, it was with the settled expectation that I would be back as soon as I had my theological credentials in hand. I had not reckoned with the West's dynamism. Never mind that *my* West was initially Central Methodist College (enrollment 600), set in Fayette, Missouri (population 3,000). Compared with Changshu, China, it was bright lights and the big time. Within weeks, China had faded into a happy memory; it would not be my future. The consequence for my career, however, was slight. Instead of being a missionary, I would be a minister.

My junior year in college brought another surprise: ideas jumped to life and began to take over. To a certain extent they must have slipped up on me gradually, but there was a night when, with the force of a conversion experience, I watched them preempt my life. Returning from a meeting of a small honor society, which met monthly for dessert and discussion in the home of its faculty sponsor, several of us lingered in a corridor to continue arguments the evening had provoked—as unlikely a knot of peripatetics as ever assembled. My excitement had been mounting all evening, and around midnight it exploded, shattering mental stockades. It was as if a fourth dimension of space had opened, and ideas—now palpable—were unrolling like carpets before me. And I had an entire life to explore those endless, awesome, portentous corridors! Unhappiness might

*Excerpted and adapted from "Huston Smith's Story" in *Primordial Truth and Postmodern Theology*. David Ray Griffin and Huston Smith, eds. Albany: SUNY Press, 1989, pp. 8–13.

return, but I knew that I would never again be bored. I wonder if I slept at all that night.

In retrospect it seems predestined, but at the time I could only see it as good fortune that the faculty sponsor of our discussion group was a protegé of Henry Nelson Wieman. Wieman was at The University of Chicago, so I naturally chose it for my graduate study. Having earlier shifted my vocational intent from missionary to minister, I now moved next door again by opting for the teaching rather than the pastoral ministry—administrative and promotional demands of the latter would leave too little time for ideas. Because these vocational adjustments were not only logical but small, they occasioned no soul-searching; but as I think back on the matter I am surprised that the collapse of my youthful supernaturalism seems to have caused no trauma either. I entered The Divinity School of The University of Chicago a convinced Wiemanite, which is to say, a naturalistic theist. Robert Maynard Hutchins, the university's president, had chosen as his motto for the university Walt Whitman's "Solitary, alone in the West, I strike up for a new world," and I responded to his idealism—with some smug elitism admixed. Hutchins insisted that the "The" in The University of Chicago be capitalized to underscore its distinctiveness, and we were fond of quoting William James's alleged observation that whereas Harvard University had thought but no school, and Yale University, a school but no thought, Chicago had both. Chicago was an exciting place, and despite World War II—I had ministerial deferment and was headed for the chaplaincy—the early 1940s were a heady time for me. Through naturalistic theism, the two most powerful forces in history—science and religion—were about to be aligned, and it would be my life's mission to help effect the splice. I was a very young man and fresh to the world's confusions.

I can remember as if it were yesterday the night in which that entire prospect, including its underlying naturalistic worldview, collapsed like a house of cards. It was five years later, in Berkeley—but before I relate what happened, I need to explain how I got there. Chicago proceeded as planned, with one major surprise. Although in my first year I would not have believed that such a thing was possible, in the second year I discovered something better than Wieman's theology, namely his daughter. Two years later we were married, and for forty-five years she has been a delightful and stimulating companion.

That year, I bumped into the question of how a philosophy that placed the premium on quality that contextualism did would handle the quality called *pain*, and having given pain little direct thought up to then, I set off to the library for instruction. Rummaging under *pain* in the card catalogue, I found four titles that looked as if they might be relevant. One of them— Gerald Heard's *Pain, Sex and Time*—carried the most interesting title of the four, so I began with it. It proved to be one of the two most important reading experiences of my life. By page two, I discovered the book had nothing to do with my dissertation, but I kept reading. When I finished, I made two resolves. First, I would not read another line by this author until I had completed my doctoral studies—I obviously feared that if I did, I might quit the university. Second, when my diploma was in hand, I would read everything Gerald Heard had written.

What "grasped" me that night, as Tillich would say, was the mystic's worldview. Never before—not during my four years as an undergraduate religion major, nor during the four subsequent years as a graduate student of philosophy and theology—had mysticism been sympathetically presented to me, and when it was, I instantly cathected. The naturalistic world I had loved and lived in since my mind's arousal was, with a single stroke, relativized. It was but part of the whole. An island—lush to be sure, but rimmed round about by an endless, shining sea.

After graduate school and various teaching jobs, I moved to Washington University in St. Louis in 1948. Before the move, however, I decided to visit Gerald Heard who I had learned was living in southern California. During the course of the visit, he introduced me to his friend and neighbor, Aldous Huxley, whose *The Perennial Philosophy* had been under my arm on the journey. On seeing me off for my return journey, Heard remarked: "So you're moving to St. Louis. There's a very good swami there."

Swami? I'm not sure I recognized the word. At that point, however, Heard and Huxley were my guiding lights, so I asked for the swami's name and I looked up *Satprakashananda* in the St. Louis telephone directory the week that I arrived. He turned out to be with the Ramakrishna Order of Vedanta, which Swami Vivekananda had established in America after taking the 1893 Chicago Parliament of Religions by storm. Learning that he was conducting a Tuesday evening discussion group on the Katha Upanishad, I dropped in on a session and returned home with a copy of the text. It occasioned the second of the two distinctive reading experiences I alluded to above. I have met teachers of world religions who confess that after fifteen years they still do not understand the Upanishads. For me it was otherwise. Their teachings were self-evident, including their insistence that there was more to be comprehended than could be rationally conceived.

For ten years, my Western philosophy marked time as I apprenticed myself to my new-found mentor. In weekly tutorials he taught me the Vedanta and at the same time set me to work meditating. There was a time—about five or six years into this regimen—when in return for a monthly sermon I was listed associate minister of my local Methodist

Church and while (less publicized) I served as president of the St. Louis Vedanta Society. While this might have seemed odd, I experienced no conflict. In addition to keeping my ancestral ties intact, my church connection kept me "in love and charity" with my ostensible community and offered outlets for good works. To add, though, that the theological concerns of my congregation did not run deep enough to satisfy me would be to put the matter mildly, and its spiritual exercises stopped with pietism—in Vedic idiom, *bhakti*. There was one day each year when the two poles of my religious life were sharply joined. The church pageant on Christmas Eve was pitched early to accommodate young children, and its magic regularly worked to rebind me to my family and heritage, for what can rival a "Silent Night" that is imprinted in memory's deepest recesses? I could *sense* the mystery of the Incarnation in that service, but nothing in its ambiance underwrote for me the ontological foundations of that mystery to the extent that Swami Satprakashananda's annual meditation on "Jesus Christ, the Light of the World," delivered late at night after the children were put to bed, did. That Christ was one of multiple avatars for him was incidental compared with his certitude that in Christ's birth something ontologically dramatic had *happened*.

A move to the eastern seaboard (M.I.T.) added Buddhism to the Vedantic foundation St. Louis had laid down. Before leaving Washington University I had brought to its campus D. T. Suzuki and then a Zen priest, who was a Fulbright exchange scholar, with whom I taught a semester's course on Zen. The experience "hooked" me and, because the priest insisted that Zen could not be grasped by the rational mind alone, I decided to go to Kyoto for a summer of meditation, *ko'an* training, and residence in Myoshinji monastery. Thus it was that Zen became my contemplative practice for my M.I.T. years. In switching, I did not feel as if I was deserting Vedanta. Śunyata seemed very similar to nirguna Brahman and the Buddha-nature similar to Atman—so much so that I felt I was encountering the same truth in different idiom. Another sea-change of the same order—same sea—occurred a decade or so later when Seyyed Hossein Nasr introduced me to the mystical dimension of Islam in pre-Khomeini Iran. Again, it felt as though I was learning yet another language in which the same truths could be couched.

Only one more episode needs telling. In my introduction to Frithjof Schuon's *The Transcendent Unity of Religions*, I relate how, while conducting students on an academic year around the world, I chanced in Japan, India, and Iran successively upon books of his that dramatically deepened my understanding of the religions at hand. Pursuing Schuon's writings after I returned home, I discovered that he situated the world's religious traditions in a framework that enabled me to honor their significant differences un-reservedly while at the same time seeing them as expressions of a truth that, because it was single, I could absolutely affirm. In a single stroke, I was handed a way of honoring the world's diversity without falling prey to rel-ativism, a resolution I had been seeking for more than thirty years.

Magic Mountains and Matrimony

WALTER B. GULICK
Eastern Montana College

"My God, I'm married to a philosopher!" Barbara bolted upright in bed with the impact of her sudden discovery. As the early morning sky began to lighten, my wife perceived my identity with a clarity that was often lacking in my own self-assessment.

Unfortunately, I can no longer recall accurately how I actually responded (if at all) to Barbara's recognition those many years ago. In retrospect, though, her dramatic pronouncement, animated to the point of exaggeration, suggests that there is something strange about being a philosopher (or being married to one). It involves more than just fitting into an occupational role. Certainly I've had to struggle to see what is implied in thinking of myself as a philosopher. Some of the possibilities can be suggested by imagining different responses I might have made to her.

Had I been feeling alert and clever, I might have replied to her exclamation in kind: "My God, so am I!" That comment would have addressed the fact that she too was, like all of us, a philosopher in a latent sense. But since she was not making a discovery about how philosophical assumptions are embedded in everyone's consciousness, no doubt she would have dismissed my remark as a wisecrack fogged by pre-dawn incoherence.

Had I been puzzled and even irritated by the tardiness of her discovery, I could have admonished her: "You *know* you're married to a philosopher; I've taught philosophy for several years now." That response would have addressed the sense in which the philosopher may be understood as a certain type of professional employed in an institutional setting. Ever since the eighteenth-century Enlightenment, when disciplines were captured by the academy, it has been presumed that if you teach biology, you're a biologist; if you teach mathematics, you're a mathematician, and so on. I taught philosophy.

Had I been honest about my own feelings, however, my retort would have been something like this: "My God, even you, my wife, think I'm a philosopher, and yet I myself am not sure if I fit that designation." My uncertainty had to do with whether I could find a way to reconcile my ideal image of philosophy with its practical realities. I admired those in ancient Greece who were literally "lovers of wisdom" and who forged a seamless unity between who they were and how they lived. But I was leery of identifying too closely with contemporary professional philosophy as it extended beyond the classroom. Its practitioners appeared to me, perhaps without good cause, to be more concerned with technical minutia and competitive self-advancement than with wisdom, Sophia.

How did I manage to pick a career that was at once so attractive and so confusing to me? Not easily or directly. I sensed from an early age that my personal career should involve doing something socially or intellectually meaningful with my life—perhaps because so many of my ancestors had been doctors and missionaries. I was happiest when, if not reading or playing games, I could escape to the desert, with rockhounding providing the excuse. So I went off to Pomona College convinced that a career in geology was justifiable and right for me. It was sometime during the summer of 1959, when engaged in a summer job with the U.S. Geological Survey mapping in the Salmon River Mountains of Idaho, that a geologist died and a nascent philosopher struggled toward birth. I recall contemplating whether I really wanted a career where I was so isolated from other people. And of what significance were the geological maps I was producing? The only people who cared about the maps were the mineral extractors who might exploit and ruin the land I loved.

I returned for my senior year knowing that I should complete my major in geology in order to graduate, but also knowing that I would not become a geologist. I decided to sample courses widely that year in order to uncover a career that satisfied my desire to do something useful with my life— something that helped other people or improved society. Thus I took my first and only undergraduate philosophy course.

I can't say that my life was immediately changed by exposure to contemporary philosophy, although I found it interesting. However, too often the summaries of Dewey and Whitehead or Heidegger and Sartre seemed to me only abstractions that obscured the human significance of what these philosophers were trying to say. Moreover, the analysts entirely ignored what was fascinating to me. On the other hand, Tolstoy, Dostoevsky, and Mann charmed me in another course. They created concrete human worlds that were magical in their power to evoke reflections and emotions I might not otherwise experience. In *Crime and Punishment* I considered with Raskolnikov the worth of a seemingly expendable human life. Is it conceivable that the murder of a miserable old woman might be justified because one could make far better uses of her resources than she could? Through *The Magic*

Mountain I entered a timeless sanatorium high above our everyday world of projects and deadlines. Here the incursion of disease was rendered almost attractive, because a sick person was freed from mundane responsibilities and allowed to fantasize and speculate. Perhaps this magical world was the true home of philosophy. If speculation in hermetic isolation was all there was to philosophy, however, then it did not offer the opportunities for service and contact with other people that I sought.

The dilemmas posed within these and other works of literature awakened my imagination and cried out for philosophical reflection in response. Curiously enough, I never even considered teaching literature, perhaps because it was the speculation rather than the written expression that intrigued me. In any case, with graduation imminent, I felt I needed to find a position that would allow me time to reflect—upon life, and upon career alternatives. A position overseas teaching math seemed to offer that opportunity, so I became the thirty-third Gulick to embark upon a venture supported by a missionary board.

Turkey confronted me with a whole new appreciation of human history. The school was reputed to be built upon the site of an old Roman hippodrome, and just beyond the school walls one could dig up neolithic relics. Tarsus was where Antony had met Cleopatra and where St. Paul had been educated. To live in this land of Crusader castles and ancient mosques enlarged my vision of what wisdom must encompass.

The person who had been teaching the philosophy class was to go on leave my third year in Tarsus. On the basis of my one course experience in philosophy, I seized with relish the opportunity to take over the course. Maybe I could recapture the intense pleasure I found in considering life's most significant questions. That hope was not fully realized, but I came to see how teaching philosophy allowed one both magical moments of speculation and meaningful wrestling with the concerns of the day. I decided to do graduate work in philosophy and religion, and so traveled to New York City to see if a joint program at Union Theological Seminary and Columbia University would allow me to explore the wisdom of the ages. It did. It was there that I came to admire the lovers of wisdom. At Union I also began dating a young woman, and within three weeks I asked her whether a joint marital venture suited her. It did. It was she who would, one night some years later, bolt upright in awestruck recognition.

I now needed to support a wife, and an M.A. in comparative religion was not a very marketable degree. I found employment as a group insurance administrator for Teachers Insurance and Annuity Association. I thereby served philosophers rather than taught philosophy (the missionary impulse does not die easily). An insurance administrator may be called many things, but "lover of wisdom" is not likely to be one of them. After a couple of years of reading Plato and Polanyi on the train while the other gray-suited commuters read the *Wall Street Journal*, it was clear to me that I was called by headier claims than working my way up the corporate ladder.

Still, it was a shock to Barbara when I announced my desire to return to graduate school for a doctorate. She well could have exclaimed then, "My God, you're really married to philosophy!" And so, in a way, I seemed to be. Yet my courtship was never simple and direct, nor has the consummation been as I expected. For instance, since I saw no point in submitting to the Wasserman test of symbolic logic, my marriage to philosophy has never been legitimated by a doctorate. Instead, I earned a Ph.D. in religion. And in recent years I have increasingly incorporated into my teaching the sorts of materials that initially excited me. My anxieties about professional philosophy dissolved as I engaged philosophically the literature of ancient civilizations, the novels of modern seers, and indeed all that wisdom touches.

Some might say I enjoy something akin to a common law marriage with Sophia. On the other hand: "Marriage to philosophy?" The metaphor doesn't seem quite right. I am married to Barbara, I teach philosophy, and sometimes, in magical or even holy moments, I encounter Sophia. When all goes well, those moments of enchantment occur not only on mountain tops, but in the classroom and my office, too. And then personal and professional identity are one.

The Education of a Philosopher, of Sorts

HENRY ROSEMONT, JR.
St. Mary's College of Maryland

My earliest education was rather unusual. Neither my father (a printer), nor my mother (a musician) attended school beyond the ninth grade. They were nevertheless widely read and multi-talented, which, when combined with their strong identification with the working class, made them—and hence me—oddballs in the middle-class neighborhoods of Chicago where we lived.

Following in the footsteps of Jeremy Bentham and James Mill, they began my formal education before I can remember. The curriculum included the reading, writing, spelling, and grammar of my native tongue, plus U.S. and English history, learned from my father. Mother taught arithmetic and music, the latter including not only Beethoven *et al.*, but Bessie Smith, Ella Fitzgerald, Charlie Parker, Slam Stewart, and other blues and jazz artists, which opened the door of Black American culture to me.

Excellent and enjoyable though this education was, it ill-prepared me for life outside the home when I was finally obliged to enter the public schools at age seven. The world was turned upside down. Most of my heroes—Big Bill Haywood, Joe Hill, Kropotkin, Malatesta—were seen as villains, and *my* villains—Rockefeller, Morgan, Gould, Carnegie, etc.— were to be revered; Negroes had rhythm, but little else; Wobblies and other left-wing groups would destroy us all were it not for the vigilance and dedication of the F.B.I. Worst of all, reading was reduced to Dick and Jane, writing to penmanship, and math to rote memorization, all the while insisting on good personal habits, such as punctuality and respect for authority.

It took me almost eight years to effect an escape from this regimen, which necessitated my leaving home as well. My path was Route 66 West, my method a thumb in the air and two dollars plus change in my carrying bag. For the next three years I lived alternately on the road and at home, holding a succession of undistinguished jobs ranging from brush packer to newspaper subscription salesman, kick-press operator, and grease monkey. Here, too, I received a solid education, although it was neither as exciting nor as profound as the wandering American life Kerouac would later chronicle.

One of the lessons I had not yet learned anywhere was humility, which, alongside a macho sense I had absorbed from the Chicago streets, led me to forget politics for a while, and to volunteer for the Marine Corps, for Korea, and for the infantry. Not surprisingly—it was late 1952—all three wishes were promptly granted, but my luck held, and I even managed to continue to learn a few things, paramount among them being: (1) that the effectiveness of the Corps was due to its inculcating communal values in its members—like a union brotherhood—rather than the capitalist values of rugged individualism it was designed to protect; (2) war is insane; (3) East Asian cultures were ancient, mysterious, and beautiful in their own right, and fascinating because they obliged others to confront their own culture(s) in a very different way.

Following my discharge I returned to the railroad job I held at the time of enlistment, and spent the next three years in a Chicago switching yard. I enjoyed the freedom and camaraderie that comes with being a rail and became active in the local union. I thought about college occasionally, but not seriously, because I had never secured a G.E.D., and my meager high school transcript ended with the notation, "incorrigibly truant."

Through the good offices of a close friend and fellow ex-Marine, however, I learned that veterans over twenty-one could sit for special entrance examinations at the Navy Pier branch of the University of Illinois. I took them, was admitted probationally, and returned, after almost a ten-year absence, to school.

Initially interested in U.S. history, a course in formal logic followed by one in Greek philosophy inclined me to pursue that subject further. In philosophy—unlike the other disciplines I was studying—it appeared as though you could think about anything at all and get away with it if you were clever enough. But my path to philosophy was still not clear, because I had had experiences in East Asia which no Western philosopher spoke to, or about, nor did they even provide me with a vocabulary for describing those experiences accurately. I began to read some Chinese philosophical texts on my own and became enamored with the Daoist sage, and, for very different reasons, his Confucian counterpart. Both of them struck me as true philosopher-kings, but of a rather different kind than Plato's: they hadn't lost touch with the world of flowers, food, drink, conversation, dancing, and love-making. Unfortunately, studying philosophy in U.S. universities in the early 1960s meant studying analytic philosophy only; Chinese thought was scorned, when not excoriated. As a consequence, I took only the minimum requirements to major in philosophy while devoting much of my time to the study of Chinese language, history, and politics. I was determined to be both logician and lotus-eater, but the task proved more difficult than I anticipated; it was only by the skin of my teeth that I completed the Ph.D. requirements at the University of Washington and embarked on a professional career.

Although I had no difficulty securing a decent position, most philosophy departments—then and now—had no use for a person who thought Confucius or Lao Zi might have important things to say; I would surely never rise in the profession. But at the time (1965) I wasn't concerned, because my education had again returned to the streets in the escalating civil rights and antiwar struggles for peace and justice. In 1969 I had the great good fortune to spend two years studying with Noam Chomsky at MIT, and again, I learned much, doing linguistic theory from nine to five, and politics from six until midnight. The linguistics impressed me significantly, because the elegance of its abstract formalism (logician) was combined with equally abstract speculations about human nature (lotus-eater). The combination convinced me once and for all that analytic philosophy could only assist in the rephrasing of premises, and that much more was needed if conclusions were ever to be reached. The politics, despite some ups and downs, reaffirmed my faith in, and affection for, communal anarchists and the peoples and cultures of Black America and East Asia. And Chomsky was living proof that intelligence could serve conscience as well as abstract theory—in the best tradition of the Confucian sage.

Many other people, of course, also contributed to my education over the years—wife, children, friends, and students—most of whom taught me as much as they did because they had even less formal training in philosophy than myself. It takes many years of schooling in the discipline to stop asking questions like "What is it to be fully human?" or "How should I live my life?" But it was just those questions I had been asking for many years and had been regularly obliged by others to confront afresh. The opportunity of getting paid for pondering those questions, even though it required joining the ranks of an increasingly corrupt U.S. intelligentsia, was a temptation I could not resist. The alternative was to altogether forswear my heritage; and all of my teachers had contributed to my conviction that a fully human life could not be lived if I did that.

Thus my education, of sorts; which led to my becoming a philosopher, of sorts.

In Search of Self and Cultural Coherence

E. M. ADAMS
University of North Carolina,
Chapel Hill

I was born and reared in the Protestant Reformation and educated in the Enlightenment. Driven by these internalized cultural contradictions, I have struggled all my life toward an integrated cultural perspective and a unified worldview.

The culture of my home and church was Biblical, God-centered, authoritarian in approach, emphasizing the virtue of belief and the wickedness of doubt; the culture of my education from high school onward was largely liberal and scientific, both in method and content, emphasizing the freedom of the individual, the powers of the human mind, and the virtues of questioning and inquiry. I began to feel some pangs in high school, but before the end of my first year in college my intellectual cramps were severe. Like so many others, I had internalized the basic logical tensions of Western civilization in the modern era: the contradictions among Biblical religion, democratic liberalism, and modern science. These conflicts within the culture had become deeply disturbing personal problems for me.

My identity was first formed in terms of Biblical religion. By the time I was thirteen I had read the Bible through twice. I read it every day. It was the major literature of my childhood. In the fall of my first year in high school, each of us had to give a talk before the class on his or her chosen vocation. By this time, I was thoroughly committed to being a Baptist minister. The teacher was so impressed with my talk on why I was going to be a minister that she arranged for me to give it before the whole high school assembly. At the University of Richmond, I was a ministerial student; but, in my college years, I had to do some serious restructuring of my thought.

I was wrestling with philosophical problems before I discovered philosophy. How could I reconcile the authoritarian approach and the values of my religion with the freedom of thought and inquiry and the values of democratic liberalism? And how could I reconcile either of these humanistically-oriented approaches with the naturalistic view of knowledge and the world presupposed in modern science? In the spring of my freshman year, I discovered some philosophy books and read them hungrily. In the fall of my second year, I took a course in philosophy of religion, and went on to major in philosophy. Since my first year in college, there has probably not been a day without some philosophical problem weighing on my mind.

When I finished college, I knew that I had just begun to grasp the magnitude of the problems that bothered me. The further I went in my education, the stronger my commitments to democratic liberalism and scientific naturalism became. By the time I entered Harvard, the religious culture of my upbringing had been largely dislodged from my mind, at least at the intellectual level. My identity was then tied up with democratic liberalism, just as it had been with Biblical religion earlier. The troubling tensions of these years were between democratic liberalism and scientific naturalism. I felt the tensions primarily between humanistic ways of thinking about people and their behavior and the scientific view of knowledge and the world. My work at Harvard concentrated on epistemology, philosophy of science, and value theory and ethics. I had written a thesis on Russell's philosophy of mathematics, and a dissertation on scientific explanation. Metaphysically and epistemologically, I was a scientific naturalist, but in a phenomenalistic mode.

Accepting the modern scientific view that there are no ends or normative laws in nature, my dominant interest was in trying to work out a value theory and moral philosophy that would be supportive of democratic liberalism. I thought that only some form of ethical naturalism that interpreted value judgments in terms of scientifically confirmable factual statements would suffice, since either an emotivist or an existentialist theory of ethics, if true, would preclude the possibility of a reasoned moral consensus on issues of government.

In the early 1950s I undertook to write a comprehensive book on ethical naturalism in which I would try to develop a version of cognitive naturalism that would be able to withstand the attacks of its critics. But some of the arguments against the position proved insurmountable. Then on one February night in 1955, just when all seemed lost, I had the most dramatic and exciting experience of my philosophical career. I realized for the first time that most naturalistic theories of value language accepted a view of value experience much like the view phenomenalists had held about sensory experience. So I asked the same questions of value experiences that, when asked of sensory experiences, had opened the way for a realistic theory of physical-object language. I saw immediately the possibility of a similar realistic but nonnaturalistic theory of value language. My whole worldview was transformed in a flash. It was a genuine epiphany that opened up the possibility for the integration of the culture on the basis of a wider view of the knowledge-yielding powers of the human mind and a richer worldview than had been thought possible under the assumptions of modern naturalism. My major philosophical work for the past thirty-five years has been toward fleshing out and defending the world-transforming intellectual vision of that night.

I feel that I got pulled into the vortex of the deep intellectual and cultural contradictions of modern Western civilization at a very early age. It has been an exciting and challenging struggle. At times, it has seemed that nothing was grounded or secure, that everything solid would melt into thin air. In time I became convinced that there were groundings and directions, if we only knew how and where to search for them. For me, philosophy was the only way that offered help in the midst of the conflicting cultural claims and contradictions that no one in our civilization can avoid without closing one's mind. Philosophy is, indeed, our only disciplinary approach to these profound and vitally important problems in our culture.

On Becoming a Philosopher

ROBERT BAIRD
Baylor University

An amazing confluence of four experiences occurred during my sophomore year in college. Those experiences did not, of course, make me a philosopher, but they dramatically turned me in that direction. Thirty-three years later, I still marvel at the simultaneity of the events, events that, even at the time, I knew were changing my world.

The first experience followed a history class discussion of the Cold War between the Soviet Union and the United States. After the session, I approached the professor and made what seems to me now an incredibly naïve statement, even for a college sophomore. "The thing is," I recall saying, "the Russians know that the United States is *not* going to attack them. But we don't know that they will not attack us." My unstated assumption, of course, was that we were the "good guys" and they were the "bad," and furthermore, everyone knew it, even them.

My professor turned to the wall and pulled down a map of the world. "With this chalk," he said, "I am going to place an *x* everywhere the United States has missiles aimed at the heart of the USSR, and an *x* everywhere Russia has missiles aimed at us." When he finished, I stared at a map which had Russia virtually surrounded by U.S. missiles and a United States wholly unthreatened. What a moment of insight! The scales fell from my eyes. All of a sudden it seemed clear to me that if I had been a sophomore at the University of Moscow that morning, I would have been petrified of the United States, terrified that the country that had dropped *the* bomb on Japan might do something comparable to us.

Even during the experience, I knew that the lesson I was learning, the insight I was gaining, had to do with much more than the Cold War. For the first time in my life I was experiencing that we see things through "colored glasses," through assumptions and presuppositions received from our surroundings. But if our conclusions are colored and thus distorted by where we live and who we are, how can we ever be sure that we have the truth? The door to philosophy cracked open.

That semester I was also taking a basic course in communications. In the process of reading some old speeches, I came across an oration written by a 1936 Baylor University undergraduate student. It opened as follows:

On a sabbath morning in 1914 (the great conflict had just begun), they held a prayer service in Berlin. The Kaiser was there. The aisles were jammed. . . . A German minister mounted the stand and, reading from the Old Testament the account of the battle between Gideon and the Midianites (and how God favored. . . [Gideon]), drew across the centuries a 1914 parallel; and then they said . . . , "Our strength is our God." Then they prayed, "God of Germany, give the victory to Germany. God of righteousness, give the victory to right."

On that sabbath morn they held a prayer service in Paris. The war ministers were there. The aisles were packed. A French priest mounted the stand and, reading from the Old Testament the account of the battle between the Israelites and the Philistines (and how God favored the Israelites), drew across the centuries a 1914 parallel; and then they [said] . . . , "Our strength is our God." Then they prayed, "God of France, give the victory to France. God of righteousness, give the victory to right."

On that sabbath morning they held a prayer service in London. The King was there. The aisles were packed. An English bishop mounted the stand and, reading from the Old Testament the account of the battle between David and his enemies (and how God favored David), drew across the centuries a 1914 parallel. [And then they said, "Our strength is our God."] Then they [prayed], "God of our fathers, God of England, give England the victory. God of righteousness, give the victory to right." [PAUL GEREN, AN UNPUBLISHED ORATION.]

The Germans see God through German eyes. The French see Him through French eyes; the British through British eyes. And we, it seemed to me surely to follow, see Him through our own eyes—and all of us see through a glass darkly, through a glass well-smoked by environmental and hereditary factors that influence who we are. Where is truth in all of this? The door to philosophy opened further.

In a literature course I was taking that fall, we read "The Grand Inquisitor" passage from Fyodor Dostoevsky's The Brothers Karamazov. I encountered in that story the dramatic claim that Christ came bringing freedom with its accompanying uncertainty, ambiguity, and doubt. Furthermore, the passage seemed to suggest that we humans are so frightened of the anguish that goes with uncertainty, ambiguity, and doubt that we are eager to forego freedom for the sake of certainty and security.

My life to that point had been a quest for certainty, a quest for Truth (with a capital *T*). Was such a quest an attempt to avoid freedom and associated mental anguish? Perhaps assuming responsibility for one's choices inevitably involved uncertainty, ambiguity, and doubt. Perhaps truth was not a matter about which one could ever be absolutely certain. The door was more than half open.

Finally, and most importantly, I was taking my first philosophy course that semester. John Stuart Mill's essay *On Liberty* got inside my mind like no other text ever had. I still remember the power of one particular passage. "It never troubles him [the religious dogmatist]," observes Mill, "that mere accident has decided which of these numerous worlds is the object of his reliance, and that the same causes which make him a churchman in London would have made him a Buddhist or a Confucian in Peking." [LLA, pp. 22–23.] Disturbing though this thought initially was, Mill persuaded me to be honest enough to acknowledge that if I had been born in a Buddhist culture, the odds are I would see God through Buddhist eyes; and if I had been born in a Moslem country, the bet is that I would make pilgrimage to Mecca. The question of truth and our ability to grasp it had again been raised in a dramatic way. The door was now wide open.

Not only were these four experiences decisive in turning me to philosophy, they were formative for my later philosophical development. Philosophy has become for me not only an activity of critical reflection and examination, it has become an attitude toward life or, perhaps better said, toward the experiences of life. Whatever else human fallibility means, it means that we can never be certain about our truth claims and that to assert such certainty is to worship truth claims in an idolatrous way. Acknowledgment of human limitations and acceptance of uncertainty as an inevitable corollary of human finitude are for me two defining characteristics of the philosophical attitude.

On the other hand, acknowledging finitude, accepting uncertainty, and experiencing doubt need not preclude reasoned commitment to conclusions, ideas, principles, and values. In fact, reasoned commitment in the face of uncertainty is for me a third defining characteristic of the philosophical attitude.

Perhaps Bertrand Russell had something like this in mind when he maintained that "to teach how to live without certainty, and yet without being paralyzed by hesitation, is perhaps the chief thing that philosophy, in our age, can still do for those who study it." [A *History of Western Philosophy*, p. xiv.] This is fundamentally what philosophy has become for me since I first entered its door those thirty-three years ago.

From Strange Causes
to Strong Causes

"All at once there came to him another dream, in which he thought he heard a loud and piercing sound which he took for a peal of thunder. . . . And having opened his eyes, he perceived a multitude of sparks of fire about the room."

(FROM RENÉ DESCARTES DREAM ON NOVEMBER 10, 1619, IN WHICH HE CLAIMED THE DISCOVERY OF THE UNITY OF ALL THE SCIENCES; BAILLET 1, 82.)

First Philosophy

CHARLES HARVEY
The University of Central Arkansas

I can't isolate the cause or causes that pushed me to philosophy. However deeply I probe into my past, whatever event I dredge up seems already to be an effect of a philosophical bent. So the account I give here is an account of the first and strongest experience that I now associate with my life in philosophy.

One day in second grade, I was walking to school with a group of classmates. We were about to cross over a causeway built above a swampy woods. Suddenly in the middle of the normal hullabaloo that consisted of shucking and shrieking and jiving and jabbing, I was struck silent by the realization that I was I. I wasn't seamlessly melded to my friends, I wasn't even capable of experiencing what they experienced. "I am I" I kept repeating to myself, like a fool struck dumb by a fact that was universally obvious. I remember looking at my circle of acquaintances (they had suddenly devolved from friends to acquaintances, from things with *whom* I had internal connections to things *that* I experienced on the outside alone), unable to shake the knowledge that I was not them, they were not me, and that I was *stuck in myself*; that I *was*, somehow, myself; that I was nobody else, that I never could be, and that suddenly there was a gulf that could not be crossed between me and those others.

"I am I," "I am I," "I am I," the silent voice kept repeating. I lingered behind my advancing acquaintances, falling further and further behind. I didn't experience this disconnectedness in moral or evaluative terms at all. It was simply a shockingly clear realization of what I would now call a problem in epistemology or metaphysics—the problem of the self, the problem of personal identity. No matter how much I shucked, shrieked, jived, or jabbed, I knew with a knowledge deeper than words that I couldn't get through the barrier that had suddenly appeared before me. Yet it was a barrier composed of "nothing" (as another voice would later inform me). I was in a sack, a sack of selfhood, and I knew right then, with a clarity I never wished for, that there were no borders I could cross to escape it.

I walked off of the causeway into the woods. "Where are you going, Harvey?!" "You're going to get your ass beat from Mr. ———— when he hears about this!" "Come on! We're just about late already!" "Your ass is grass Harvey! The student patrol saw you!"

All of these words were mere sounds. They were suddenly as strange and insignificant as was the school, the principal, the rules, or my friends. I went into the woods. I found a log at one of my favorite spots in the swamp. And I sat. And sat. And sat. "I am I," I kept thinking, "I am I." The repetition, I guess, and Mother Time, diminished the effect. I couldn't forget it, of course, but it no longer paralyzed me. The *Augenblick*, Goethe or Heidegger would say, had passed.

I walked home. Mother was waiting. Her verbal (and only mildly physical) assault was unpleasant. My attempts at explanation generated more suspicion and anger than anything else. "Are you smoking?!" "Who did you meet there?!" "What are you up to?!" "Are you seeing———— again?!" "Your sister never did this!" "How will you amount to anything?!" "Skipping School!" "The police are out looking for you!" "Your principal called!" "What am I supposed to tell them?!" "Your father left work and is looking for you now!" "Where did you go?!!"

I don't recall what immediately followed. I have no memories of the principal, teachers, police, or friends. But I do recall what is perhaps the fondest memory I have of my father. The next weekend (I guess, since weekends were the only time he wasn't working, and were always the time of the ritual here described), we were on our way downtown. I remember sitting, minuscule, in the passenger's side of the great De Soto he then owned. He would make his weekly perusal of the book and magazine shop, while I looked at the newest items of childhood interest in the five-and-dime store attached. This day he asked me as we drove along (me, bouncing with each bump, unconsciously proud to be riding alone, riding "shotgun," going downtown with Dad): "What happened that day when you didn't show up at school?" "What was going on?" "What were you up to?"

I'm not sure just what words I used, but they were something like these: "Did you ever think of yourself as being *only* yourself?" "Did you ever think that 'I am I'?," I asked. "Nobody else, but just yourself?" "I just started thinking about that," I said, "and I couldn't do anything." "I just went into the woods and kept thinking about it."

He looked over at me, expressionless. Dug deep into what always seemed his bottomless pockets. Pulled out a fifty-cent piece (a rare and special prize for both its physique and for its purchasing power). He flipped it to me and said: "Buy some men." "Men" were my favorite objects of occupation—

those tiny human replicas that could consume days and weeks while I ar-ranged and rearranged them into multiple and sundry worlds.

I still wonder if he was rewarding me for discovering that I was I, and for acting on it. Or if he was attempting a preemptive strike against some bizarre aberration of the childhood mind that only good honest play could obliterate.

Synergism of Text and Vision

GRAHAM PARKES
University of Hawaii

They would meet every other Thursday evening in the Prefects' Room, a small eyrie-like chamber in a building across the street from the main part of the school. (Glasgow Academy was one of several private schools in Scotland whose pretensions to being what in England is called a "public school" consisted in an emphasis on rugby and cricket and service in the Combined Cadet-Corps—a kind of ROTC—as ways of strengthening the physical and moral fiber of its pupils.) Regulations concerning uniforms prescribed grey flannel trousers, but the members of this group were distinguished by their sporting black—one of their number having astutely forestalled the suppression of this trend by arguing that the proper sartorial term for this apparently nonconforming color was "charcoal grey." The school tie, diagonally striped, was worn narrow with the edges more or less parallel: if one's mother refused to perform the necessary alteration, and the more conservative did, then a friend's more liberal parent might oblige with the sewing. The closer the shape of the shoes' toes to that of a chisel, the greater the approval they would command from the group. As if to assert their difference from the conforming majority, these rebellious young aspirants went by the defiantly secular name of "The Humanists." Their primary activity was the fortnightly discussion of an agreed-upon text of heavy intellectual weight.

The invitation at the age of fourteen to join this select group, this elite corps in the vanguard of the struggle against the philistines, was for the young Parkes an unexpected joy and honor that more than compensated for humiliations suffered in connection with rugby teams and cricket elevens. The first month's text was to be *The Rebel* by Albert Camus. It was not the first time Parkes had found a book hard to understand—but before it had been because it was written in some foreign language. (Shakespeare could present problems, of course, but then, that was poetry.) But here was a book in English of which it seemed impossible to make any sense whatsoever. What *were* these things—nihilism, dandyism, deicides? Who were all these people with such unpronounceable Russian names? It was a rude shock to find oneself so helplessly at sea in an expanse of English prose. In retrospect, however, it was an important initiation into the experience of finding a text at first incomprehensible, that would on rereading turn out to contain worthwhile ideas.

The next month, however, brought a revelation of a very different tenor. The author of the assigned text was one Friedrich Nietzsche, and its title *Thus Spoke Zarathustra*. This text—while still obscure—was clearly something important. The style was overwhelming, though it was hard to say in what its power consisted. The book somehow intimated a life that was freer and more vital than the callow reader had imagined life could be. Again, the important thing may have been an engagement with a book that demanded repeated reading, accompanied by the sense that there were layers of meaning here that would take a long time to fathom. (The paperback Parkes used at the time has since been lost, but a perusal of it fifteen years ago, before it went missing, showed it to contain a good many inapposite inscriptions. Many of the zealously underlined passages were of minor import and a good number of the marginalia quite embarrassing in their naïveté. The markings in more recent editions of the text in his possession suggest, as one might expect, a somewhat deeper understanding of this seminal work.)

However poor Parkes's understanding of the text may have been, the reading stimulated inquiries into the vocation of philosophy, the results of which somehow led him to believe that philosophers "got paid to sit around and think all day." And if *Thus Spoke Zarathustra* was, as the blurb on the back cover assured the reader, a consummate work of philosophy, then a career oriented toward that discipline might be worth investigating—especially if there was indeed a chance that one could make a living at it. (The discovery that it actually cost Nietzsche money to publish his books after *Zarathustra* did not come until much later.)

None of the subsequent books discussed with the Humanists had anything like the same impact, though the continuing experience was valuable for a number of reasons. There was a sense that something subversive was going on, something that ran obliquely across—if not counter to—the direction in which the "old school spirit" so solemnly proceeded. It no longer mattered when one was humiliated by the members of the elite rugby teams (since rugby was compulsory, such humiliation was more or less unavoidable— short of acquiring the physique of a bear and the disposition of a bull). And the air of conspiracy that surrounded the evening discussions, suffused with cigarette smoke and the smell of strong, black coffee, provided an excitingly decadent alternative to the sweaty camaraderie of the locker rooms. Zarathustra's dictum that "thoughts that come on doves' feet guide the world" began to seem gradually more plausible.

Although school reports had for some time praised his "initiative," Parkes's *modus vivendi* had in fact been to follow dutifully the paths prescribed to him by others, by parents and similar figures of authority. Since he had shown some aptitude for the study of languages, it was decided by his mentors that he would join the select few who were to be prepared for the scholarship examinations for Oxford. And since he did better at modern languages than at Latin and Greek, he was instructed to study classical French and German literature. Protests to the effect that he ultimately wanted to study philosophy were simply ignored. If French and German literature were what he was being trained in, then those were the subjects to pursue at the university. Besides, there were "connections" with a modern languages don at a certain College.

The training proceeded remorselessly, batches of examinations were taken, and finally there came a call for an interview at the College in question. Direct communication with the appropriate officials—the first spark of genuine initiative on Parkes's part—resulted in the addition of a member from the philosophy faculty to the interviewing committee. So while most of the discussion centered on motives of Racinian heroines and fatal flaws in Schillerian protagonists, the last part of the interrogation was left to the philosopher.

PHILOSOPHER: Now tell me, Mr. Parkes, just what is it about philosophy that makes you so eager to study it?

PARKES: Well, I'm not really sure. It, uhm . . . well, I suppose it seems to address the basic problems . . . I mean, the fundamental issues of existence.

PHILOSOPHER: (*with raised eyebrow*): Does it really seem to do that? And what, may I ask, might these "fundamental issues" be?

PARKES: (*flustered*): Ohh . . . uhm, things like . . . the meaning of it all—I mean, whether there *is* any meaning to it . . .

PHILOSOPHER: I see. I'm afraid, Mr. Parkes, it's rather unlikely you'd find many people dealing with *those* sorts of issues here. But thank you so much for coming to talk to us

Joyful surprise at the news that the scholarship had been won was tempered by the discovery that it was impossible to do a degree in philosophy *simpliciter* at Oxford: It had to be combined with the study of such disciplines as politics and economics, or physiology and psychology. The wooing of wisdom would apparently have to be undertaken in concert with more mundane pursuits. The first term yielded the discovery that the pain of studying politics and economics more than outweighed any pleasure to be gained from initiation into the mysteries of philosophical logic and the predicate calculus. A subsequent switch of subjects meant catching up on what had been missed concerning the neurophysiology of cats contemplating light bulbs and the psychology of rats running mazes.

It was something of a surprise for the youth from north of the Border to discover that sherry and port were supplemented in some undergraduate circles by hashish and hallucinogens, and Bach and Mozart by the Doors and Captain Beefheart and His Magic Band. Nor were Parkes's initial tutors in philosophy quite as he had expected. The first was a brash Canadian, whose style—modern, verging on hip—aroused the freshman's curiosity about the other inhabitants of North America. The second was a brilliant young Englishman, whose style provided reassurance that the British could be cosmopolitan when they chose. Arriving for the first tutorial with this latter mentor, Parkes found him cleaning out his pipe to the accompaniment of an up-tempo number by Cannonball Adderly. The mental acuity of these men not so much older than oneself was inspiring, and their personal style suggested that Oxford philosophy might be less stuffy than one had been led to believe.

The following year brought the tutelage of two senior dons. Parkes attended the tutorials of the first together with another undergraduate, with whom he would take turns in reading the essay on the week's reading assignment. This tutor would occasionally disconcert by wandering off into an adjacent room during the reading of the essay. Any pause in the recitation, prompted by the suspicion that the audience had defected, would elicit the exclamation from afar: "Do go on!"—which one then felt obliged to do at considerably higher volume. On one occasion the exhortation to continue seemed to waft in from a still farther room, accompanied by the gentle lapping sounds of bath water. The intermittent withdrawal of the listener actually had a salutary effect on one's writing: The knowledge that his reflections on certain aspects of ethical theory might have to be loudly declaimed encouraged the writer to pay special attention to how well the prose sounded.

The second senior tutor was the epitome of urbane intelligence and wit. Tutorials alone with this tweed-suited thinker in his wood-panelled, book-filled study, through whose leaded windows one looked out on a tree in the quadrangle (perfect for discussions of Berkeley's idealism), seemed consummate paradigms of the institution—except for the don's unnerving habit of perusing the day's correspondence during the recitation of one's essay. This practice, too, turned out to be pedagogically effective, insofar as it encouraged the student to try to make his side of the dialogue so forceful as to impede the superior interlocutor's reading of his letters (a feat that Parkes never managed to accomplish, much to his chagrin).

It was inspiring to be in the presence of figures who were devoting themselves with style and success to the life of the mind, and Parkes was thereby encouraged to follow through on his decision to pursue the study of philosophy. However, in spite of the benefits resulting from the sharpening of his analytical skills, there was a growing feeling underneath it all of, "So what?"

Then one day a series of events occurred that were to bring about a major change in perspective.

It began with a most unusual experience at breakfast in the College Hall, a cavernous place from whose high walls lugubrious portraits of past provosts and other dignitaries stared down with disapproval on the affectations (this was the late 1960s) of the newest generation of undergraduates. As the somnolent Parkes gazed upon the familiar scene—disheveled students struggling to prime themselves with mediocre coffee and less-than-appetizing food—it began to become strangely *un*familiar. The condescension on the faces of the portraits appeared transformed into compassion for the vain strivings of the youths below. It became painfully clear that there was ultimately no point to any of the exertions of student life, nor any ground to its anxieties. The refrain "Vanity of vanities! All is vanity!" blared forth from the venerable surroundings with a vengeance.

If Sartre's Roquentin was assailed by nausea at the sight of the roots of a tree, imagine what depths of existential despair were engendered by the spectacle of a grease-coated strip of bacon's being pursued around the plate by the unshaven, long-haired undergraduate sitting opposite. The desolate morsel evoked a painting by Francis Bacon that Parkes had seen the previous week in London. And from a sudden fear that, on finishing chewing, the desultory eater might look up and open his mouth in the silent scream of a caged pope—the anguished observer fled the hall.

More and more it seemed like a matter of downright poor acting. At first Parkes had thought that his fellow students were simply not putting their hearts into their roles, thanks perhaps to the oppressive presence of the audience of painted provosts. Remembering that the role-playing Sartre saw through so easily had been on the part of a waiter in a café, he thought that a move away from the institution of eating might yield some more convincing performances of the drama of life. But outside on the High Street things were just as bad. The conversations of the gowned undergraduates as they walked to lectures appeared as unnatural as those of extras in low-budget films. The ministrations of a young mother to a baby in a perambulator seemed so forced that the concerned student feared for the child's survival. However nauseating the tree roots may have appeared, at least neither Sartre nor his character suspected them of bad acting. The only option left open, it seemed, was to escape the trappings of culture and seek solace in the bosom of nature.

Walking in the direction of the meandering river, the dazed fugitive paused for a while in the open of The Meadows to contemplate the further turnings of the world. There were some other people in the vicinity, but now, instead of poorly playing their parts, they seemed perfectly poised in the greater ensemble of things. After a while the realization dawned as to why this apparently novel ordering of the world was after all somehow familiar: It was the world as painted by Seurat. The landscape was only superficially similar to La Grande Jatte, and people's clothing quite different from *fin-de-siècle* Parisian attire, but the mood and disposition were the same. The fleeting moment became fixed, as if eternal, and the everyday scene suffused by a deeply hieratic atmosphere.

Or was it the world as imagined by Virginia Woolf? All the interrelations were just right: the distance of the seated couple from the bending tree, the orientation of the man lying on the blanket, and the triangle formed by the children searching for something lost in the grass. The dynamism of the scene—soccer players running, a cyclist coasting by, a pair of dogs bounding—seemed only to intensify the stillness of it all. *"Still! Didn't the world just now become perfected?"* As Zarathustra's words floated up from the depths, all that talk about dropping off into the well of eternity and the abyss of midday became suddenly comprehensible. This was it—whatever that was.

As the bemused viewer looked back at the city, it appeared as if rendered by Cézanne, with every bulk of every building and every angle of every roof contributing to an overall synergism. Moving on under a sky worthy of Van Gogh, it was with only mild surprise that the wanderer began to hear—the source unclear—an internal monologue *à la* Samuel Beckett. On and on, still going on. If these painters and writers weren't philosophers, they had at least traced some things in which philosophers would do well to be interested. After negotiating a path through to the Cherwell, contemplation of the reflections of the sky in its flowing mirror served to shift the scene to another dimension.

Little by little things began to slip away, while at the same time the spectator seemed to be sliding back away from it all. A chasm opened up that was at the same time an impenetrable membrane: the temptation to reach out was checked by the terrifying prospect that the whole show might shatter at the first fingernail's tap. There would be nothing left but shards with nothing to reflect. But somehow, strange to relate, distance turned out to be immersion, and reflection the pulsation of life itself. Zarathustra again: "Night is also a sun. . . . The world is deep, deeper than the day had thought."

Perhaps it is always these ways—the thought reverberated—and we simply don't realize it. What *is* going on, anyway?—*that* became the question!

The inquiry became charged with an urgency pervaded by a strange calm. There was hardly any time—it was all over any moment now. If understanding was to be sought through philosophy, it had better be through philosophy in concert with the arts and literature. That much had become clear. The moment had passed, but the memory persisted and continued to provoke wonder.

Subsequent research unearthed some enlightening passages in Plato, allusive accounts in texts from Asia, and gnomic utterances in Heidegger. But how to proceed? This would take time. A friend who had been there suggested the possibility of graduate study in America—a salutary change of perspective, perhaps. By all accounts a great deal was going on in the United States in 1968. It would be better to go sooner rather than later—while the place was still in one piece. But doubts arose as to whether the study of philosophy in an academic setting would assuage the desire to understand. Was there not a need to convey that enigmatic *vision* first, before inquiry through the medium of language could be fruitful?

A summer job with the B.B.C. sparked the ambition to make films that would do for painters what Ken Russell's earliest works had done for composers. That way the enigma could begin to be addressed. But there seemed no way for a novice to gain financial support for film school, and so, with an eye cocked toward the western horizon, Parkes hopefully sent out applications for graduate study in philosophy. Several possibilities opened up in response, and on the basis of very little of the relevant information (the friend had given a glowing account of the cultural life of the San Francisco Bay Area) Parkes opted for Berkeley, California. The next summer, buoyed up by the prospect of returning—via film school, somehow—to Britain and making films that would change people's understanding of the world, the might-be philosopher launched himself out across the Atlantic, bound for the far side of the unfamiliar continent beyond the ocean.

Once there, the projected return was forestalled by the unexpected discovery, while acting as a graduate assistant, that the attempt to teach philosophy could be a seductively fulfilling occupation after all. The joy that comes from seeing the occasional inquiring soul fired by a passion for understanding appeared to be infectious, and capable of inspiring other souls to open up in sympathy. Decidedly out of place in a department with a predominantly analytic orientation, Parkes was delighted to discover, after a while, the joys of philosophical conversation among several fellow graduate students. At least some of the vision was shared after all, and that seemed to allow a confluence of streams of inquiry and a pooling of philosophical reflections capable of nourishing the life of the intellect. That kind of conversation with peers, ongoing in the fertile cultural medium of the Bay Area at the time, cultivated in the now resident alien a love of the spirit of inquiry that was to endure.

In retrospect, all three factors appear to have been necessary for this philosophic initiation, each in its place: The encounter with *Zarathustra* in Glasgow and the vision of the world transfigured at Oxford together sparked the desire to understand more—which might not have endured, had it not been fueled by the joys of conversation discovered in Berkeley. At the same time the whole thing was a matter of chance, with which I had very little to do. What prompted the Humanists to suspend protocol and issue an invitation to the unfledged fourth-former? It was surely through no conscious resolve on his part that the young Parkes landed a place at Oxford. And if the move to the New World was a result of the first real decision he ever made, then the choice of Berkeley was quite fortuitous.

One thing cannot be left to chance, however: should a film be made, after all, the protagonist will wear chisel-toed shoes.

Faute De Mieux

LEON ROSENSTEIN
San Diego State University

It was a case not so much of reason being a slave of the passions as its being a willing accomplice that transformed my well-intentioned studies for a career as a nuclear physicist into those of a philosopher in the middle of my freshman year at Columbia in 1961.

Though I had read Camus my senior year at Weequahic High School and for some unknown reason was fond of Absurdist drama, it was surely the *facts* of my impending failing grade in Physics 101 together with my impending A in Richard Kuhn's "History of Aesthetics" course that "turned me." As "counsels of prudence," grades are great stimuli to action for eighteen-year olds. On the other hand, I don't really recall why I took the philosophy course in the first place—it was upper division, filled with awe-inspiring graduate students, and in no way "required" for my course of studies. It may have been pretention as much as anything, I suppose; for I was very pretentious in those days—my trench coat, flowing white oversized silk scarf, and hideous-tasting black-gold Russian "Sobranie" cigarettes. Had I known J. K. Huysman's À *Rebours*, I would have found in its hero, with his arch contempt for the ordinary, a kindred soul. Since the very title "Aesthetics" sounded sufficiently effete and arcane, it no doubt enticed me. In any case, I did well there and not at all where I had intended. I well recall now my conscious justification for the change in major (for certainly the crassly pragmatic one of A versus F was not at all appropriate): As it was the primary function of education to enable one to understand "what it's all about," and as physics was not adequate to this task while philosophy pre-sumably was, I should offer my intellect to this higher, worthier god. (As for God himself, I had quite naturally converted to atheism by that time.) I proposed this justification to others in the spirit of a lie, but I did, in part, believe it myself.

There was the passionate element, too. Love and hate, thirst for life and experience, awe of death and fear of pain, and all the juices that ran with the passions attendant thereto. For in those days of my unrestrained Byronic and sybaritic self, there was so much unrequited and unrequitable love. *Weltschmertz* and world-weariness and occasional thoughts of suicide. And I was lonely, for I lived only "in-the-midst-of" the many people I had daily intercourse with; and all the world, all the courses and individuals and imaginable ways of being my future self often seemed so utterly detestable then. All, except philosophy. Somehow it alone seemed virginal and worthy of love as an end in itself—or, at least, it could find nothing there to despise. Not, of course, that philosophy soothed my savage breast or gave me a reason for living, but it was capable of distracting me from those violent passions and depressive states of ennui. And it enabled me to believe my quest for understanding my state of being was not chimerical—or, at least not a solitary delusion. In the end it may well have been this belief or faith in the universality of reason that led me finally to accept the community of human beings.

That was the origin of my becoming. It explains how I turned to philosophy—not really how I became a philosopher. It also suggests a further consequence for my life—how I became "civilized." Full *humanitas* did not arrive until many years later and far away from New York under the more genuine passion of *caritas*. I do not know what I would have become were it not for philosophy—surely, I wouldn't have become a nuclear physicist—but I shudder to imagine my plight.

Always the Philosopher

ROBERT SOLOMON

University of Texas at Austin

In the Fall of 1963, I was a medical student at the University of Michigan, Ann Arbor, bored to tears with the tedious memorization, disturbed by the hospital wards, and unmoved by the promise of a vast and well-deserved future income. Across campus, a young philosophy professor was making waves and a nationwide reputation (even a profile in *Esquire* magazine). Frithjof Bergmann's "Philosophy in Literature" course was something of a campus phenomenon. A young woman I knew suggested to me that I attend the class, which not so inconveniently conflicted with my gross anatomy lectures. I did not need persuasion, and I became a regular but silent auditor in the class.

I think it was already the end of November, and the world was in turmoil. John Kennedy, who had not long before appeared on the steps of the Michigan Union to announce the formation of the Peace Corps and for whom I had campaigned in college, had been murdered in some city I had hardly heard of in an Edna Ferber state known only for oil, nuts, and cowboys. Twelve thousand miles away United States Marine "advisors" were getting increasingly bogged down in an undeclared war whose seriousness I was just beginning to appreciate. And I was plodding through my chosen "career" in cardiology as if I were walking into a black hole. It was about that time in the semester, too, when Professor Bergmann was warming up to one of his favorites, a German exile and eccentric named "Nietzsche." I remember reading *On the Genealogy of Morals* in particular with the feeling that I was participating in some very special, very private, very personal liberation. This had none of the immediate consequences often promoted by Nietzsche's detractors. I attempted to break no moral or social taboos and desecrated no churches. Neither my dating behavior nor my attitude toward the law significantly altered (except, of course, in conformity with those widespread shifts due to "the pill," and in reaction to the ambiguous role of the police in controlling anti-war activities, respectively.) What did change, and I think it was "once and for all," was my sense of enthusiasm about my own life. During a period of profound personal unhappiness, national confusion, and international intrigue, I nevertheless felt "clarified."

It was early December when the lectures on Nietzsche reached their climax in the idea of "eternal recurrence," the wild notion that everything that has happened, including the whole of one's own life, has happened innumerable times before and would happen indefinitely many times again. My gross anatomy class, meanwhile, had only just reached the navel (it was a full-year course). As a life-long science student, I found the physical hypothesis of recurrence nothing less than laughable, but the *moral* impact was an entirely different matter. Bergmann emphasized and dramatized the implications of the "terrible thought" so persuasively that my memory of that particular class is a brilliant blur, much like the memory of a most wonderful romantic evening or, I suppose, a true believer's memory of the moment of conversion. Bergmann was going on about the idea of repeating the days and hours and minutes of one's life, this very minute in particular, over and over again, quoting Nietzsche's demon, "would you not throw yourself down and gnash your teeth, and curse the demon that spoke so? Or have you once experienced a tremendous moment in which you would answer: 'You are a god and never did I hear anything so divine!' "

I thought about this moment itself, already so recursive and convoluted as I thought of myself thinking this thought about thinking this thought about thinking this thought forever, but I have never been all that fascinated by the self-referential paradoxes that fascinate so many of my colleagues. I did wonder, for just a moment, whether Nietzsche thought about the eternal repetition of his own aphorism. But what I mainly thought—or rather, what thought overwhelmed me—was that the scope and enthusiasm of this very moment was such that I would gladly have answered the demon "Yes! I'll take this recurrence!" I remembered, however, that not just this wonderful moment but all of my moments, including the histology lab at 7:30 this morning and the physiology lecture to follow, would be repeated a virtually infinite number of times. I spent the rest of the lecture dwelling on that awful hypothesis, and at 3:00 that afternoon I walked into the Dean's office in the medical school and resigned. (I never did find out what's below the navel.)

There is currently a scholarly dispute in Nietzsche circles, in which the very notion that Nietzsche intended to change lives has been thrown open to question. He is rather depicted as something of a proto-deconstructionist, an end-of-the-line metaphysician, an isolated writer who sought to create for himself a persona, an "author" who would be as noble, exciting, even dangerous, as the sickly, lonely writer was not. Bernd Magnus has rescinded his old defense of "Nietzsche's Existential Imperative" with eternal recurrence as its core, now insisting that eternal recurrence is an "impossible" thought; and Alexander Nehamas has argued with great flair that Nietzsche did not intend to give "moral advice" or tell us "how to live." These are two dear friends, but I must say that they are, in my own experience, just plain wrong. It is true that Nietzsche does not tell us to be kind to strangers or to join the military or to quit medical school, but he does something far more powerful and effective, as the best philosophers always do. He throws us back to ourselves (and into our times, too) and teaches us to "see" a whole new way, or many ways. His philosophy is not that delight in the logic of counterfactuals and self-referential paradoxes that draws us away from our lives; rather, it is that uncompromising reflection that is always personal and, if the word makes sense in this context, practical. It concerns hard decisions and one's place in history and the construction of a self one can be proud of. It is not just a game or—worse—a career. It is an invitation to live, and if the form of the invitation is often vacuous, its meaning is not. I understood that before I became a "scholar," when I walked into that Dean's office and, fifteen minutes later, marched over to the Dean of Arts and Science and announced my intention of becoming a philosopher. I hope that my half-hearted attempts to be scholarly never allow me to lose that awareness that, even when what I say is vacuous, I may well be changing lives, including my own.

Of course, no "existential" decision happens in a vacuum. I had always been a brooder, a talker. I loved to argue, to push the perverse sides of an argument, to imagine new worlds and convince my playmates that they were or could be "true." I could talk my way out of—or into—almost anything. (As a diminutive juvenile gang leader in elementary school I already earned my street name, "the mouth.") Now that I look back on the narrative of my life I can easily construct an almost linear path from birth to philosophy, expressed for many years through my fascination with science and only briefly side-tracked by a brief deviation through misplaced professionalism. (Of course, in medical school I had an equally plausible narrative about having always wanted to be a doctor.) In high school I had had a similarly euphoric philosophical moment, during a lecture on Parmenides and Heraclitus given by an unusual and superb history teacher. I later had another such experience (this one aided by a now-controlled substance) in which I comprehended— "embraced" would be a better word—the previously incomprehensible thought of Hegel. My life, in this construction, has been punctuated with philosophy, coupled with the meta-thought that it all could have gone another way. The narrative may be imaginary, but it is not fictitious, and I now have a great deal of difficulty thinking of myself as anything other than "always the philosopher"—as one of my more sarcastic juvenile delinquent friends used to say. And, I can honestly say, I have never once regretted it.

Finding Philosophy

ALBERT BORGMANN
University of Montana

I was born and raised in Freiburg, in the shadows of a Gothic cathedral, the Black Forest, and the university where Husserl and Heidegger had been teaching. My parents were part of Freiburg's Catholic intelligentsia and acquainted with Bernhard Welte, Karl Rahner, and Max Müller—liberal Catholic thinkers who had come under the spell of Heidegger. Soon after the war, my mother pointed out Welte in a Corpus Christi Procession as the one who would make Heidegger's thought fruitful for theology. My father would reenact his life as the editor of the journal *Caritas* and as a Catholic activist at the family table. Philosophy, theology, and Heidegger's name were vague and venerable presences in my youth. If I showed philosophical inclinations, it was in German composition where I had a penchant for the analytic and the ponderous. With nine years of schooling in Latin and six in Greek, ancient philosophy, though we read little of it, was ever in the vicinity.

When I began to study at the University of Freiburg in 1957, I was enamored with the grandeur of philosophy but knew little of substance about it and was uncertain of my abilities and unfocused in my habits. When Heidegger put in an appearance at the University to give a lecture series in the *auditorium maximum*, I would attend the lecture preceding his to be sure of a seat. I felt Heidegger's claim strongly, but my awe was inarticulate.

Conditions in Freiburg were rich and favorable to the point of being oppressive. I lived in an affectionate and well-educated household in a town of liberal and venerable traditions; yet I felt more burdened than favored. In 1958, I left for the University of Texas, where conditions were bracing and invigorating to the point of being exhilarating. I loved the clear and fair demands of American academic life and fell in love with the popular culture of the United States in the last years of its arrogant innocence. To see more of it, I went to the University of Illinois, and after two years finished with an M.A. in German literature. And there I fell in love with Nancy.

As my habits became more disciplined and my ambition more vigorous, my desire for the free and imperious ways of philosophy grew stronger, too. Youthful arrogance made me impatient of service to literature. I wanted to speak in my own right on whatever I thought was important. In 1961 I followed Max Müller to the University of Munich where Wolfgang Stegmüller was teaching as well; thus, I became the student of a student of Heidegger and the student of a student of Carnap. In one year of monastic devotion and another of Nancy's companionship and help, I acquired the rudiments of philosophy and wrote a dissertation under Müller. However, he had students of longer standing and more evident talents and did not want to take me on as an assistant, thus barring me from a university career in Germany.

Nancy and I got married in 1963. We were unwilling to try and change Müller's mind or try another apprenticeship with uncertain and distant prospects elsewhere in Germany. I taught high school for a year in Freiburg and applied blindly and ubiquitously for a philosophy position in the United States. Only the German department at the University of Illinois would have me, and that is where we went.

I was sorely tempted by the generosity of my colleagues and former teachers and the superb working conditions in Urbana to stay with German literature. I could not let go of the freedom and adventure of philosophy, however, and once more we flooded the realm of American philosophy with applications. To hear of a student of Max Müller must have been disorienting at best and likely unhelpful if it was clear that Müller was a Catholic follower of Heidegger. When I gave a lecture to the Philosophy Club at the University of Illinois in 1965, I was told politely that Heidegger's thought was nonsense and told bluntly that it was fascist. I keenly felt my inability to answer my well-trained analytic critics. Had I drawn on my teacher's Catholic sensibilities and vocables to defend my position, everything would have been worse and I would have been swiftly told to seek employment in one of the unfortunate Catholic philosophy departments that were moving from the barren ghetto of Thomism to the swampy ghetto of existentialism.

Yet had it not been for one such department and its brave supportive chair, I would have abandoned my search for philosophy then and there. In the fall of 1965, I accepted a position at DePaul University and began to publish articles on language and on Heidegger, the kind of studious and clumsy pieces that gave a young person, struggling with a still foreign tongue and idiom, some room to gather his thoughts. In 1967, we moved to Hawaii where I had John Winnie as a colleague in philosophy. John's is the most powerful intelligence I have known first-hand, and it is well balanced by an engaging personality. He was a relentless and resourceful antagonist and forced me to reconsider and recast everything I had known in philosophy.

I began to feel at home in philosophy and at ease with its local idiom. Toward the end of our three years in Hawaii I wrote the first piece of any significance, "Technology and Reality." I thought I had found philosophy at last.

No one can escape the sweet charms of Hawaii, and yet we began to suffer from the unreal confinement of place and season on Oahu. We became distressed at seeing our three daughters grow up unacquainted with the brilliance and tumult of fall and the rigor and splendor of winter. We moved to Montana and were captivated, forever it seems, by the mountains and the seasons. I continued my critical analyses of technology and of standard professional problems, of mind and body, of freedom and determinism. Things went along well enough, but I was working without final orientation and in relative seclusion. Henry Bugbee helped me find the former, and Carl Mitcham helped me overcome the latter. In reply to my reading "Orientation in Technology" before colleagues from Missoula and Bozeman, Henry took me to task for analyzing and criticizing technology without letting on where I really stood. The author of *The Inward Morning* was well placed to reprimand me, and I began to work on locating in philosophy the focal things and practices that had been centering my life.

All of us at the University of Montana are too remote by many hundreds of miles to be casually invited for lectures or to conferences, and most of us are too insignificant to be invited as stellar speakers or participants. We center our professional lives here on campus. We are resourceful teachers and steadfast colleagues, and in philosophy we are cordial friends, too. At the same time the resonance of one's scholarly work is muffled by distance and muted by the narrow circle of listeners. I was beginning to doubt my work when Carl Mitcham invited me in 1975 to the founding conference of the Society for Philosophy and Technology. There, I was introduced to the far-flung group of colleagues whose interest helped me to expand and focus my thoughts on technology.

Also in the mid-1970s, I was introduced to liberal democratic theory and to Rawls in particular. The *Theory of Justice* made me rethink my position once more. It also made me grateful to be an American philosopher. To this day I am deeply moved by the generous and compassionate attitude of the book, by its masterful development of the material, and by the measured and even pace of its prose. Heidegger had shown me the problem that needed attention. Rawls set the standard for solving it.

I am not sure I was equal to the task when I wrote *Technology and the Character of Contemporary Life*, but after initial stiffness and apprehension I began to enjoy working out the argument and attesting to what really matters. I was grateful for the chance to say my piece and for having it published well. In retrospect, the book seems overly long and difficult to me. It had looked transparent if not simplistic upon completion. At any rate, it did bring up problems that had been bothering people and things that had sustained them. The common recognition of these things and problems has since been the occasion for many friendships.

The book that helped me find a voice, however, also opened up a troubling rift between the instruments of thought and what matters in thought, between the discipline of philosophy and the task of philosophy. The latter, I thought, was a matter of helping people become more conscious of the distractions of the culture of technology and more confident of the focal things and practices that can center one's life. I had engaged the arguments of the discipline to advance the task. The clanging and grinding of the disciplinary machinery was music to some colleagues, an ordeal to others, and incomprehensible noise to all non-philosophers. Where, then, is philosophy to be found, in the discipline, or in the task?

Per Iram ad Philosophiam*

THOMAS S. VERNON
University of Arkansas, Fayetteville

I suspect that philosophers commonly become such as a result of anger. People who should know better say outrageous things; this ignites the flame. One's sensibilities continue to be assaulted by wrong-headedness, and this keeps the flame going. I can see in retrospect that this was true in my case.

I graduated from the University of Chicago Divinity School in 1938 and was cast, dewey-eyed, into the world of closed-minded parishioners and ecclesiastical power-politics. How I stood this for twenty years I do not know. Perhaps it was because my illusions were so deep-seated. At any rate, I gradually became aware that a church was not, as I had fondly supposed, a body of people engaged in a shared quest for truth, as well as being a way-station for the afflicted. I began to see that a major function of churches was to *protect* people from the truth, and that ecclesiastical establishments were business organizations driven by the profit motive.

I was a Baptist minister (ordained with some difficulty) for four years before seeking what I supposed was a more hospitable milieu in the Congregational Christian denomination—which has since merged with the Evangelical Reformed to become the United Church of Christ. I shortly discovered that something called "neo-orthodoxy," a sort of Calvinist revival, was becoming the dominant ideology in the Congregational superstructure. That and the "ecumenical movement," which was also theologically regressive, opened my eyes. By 1950 liberal had become a dirty word in the denomination that I had joined because I thought it was liberal.

In an effort to grasp what was happening, I began to read such leading Protestant gurus as Reinhold Niebuhr and Paul Tillich. That was when my blood pressure began to rise. These guys were thinking up new and sophisticated ways of marketing the doctrine of Original Sin, and the idea that we

---

*An earlier version of this material, entitled "The Blossoming of a Philosopher," appeared in the March/April 1990 issue of *The Human Quest*.

all need a "crisis" conversion so we can turn the task of saving ourselves and our world over to God. Coming as it did when we were all having nightmares over the discovery of the atom bomb, this upsurge of Barthianism, neo-Calvinism, and evangelicalism struck me as both irresponsible and danger-ous, a loss of nerve as it were.

To cap the climax, a group of my parishioners succeeded in bringing myself and the liberal members of my flock before a denominational tribunal, charged with deviating from the doctrines and policies of Congregationalism. For example, our congregation had withdrawn from the local Council of Churches when that organization imposed trinitarian doctrinal requirements for membership. As the proceedings got under way, it became apparent that it was "yours truly" mainly being raked over the coals in what was actually a heresy trial. I was charged with propagating unitarian liberal ideas, as well as promoting the brotherhood of man and other hurtful notions associated with the "social gospel." And I had thought heresy trials were a thing of the past!

In the meantime I had come to realize that, in order to do battle with the likes of Niebuhr and Tillich, I would have to acquire a richer background in philosophy and the history of thought. I realized, in other words, that an honest search for truth could not be carried on within the confines of the religious establishment. I resigned as minister of the Congregational Church and started a Unitarian Fellowship. I also enrolled, in 1958, at the University of Michigan for graduate work in philosophy. I was fortunate enough to be granted a teaching fellowship, while my supportive wife worked as a librarian. We managed to keep the wolf from the door—barely. In addition to studying and teaching in Ann Arbor, I made the 100-mile trip to Bay City every Sunday for three years to minister to my Unitarian flock. A small stipend from this group of friends helped further to ease the financial strain.

My wife was earning a library science degree, also at Michigan, so we were both carrying the double load of work and study. She obtained her MLS degree and I an MA in philosophy during that three-year period. We used to say that we didn't know where we were going but were getting there by degrees. During my fourth year at Michigan I left my Bay City Unitarians to carry on by themselves so that I could concentrate more fully on my quest for a doctoral degree.

In 1962, having passed the doctoral "prelims" and begun work on a dissertation, it was time to look for a job. In those days, "ABDs" were employable. I was hired as an instructor at the University of Arkansas in Fayetteville. I managed to complete my dissertation and received my degree at Michigan in 1963 at the same ceremony in which our older daughter received her AB. Thus, at age forty-eight, I found myself launched on a new career as a teacher of philosophy. I remember saying to myself that I wanted to become a philosopher as well as a teacher of philosophy. Among other things, my four years of graduate work had helped discipline me in the habit of critical thinking. In the process, I had cast aside the last remnants of religious belief and become what we now call a secular humanist. The former Baptist minister had become a Humean skeptic. Some years later I was to learn, to my astonishment, that several members of the Michigan faculty—men who had enabled me to accomplish this drastic surgery—were themselves devout Christians. Thus, my escape from prison had been aided by men (I had no female instructors) who were still there.

My second career lasted a little over nineteen years; I retired in July of 1981, having gradually achieved full professor status. During that time, I became better acquainted with academic philosophy as well as with academia in general, and in the process had become somewhat disillusioned with both—my second experience of occupational disenchantment. Academic politics, I discovered, are of a calibre not much higher than that of church politics; university management (aka "administration") is controlled by chamber-of-commerce types for whom "the bottom line" is government contracts ("grants") and athletic revenues.

I came more and more to sense that academic philosophy was an ingrown discipline that fed on itself. Still, if I had to choose between the church and academia, I would take the latter as much the lesser of two evils. Though it is not encouraged in a university, one does have the opportunity to teach and to enjoy dealing with young minds. To the credit of the University of Arkansas, I always felt free to speak my own mind, though this might not have been so had I been a Marxist. The academic community is tolerant of atheists.

My conception of being a philosopher is being engaged in the search for truth—wherever one feels that honest inquiry is most needed. The requirements of academic publishing do not allow much scope for this freewheeling approach. Consequently, it was not until after I retired that I could begin to blossom as a writer. In the ten years since my retirement I have published more (four books and over two dozen journal articles) than I did during my academic career.

While being introduced to academic philosophy at Michigan, I was impressed by someone's comment that the proper business of philosophy is to "resolve linguistic muddles." In time, I came to believe that there is more wisdom in this than I at first supposed. My training in philosophy, combined no doubt with my years of writing sermons, developed in me a fascination with language and its intimate involvement with the thought process. Insofar as I developed any "specialty" in philosophy, this was it. In the course of my sojourn in academia I have become convinced that philosophy, more than any other discipline—the English department not excepted—develops *linguistic sophistication* in its practitioners.

The rise in recent decades of anti-intellectualism in general and the upsurge of religious fundamentalism in particular has made me aware, nevertheless, that linguistic muddles are not the only muddles with which philosophers ought to be concerned. I have come to believe that one of the most pervasive and lingering effects of Christianity is its interference with clear thinking. It was anger and exasperation that nudged me into philosophy, and it is anger and exasperation that keep my pen busy now. My situation as an emeritus professor of philosophy has given me the opportunity to resume, in a sense, my original career as a preacher. I am now, so to speak, a minister without portfolio, and very happy.

Finding My Voice:
Reminiscence of an Outlaw

CLAUDIA CARD

University of Wisconsin, Madison

Becoming a philosopher can be a life-long process. My story is how, having chosen philosophy, I learned to speak with my own voice. It is not how I first chose philosophy—a tale, in my case, of adoration for teachers and texts. I have had to find and help maintain communities of women in order to continue growing philosophically.

This year (1990) I will be fifty. My story begins in my early thirties, when, while tenured at a large midwestern university, I developed a writing block. I had taught and written through reflection upon the written word, not otherwise out of my life experience. Specializing in criminal justice, I taught an undergraduate course called "Crime and Punishment," which seemed highly successful.

I had never been inside a prison. I had never witnessed an execution. I had never even attended a criminal trial. I was not aware of knowing people who had done such things. None of that worried me. I had learned to identify with the perspectives of lawmakers who may never have had such experiences, either. Personal and public events of the 1960s and early 1970s let me see that I did not yet have, or know, my own philosophical voice. I did not yet speak from my position in the wider universe of space and time, but at most from my position in the universe of books.

During that time two things sent young white middle-class Americans to prison, mostly men who might otherwise have arrived at my point in their careers with no more knowledge of prisons than I had. The two things were war resistance and marijuana. Soon, my "Crime and Punishment" was populated by students with first-hand experience of the criminal justice system, as I learned when several voluntarily presented their papers to the class. I had asked them to begin with the point of view of someone either accused of a crime or fearful of being victimized by a crime and search for a solution acceptable from both points of view. I sought wisdom through imaginary perspectives of ideal legislators who would take up both standpoints, since in reality, anyone might be accused or victims of crimes and be unable to insure against either.

The students' presentations were autobiographical, highly personal, and very moving. They were not typical philosophy textbook examples. One man had been sentenced to a drug rehabilitation center. Another was confined in a Navy brig for the crime of smoking grass. One was assigned guard duty at the Camp Pendleton prison. Others were arrested in war-related protest demonstrations. One was assigned alternative service as a Conscientious Objector. Encouraged, others spoke up who might otherwise have kept silent. A woman institutionalized at thirteen by her father for being out of his control was released *in her mid-thirties* thanks to the efforts of a woman worker in the institution. Another, found "not guilty by reason of insanity" of the murder of her husband, had done time in an institution for persons so declared. Most disturbing was a young man convicted of child abuse who had done time in both a regular penitentiary and an institution for the criminally insane, as required by the law of his state. Not claiming innocence and yet outraged at how he was judged and treated, he appeared little more than a child himself. The class, visibly disturbed, tried to engage him in thinking how to protect children from abuse.

The students tried, with amazing good will, to take up the perspectives of the assigned journal articles and textbooks. They tried to see crime and punishment through the eyes of designers of penal institutions and to make that vision fit with that of people liable to suffer from such institutions. In doing so, they struggled with a perspective that did not represent their own well. I was struck by the discrepancy between their attempts and the original assignment. The philosophical literature was inadequate for getting at the point of view of either potential accused or potential victim, much less reconciling them. Instead, it offered the visions of men writing from the safety of not having to think much about *either* potentiality, overseers involved in neither the workings of penal systems nor the activities calling their machinery into action. Who *was* most liable to being accused of crimes or victimized by them? Not (conventional, economically privileged, mostly over forty, white male) legislators, but, rather, the very young, the homeless, the poor, (in this part of the world) people of color, women attempting to protect themselves or children against battery and sexual abuse, women (rebels) who refused the "protection" of men.

Take myself, for example—a young lesbian (thereby, outlaw) from a rural village, catapulted by scholarships from the village high school to state university and then by fellowships to Ivy League graduate school. I was living in one of the highest crime areas of the city in which I taught, without a car, with no more than the simple hard-won financial security of a monthly paycheck, and with an abusive lover in a closeted relationship. I knew first-hand the fear of murder. How did my philosophizing connect with the realities of my life outside the classroom and the library? It was surely an escape. I began to suspect that it also served interests opposed to my own. How could I avoid abandoning or compromising my truths while making "satisfactory progress" as a philosopher? I had reached a point where I seemed unable to do either.

Simultaneously with the preceding events I experienced the first of two stages of feminist awareness. Both stages required intellectual interaction with women. I was in contact with no other faculty women; there was no Women's Studies. My first intellectual community of women was a Consciousness Raising (CR) group that met weekly for three years, mostly grad students in philosophy and computer science. The non-hierarchical structures, narrative style, and respect for emotion, characteristic of such groups, were things many of us later tried to bring to our classrooms: we experimented with "rotating chair" discussions, encouraged the use of *I*, took responsibility for exploring anger and fear.

The second stage of feminist awareness occurred when I connected with the Midwest Society of Women in Philosophy (SWIP), two years after the CR group ended. This connection precipitated my exit from the abusive relationship. I was able to "come out" professionally, thereby also becoming less vulnerable to intimate abuse. I became less blocked in my writing as I began integrating my life experience with my work. The CR group, SWIP, and, later, Women's Studies helped me heal and heard me into speech, enabling me to find my voice as a philosopher who is, not incidentally, a semi-rural white-anglo woman, a woman-lover, and a survivor.

I found my (physical) speaking voice, a symbolic happening, through my "coming out" paper. On a warm day in May 1978, wearing a double-axe (labrys, symbol of ancient Amazons) that swung as I leaned over the paper, I presented my overly long "Feminist Ethical Theory: A Lesbian Perspective" to an overflow crowd of philosophers, Women's Studies faculty, students, and community dykes in a Law School auditorium at the University of Minnesota. I announced, as usual, that those in the back who could not hear should wave a sheet of paper or speak up, and I would try to speak louder. To my surprise, I began speaking from deep inside, without effort, in a large voice that I had not known was there. People later said they heard me in the hallways, even outside the building through open doors and windows. There was anger fueling that voice. There was also confidence, despite anticipation of scorn ("what has that to do with *philosophy?*") from those I had been used to identifying as my audience. In fact, this audience, highly attentive, received and discussed my presentation with more warmth and respect than I had observed elsewhere in professional philosophy colloquia.

I am no longer occupied with the perspectives of ideal legislators, nor with punishment, or even crime. My attention has turned to the goods and evils of interpersonal relationships among those whose life situations are more like mine than like those of men apt to become legislators. My vision of philosophy has changed. I no longer linger over "eternal" or universal truths. I seek wisdom not in relation to the abstraction of a human life considered simply as such, but in relation to lives fleshed out as gendered as well as members of species, as having ethnic, economic, and religious backgrounds, even sexual orientations—things *not* universal—and in relation to communities of such beings and their environments. I still teach from books— I am writing one—but I also teach from my life, and my writing flows from that life (with an awareness of its finitude) as well as from my reading (which is endless).

The primary audience I usually address has also shifted. It is no longer men who are oriented toward men conventionally selected as representative of humanity—many of whose works I nonetheless continue to read with profit. It is (what feels in certain moods like) a "jury" of those more nearly my life-experience peers: mostly women, many of them lesbians, all with points of view shaped by surviving and resisting sexism, many shaped by surviving or resisting racism and other forms of oppression. They are my "jury" in that their evaluations help keep me honest and growing. They also enable me to write, to reflect philosophically upon the data of my life, my major relationships, my perceptions and doubts, joys, fears, loves, and hates. I worry less how to make "satisfactory progress" as a philosopher. And I work productively, without fear of running out of things to say.

Up from Poverty

JIM SHELTON
University of Central Arkansas

My journey to philosophy began as the son of a poverty-stricken sharecropper of the Great Depression and "Dust Bowl" days in Oklahoma. My father became an "Okie," trying to keep his family alive by moving from Oklahoma to Phoenix. It barely worked. He returned to Oklahoma to take up farming once more and worked for the WPA to provide necessities. My earliest recollections are of life on a rented farm on Beaver Mountain in southeastern Oklahoma. Fortunately, when I was ready to enter the third grade, we moved to the outskirts of Tulsa. This provided me an opportunity to attend the Tulsa Public Schools.

Poverty leaves its marks in many ways. The necessity of work, and the lack of a vision of possibilities other than just plain work, deprived me of many educational advantages of the leisure that wealth provides. In my case, poverty brought with it a particular brand of fundamentalist religion. But forces were at work on my intellect that would eventually undermine and destroy that religion, and with that my whole understanding of the world and my relation to it.

Several books that I read as a young boy stand out in my memory for their lasting influence. One was the autobiography of Booker T. Washington, *Up From Slavery*. This story of the struggle to achieve gave me a vision of what is possible for an educated person. There was never any question in my mind from then on that I would obtain a higher education. Another book was a biography of George Washington Carver, the Black scientist who did so much for Southern agriculture. His life taught me the value of scientific thinking and led me to develop a life-long interest in science. I soon began a serious study of geology and paleontology. I read every book on the subject in the Woodrow Wilson Junior High School. I collected rocks, minerals, and fossils with a passion. Unfortunately, my huge collection was destroyed in a fire during the summer before my ninth grade, but this early scientific interest has stayed with me throughout life. A third book was read during the summer at the end of my eighth grade. It was Charles Dickens' *David Copperfield*. This further reinforced my intellectual ambitions.

My experience in geological sciences and reading in biology led me directly to accept the theory of evolution. No one in my circle of acquaintances, especially no one at the church, believed anything but that evolution was the Devil's work. I felt completely alone with what appeared to me to be a well-substantiated and rational point of view. One effect of this intellectual isolation was that I became perhaps overly argumentative and concerned with supporting a viewpoint with evidence. Another effect was to force me to adopt an understanding of the Bible that was inconsistent with a fundamentalist point of view.

Religion temporarily won out in the struggle between God and Satan for the possession of my mind. I felt God's urgent call to service in the ministry and "surrendered" to that call in the summer before my tenth year in high school. I began to shift from a scientific interest to a dedicated study of the Bible. I believed the Bible to be the divinely inspired word of God himself, though I still allowed for a nonliteral reading, not having abandoned my evolutionary views. Throughout high school I studied the Bible avidly, reading and re-reading it several times. I loved that book with a deep, if blind, passion.

But doubts crept in. During a high school psychology course, for example, I read a biography of the Depression-era preacher, Father Divine, who claimed to be Jesus Christ reincarnated. It was unavoidable that I would think about the possibility that the followers of Jesus were just as confused as were the followers of Father Divine. If contemporary people could believe that a mere man was divine, it would be easy to understand how ancient and ignorant people could accept the same mistaken notion about some wandering prophet. Such doubts, however, were largely suppressed. Upon my graduation from high school, I entered Oklahoma Baptist University to study for the ministry.

The doubts that I had experienced continued to penetrate occasionally into my consciousness during that first year in college. Still, there was no significant challenge emanating from the courses that I studied. However, by the end of the succeeding summer, those doubts had become so predominant that I had to deal with them in a direct fashion. I stayed out of school the following year, worked and spent all my spare time simply thinking about what I must believe. One after another, the doctrines that had been so much a part of my outlook began to drop away under this critical scrutiny.

Even though I did not read the Bible with a strict "literal" reading, the basic doctrinal content was not doubted. Up to this time I had not read anything that was attacking these doctrines. So my objections to them arose largely from within their context, from the grounds of consistency. A powerful book that I did read, I think while still in high school, was James Sheldon's *In His Steps*. This was an appeal for Christians to put their ethical beliefs into actual practice. It deepened my study of the ethical teachings of Jesus. This commitment eventually undermined the doctrine of Hell. The problem of evil thus came to be of great significance, though I knew nothing of the debates that had been waged and the philosophical literature that had been written about that problem. One after another, what I can now identify as types of standard moves in respect to the problem were examined and dismissed. I desperately sought some rational way to harmonize a good and compassionate God with the existence of suffering. Even the free will defense had to go. It matters not whose fault the suffering is; a compassionate person wants to ease the suffering even of his or her enemies. The ethical teachings of Jesus, as claimed in the Bible, legislated against a God who could endure the suffering even of the guilty, much less the innocent. On looking back at this, I realize that the logic is not impeccable. There may be some good reason for God's behavior. There *must* be if God is to be exonerated of what otherwise looks like unconscionable behavior. But the inability to even imagine such a reason legislated against there being one.

Hell is actually very central to any doctrinal Christianity. But Hell, as I later discovered even John Hick believed, presents the problem of evil in an especially troublesome way. I found myself incapable of believing in Hell. But that brought up the whole conception of Jesus as vicarious sacrifice. All the major doctrines of Christianity, the Christology, becomes doubtful once Hell is abandoned. All the special divine attributes of Jesus come under fire.

The historical accuracy of the Bible came to be questioned, simply from my reflection on the liability of people to make errors, to exaggerate, to select, and do other things to texts. Growing up in Tulsa, I was well-aware of evangelists, such as Oral Roberts, who were widely suspected of being charlatans. It did not take a great intellect to compare accounts of their claims to miracles with those of the Bible. When still in high school, I remembered attending a rally organized by the evangelist, Billy James Hargis, aimed at burning copies of the newly-published New Revised Standard version of the Bible. This struck me even then as representing a rather slavish fidelity to the King James version, and to a literal reading of the text. These reflections had the effect of undermining authoritarianism with respect to the Bible. And, therefore, by destroying the evidential base for many theological doctrines, they undermined those doctrines.

In September 1955, after an intense year of reading the Bible and thinking, I registered for classes at the University of Tulsa. As I chose a major, I remember reflecting that what I wanted was to learn and to think, to rebuild some kind of understanding of myself and the world. Philosophy promised that sort of possibility. So I enrolled in philosophy.

I remember with great clarity that day, when I returned home, pitched my newly purchased books onto my bed, and almost exclaiming aloud: If I can say this to no one else, I must say it to myself, I do not believe in God. Immediately, a great peace and joy flooded throughout my system as the years-long conflict that had taken its emotional toll was suddenly resolved.

For me, philosophy is a passionate pursuit of understanding the world and self. In this way, I view philosophy much more akin to science than to art or literature. Literature presents important understandings, of course, but the activity of literature does not have understanding as its primary or even essential goal. Philosophy is not properly seen as one of "the humanities." Yet it is "humanizing," for the attempt to comprehend reality is one unique activity, one unique hope, one unique pleasure of human beings. What is "humanities" about "the humanities" is nothing less than philosophy. Art is a humanities subject only to the degree that it promotes philosophy. The same goes for history and literature and other subjects. But science, too, is a humanities subject in so far as it promotes philosophical reflection.

My study of philosophy did not particularly reflect an occupational goal. When I graduated from the University of Tulsa, I asked myself, now what? It was only then that I thought to continue my study of philosophy. But the pressures of the need for work and, soon, marriage forced me to think about making a living. I tried the business world but was not content, finding it all rather boring. Soon I decided I would prefer to teach school. I returned to college to study more history and education. Subsequently, I taught public school for eight years at a school in Arkansas. In the first week of teaching, I was called before the school board for teaching evolution. I hoped I would be dismissed so that I could sue and test the Arkansas statute against the teaching of evolution, but a sufficient number of school board members proved to be quite reasonable. I was called up again the second semester, following the election of some new members. This time I was grilled about evolution and the accusation that I was a communist. I had given a lecture to a senior class defending the notion that the United States and the Soviet Union shared enough common interests that it was mutually beneficial to live in peace with one another. The board quickly concluded that I was not perverting their youth. Unfortunately, I perverted only too few.

During this time, I worked on a master's degree in history, completing all but a thesis toward that degree. But one year, I was able to get some time off from my teaching duties and began to study Wittgenstein, Russell, Moore, and Schlick. I wrote a short book on the four, *Wittgenstein and Three*, which I never completed enough to publish. It explored Wittgenstein's philosophy in relation to the three formative stages of his life represented by his relations with Russell, Schlick, and Moore, in that order. The significance of this work is that it brought me back to philosophy. I determined that I would go back to school to work on a doctorate in philosophy. That I did and after three years I began teaching at the University of Central Arkansas.

I Couldn't Help It

PATRICIA SMITH
University of Kentucky

For me the love of ideas was a habit of mind that I acquired at an early age. I was probably doomed to this by my mother, who read to me from beautiful and irresistible books whose strange markings formed a code that only she could decipher. Amazing markings . . . that *meant* something. I was mystified by words. My mother spent a lot of time reading to me while my father was away during World War II (consequently, I learned to read—I cracked the code—very early). She has always been a creative person who taught me that imagination is fun, questions are good, ideas are pleasurable, and words are magic.

When I was older I was influenced by my grandfather. He was a crusty old guy who scandalized his very proper family by cussing, drinking, and smoking fat cigars. I thought he was wonderful. He was, in fact, a pretty unusual man, an orphan who grew up as a farm worker and came to the city to start his own business. He was gruff, outspoken, and tough, but he also loved flowers and children (on the sly); and he was the only man I know who opened his birthday presents in the basement so no one could see him get teary. My grandfather believed in books. While my mother taught me that ideas give pleasure, my grandfather taught me that ideas have power. He was an entirely self-educated man who loved to read, who claimed that anything you needed to know could be found in a book. He often said to me, "You can ask me anything, anything at all. I may not know the answer, but I can look it up. And the next time you come over I'll tell you what I found out." So I hung around and asked questions while he worked on his garden.

"Why is the sky blue?"

"Why are you putting tobacco on the foxgloves?"

"What makes clouds stick together?"

"Why does old man Fry's stomach look like a basketball?"

"Why can't anybody fix Mary Ellen's legs?"

No question was out of bounds. It was a very liberating experience.

Nevertheless, it was my grandmother who presented me with my first sustained philosophical confrontation. This was inadvertent on her part. All she meant to do was take me to church. As I recall, nobody else in the family went to church much, but my grandmother and my Aunt Lois started taking me to church when I was three or four years old.

I loved it. Since I memorized quickly and liked to sing and recite, I was the darling of the ladies club. I got lots of attention. Because I happened to be a friendly, even-tempered, fairly generous, and sympathetic child, people told me that I was a "natural-born Christian." I eventually came to think of myself as an *especially* Christian person—not necessarily *better* than other people, but more *loving*. I did not think of that as a virtue, but as a matter of luck. I was lucky that I happened to be born loving. So, I practiced being even more loving. I was convinced that everyone has some characteristic that is good and worth appreciating and I set about finding at least one such characteristic in everyone I met.

Over time, I practiced being loving and good and Christian, and I thought that I was doing pretty well until I was about twelve and discovered that I was developing a terrible fault—the worst fault a Christian can possibly have: Doubt. Let's face it, the story of Jesus is no more plausible than the story of Santa Claus, and I had long since given up on the latter. I understood Christianity well enough to know that the one unforgivable sin is lack of faith. No matter how bad you are, everything else can be forgiven, so long as you believe. But if you don't believe, then no matter how good you are, you are not a Christian.

Well, that really put me in a bind. My entire social life was tied up with going to church. More importantly, I had worked out this whole identity thing about being good and loving and Christian. What was I supposed to do? Who was I supposed to be? Besides, I really felt that being Christian was a good thing. It encouraged people to do the right things. I wanted to be a Christian. I wanted to believe. But how do you go about doing that? How do you make yourself believe something that doesn't, on the face of it, seem to be true? I had discovered that belief is not an act of will. You can't make yourself believe something just because you want to. You have to have a reason.

So my first long-standing philosophical quest was to try to figure out how to justify belief, and more specifically religious belief. The first arguments I came up with were very similar to what I now know to be Pascal's wager. What if you are wrong? You could be in serious trouble. On the other hand, what have you got to lose if you believe? Nothing. In my case this was patently true. Anything God wouldn't let me do, my parents wouldn't let me do anyway. I had absolutely nothing to lose and everything to gain. If self-interest is a reason for belief I clearly had that reason. The only trouble was that it didn't work. I still couldn't believe it. I tried reformulating the argument in different variations over time; but it never worked, and, unlike Pascal, I had to conclude that self-interest is the wrong kind of reason for belief.

So what is a good reason? I tried consensus for a while. I said to myself, most intelligent, well-educated people believe in Christian doctrine. Do you think you are smarter than they? That worked for a while, but as I got older I discovered that there may not be a clear consensus. Some people believe this, and some don't. I finally decided that the only kind of reason you can have for believing something is that you have enough evidence to conclude that it is more likely to be true than false. That's the minimum. It's nice if you have more, but you can't have less. What I didn't realize yet was that I had acquired a manner of thinking or a set of values—the love of ideas— that I couldn't give up without giving up my identity. I found this out when I grew up and got married.

Meanwhile, high school was traumatic for me. The girls I used to play baseball with acquired "hope chests" and engagement rings, and getting married became the standard of excellence. Since I was a working-class girl, and girls in my class didn't go to college, I fell in love and married at eighteen. The prevailing attitude was that women should get married and have babies, but it never occurred to me that that was *all* women should do. *That* was certainly not the impression I got from my mother or grandfather.

My husband and I had a deal. First he would go to college, and when he finished, I would go. But it didn't work. I got pregnant and college fell through. The country was in a recession at the time and my husband had a hard time finding work. Then I got pregnant again. No matter what we did, nothing seemed to stop the babies from coming. I even got pregnant while using the pill. When I said to the doctor, "I can't be pregnant. The pill is 95 percent effective!" he replied, "Well, somebody's got to be in the 5 percent." I had to have a gynecologist who thought he was a comedian.

My husband and I moved to a little house in a subdivision that never felt like home to me. I was an outsider there, an oddball. I was definitely out of step with the world, and I was not a very good housekeeper. I just couldn't get excited about it, and the things I did get excited about, like books and ideas, nobody else seemed very interested in. My references didn't seem to refer. My jokes weren't funny. My attitudes and preferences seemed to be characterized as stupidity, or at least foolishness rather than intelligence. Intelligence, for my neighbors, was practical, common sense, which they thought I didn't have (and perhaps they were right). Some of them felt sorry for me, because I just couldn't get it together. Others simply disapproved. I was not living up to the standard and that's all there was to it. I was deficient.

Furthermore, I seemed to alienate people inadvertently in two ways. First, I often asked them why they thought the things they did. Somebody would say something, and I would say, "Well, why do you think that?" This would be interpreted as hostile and antagonistic. I didn't mean it that way. I just wondered. Second, and maybe worse, I just didn't participate well. For example, I couldn't bring myself to watch soap operas. So I couldn't participate in conversations about soap operas, which were very frequent. I was without a common ground.

I remember one day my neighbor caught me reading a book on clinical psychology. "*What*," she demanded, "is *that!*" She was a very outspoken, opinionated woman (like the Queen of Hearts in *Alice*) who found the lack of any basis for her opinions no deterrent whatsoever to holding or asserting them. She was very confident. Her children were always clean. Her floors were always shiny. She was the richest woman in the neighborhood. She *was* the standard. I was very intimidated by her. I knew that she disapproved of me. "Oh," I said with an embarrassed laugh, "it's just a psychology book. You know me. I'll read anything. Cereal boxes, labels, anything I pick up."

"I can't imagine reading anything like *that*," she snorted. "I never get past *True Confessions* myself." And with her clean little girl in hand, she sauntered back home. I found myself muttering at the clothesline. Why was *I* apologizing? Why was *I* the misfit?

I now understand this, but I never figured it out at the time. The standard of excellence in that place and time for housewives was good housekeeping and material possessions. I obviously didn't care much about either of those things. But anyone who didn't meet the standard was deficient, and intellectual accomplishments didn't count. They were a luxury. The effect on an individual outside the norm is annihilating. It is not that your neighbors do it to you, you do it to yourself. I couldn't change myself, but my attitude changed about myself. I didn't lose my values, but I certainly lost my self-esteem. Since I thought that everyone else thought that I was either stupid or crazy, I began to wonder how all of them could be wrong. After all, I was the one who was miserable and deficient. They were well-adjusted.

My husband couldn't understand the problem. Over and over he explained to me that millions of women all over the world love to live as ordinary housewives, just like our friends and neighbors. All the evidence confirmed the opinion of the others, not mine. The common consensus confirmed the norm, and I was not meeting it. I was the one out of step. I was the substandard one.

I felt worse and worse about this. The worse I felt, the more ineffective I became in all ways. Even my thinking became muddled. I was unsure of myself, disinclined to talk to others. I wonder how many housewives through history have suffered this syndrome from intellectual starvation? I became very slow, fumbling, withdrawn. I couldn't understand how it could be that I was once intelligent and now I was stupid, or perhaps crazy, or both. Well, I could understand crazy. After all, people do go crazy. You don't have to be born that way. But how could someone become stupid who was not stupid to begin with? I hypothesized that I must have suffered brain damage. After all, I had had five children in six years and was severely anemic. And I had read that severe anemia can cause brain damage. So brain damage was my theory, and it explained why I could never do anything right anymore.

My husband became increasingly impatient. He couldn't understand how I got so stupid and maladjusted either. He couldn't understand why I couldn't be like *normal* women. He couldn't understand what I wanted.

And I couldn't tell him because I didn't know. I know now, but I didn't know then. What I wanted—needed—required was just one person to talk to who reflected and confirmed in some sense the values I had developed from childhood, that made me the person I am. One person to confirm my identity as normal. Fortunately, I met that person. She lived a few blocks away. Her name was Janet. She was going to college, and her husband actually approved of it. After I met her I began to heal.

Because of Janet, and a complicated series of events including a divorce, a new neighborhood, the reestablishment of stronger ties with my parents, and the creative help of a very committed financial aid officer, I found myself, at age thirty, an entering freshman at a local community college. I was very elated, but also very frightened—still having my brain damage hypothesis to contend with. I thought I would have to work especially hard to make up for the fact that I was not as smart as I used to be. Since I had "CLEPed out" of virtually all my requirements (which I did not consider evidence that I was smart, by the way, just old) I only needed elective credits. I could take anything I wanted, and I wanted everything.

One of the first courses I took was a philosophy course, taught by a woman named Aimée Mason, a no-nonsense former marine who had also previously been a New York model. On my first day in college she walked into class with a cane (favoring an old war injury to her knee), faced the class, rapped loudly on the desk with her cane, and said, "I'm Mason, and this is Philosophy 101." After that sentence she spent the bulk of the semester asking questions. Wonderful questions. Most of them without any immediate practical use whatsoever. Questions whose only reason for being was the intrinsic intellectual interest of considering them. Questions generated by a mind that simply needs to ask. And all the books we read were full of people all through history who were doing the same thing: asking questions.

Some of the questions were much like the irritating questions I had asked my neighbors. I was delighted. Here was a respected, intelligent person asking the same kind of questions that had led my neighbors to conclude that I was nuts. Now, I realize that more than one inference could be drawn from this, but I chose to draw the affirmative one. I was not crazy after all. I was just hanging out with the wrong group.

Now I had found my group. It felt like coming home. I talked to Aimée like I had talked to my grandfather, delighting in the exploration of ideas. When the course was over I took another, and Aimée sent off one of my essays to compete for a two-year scholarship at another school.

After that I never left home again, although I traveled quite a lot. As long as I was in a philosophy department I was home. I won my two-year scholarship at the University of West Florida, and then a teaching assistantship at Arizona. I knew that philosophers are my family, and philosophy departments my home when Keith Lehrer, discussing my option to be a lawyer or a philosopher, said to me, "You know, the only reason to go into philosophy is that you can't help it." I understood exactly what he meant.

The Fragility of Freedom

DAVID STRONG

Rocky Mountain College

How did I get my start in philosophy? Probably more than I care to think—
quite by accident. One summer's day between my seventh and eighth grades
I lost control of a dirt bike while going down a steep hill, wrecked over a
small cliff, and put a clutch lever through my skull. I came close to death,
suffered some paralysis in my right hand, and had to relearn how to speak.
It put an end to playing football and other sports I loved. I withdrew from
my peers, and the seriousness with which I had always approached things
increased and became a settled disposition. From then on I spent most of
my leisure time outdoors, on the streams and in the mountains.

The accident, of course, did not create my philosophic disposition *ex
nihilo*. As long as I can remember I had an inquiring mind with a bent
toward what the American transcendentalists call "high thinking and simple
living." In fact, even *before* I can remember, I am told that I asked my
mother as she rocked me to sleep on her lap, "Do we always think?"

Thinking and conversing about philosophical issues were always engaging, but thinking, especially after the accident, was not always as pleasurable
as Aristotle made it out to be. Too often, I suppose, I was brooding and
gloomy. My grandfather one day commented to my father that he thought
he had been "happier than that thing," pointing to me where I lay on the
living room floor. It was a year after the accident, and at the time I had just
finished reading about all the vanity of vanities in *Ecclesiastes*.

> Truly the light is sweet, and a pleasant thing it is for the eyes to behold the
> sun: But if a man live many years, and rejoice in them all: yet let him
> remember the days of darkness; for they shall be many. All that cometh is
> vanity.

I had not yet felt the liberating beauty in this literature.

Of course there were other events besides the motorcycle accident; that accident alone would not have been sufficiently determinative. But accidentality itself is a motif in my life's story. Paradoxically, I was neither born to do philosophy nor did I choose it, for choice connotes an arbitrariness on my part that I never experienced. Accidents, yes. It could have been otherwise. At a very early age I had come to the conclusion that humankind's principal problem was lack of an abundant energy source and that nuclear fusion was the answer to that problem. I was fascinated by the sciences, especially physics, and so I had my heart set on becoming a nuclear physicist. Clearly it turned out otherwise. What changed my mind?

My life took a decisive turn toward philosophy during my high school years. It all began ironically in two ways. The local church bulletin one Sunday contained the famous words from the temple at Delphi: "Know Thyself." So, in a sense, my affinity for Greek philosophy, religion, and culture began unexpectedly in the Christian church. But it was ironic in another way because the bulletin got it wrong. It attributed the words to one "Socrates, a philosopher." I guess I understand what the early Greek philosopher Heraclitus means by his aphorism, "The Sibyl with raving mouth utters solemn, unadorned, unlovely words, but she reaches out over a thousand years with her voice because of the god in her." These words in the bulletin spoke to me with that sibyl's voice—I just had to know who this fellow Socrates was and what philosophy was all about.

Socrates led to Plato. Plato led to the girl who had checked out all his works from the high school library. Karen became my lasting friend. She, in turn, led to the teacher under whose guidance the books had been borrowed. Because he challenged me to reflect on philosophical themes in literature to a degree no previous teacher had, I found myself taking every English course I could from Roger Powalisz. An unforeseen path opened before me, and my interest in the humanities began to compete with my interest in physics.

In my senior year, I met a philosophy professor from the University of Montana, Henry Bugbee, who spoke at a wilderness hearing for the Absaroka and Beartooth mountain ranges near Yellowstone Park. These were mountains I had grown up alongside. I had hiked and camped in them since my early boyhood. At the hearing these mountains were being considered for legal wilderness protection. I spoke on behalf of the mountains, but, like most people who were favorable toward them, I substituted in my remarks safer, more conventional, and utilitarian grounds for my riskier but more genuine and heart-felt concerns. What Henry Bugbee said was notably different in this and other regards. I did not understand much of what he said in his brief testimony at that hearing, but his obvious brilliance and eloquence seemed to define what a philosopher was, and I knew I had to find out more. I went to Missoula for college and philosophy.

The close call with death, my initiation to philosophical themes occurring in literature, and my attraction to the nontheoretical, experiential philosophy that Henry exemplified all served to foster in me a strong desire to do philosophical work in a way that integrated my studies with my walk through life. I wanted to understand things, events, my experience, and my condition in a way I later came to realize was similar to Thoreau's profound understanding of his world.

Subsequently, I took up the study of European Continental philosophy and the American Transcendentalist tradition. These philosophies showed me that our epoch is significantly unique. I saw that the material conditions which made experiential philosophy possible were quickly disappearing, that the culture of technology which was replacing these "things" was superficial, and that on the whole, we technological citizens are making choices for an even more pervasive technological order without deliberating much about what we are really choosing in the bigger picture or whether it will turn out to be in reality what we take it to be in its appearance.

What gave me insight into the problem and made these views lastingly attractive was an unexpected encounter that affected me even more than the motorcycle accident. During my graduate school days at Stony Brook, a road was built over a favorite hiking trail of mine in a wild canyon of the Crazy Mountains (near the Absaroka-Beartooths). Discovering that road, built overnight, as it were, brought home to me the pointlessly destructive character of technology. Here, I found, were the issues of our time: Whether or not we are going to allow focal *things* such as the Crazy Mountains to be in their own right without rearranging them, and whether or not we are going to pursue the good life mindlessly with technological means. Deliberating about this choice as thoughtfully as I could became the topic of my dissertation.

I now view my overall task in philosophy as one of criticizing my time; that is, resourcefully challenging its pervasive and unquestioned views of nature and of the good life, finding appealing alternatives for the culture of technology (we do need some craziness), and incorporating the best of the tradition and the best of technology. I owe much to the Greeks, to the Judeo-Christian tradition, to the Enlightenment, and to the American West. Finally, however, it comes down to living in a way that make sense here and now. That to me is *real* progress and *real* philosophy done in a way that an Aristotle might appreciate.

What does this mean concretely? Human freedom, it seems to me, is something more and *other* than making choices in front of a vending machine. Does it really matter in the larger picture whether I choose Coke or Pepsi, this product or that product? Does it really matter that I am freed from having to turn the crank to sharpen my pencil by using an electric pencil sharpener? We seem to be seduced into our common notions of freedom by the objects that surround us in our everyday lives. These objects, these commodities exact so little of us, so little of our humanity, that we are able to pick them up, use them up, throw them away and go on to others with thoughtless impunity. These objects exact so little of us that they really have no capacity to be of lasting consequence for us. We may have plenty of choices here among these commodities, but no freedom.

There is something wilder about freedom. This deeper sense of human freedom has been brought home to me most by my encounters with things and events that turned my entire life around in unforeseeable, unpredictable ways. Human freedom depends on encountering things and events powerful enough to *evoke* that kind of enduring consequence. Freedom in this fragile aspect is endangered when we lose these significant things. Walden Pond now in its ruined state no longer has the capacity to evoke from a Thoreau a book such as *Walden*. The Crazy Mountains may meet the same fate. It is impossible to be unmoved by the loss of these things just as it is impossible, the ancient Chinese philosopher Mencius points out, for us to be unmoved in the presence of a drowning child. Feeling, reflection, and political action are continuous with one another in my life. I will not take the destruction of the Crazy Mountains lying down.

A Philosopher Gone Wild

HOLMES ROLSTON, III
Colorado State University

Philosophy as biography has roots going back to Socrates, who "loved wisdom" by living out his protest against his native Athens. Socrates' key insight is that "man is a political animal," the animal who builds a town, inhabits a *polis*. Examining the character of life in this built, cultured environment is the time-honored mission of philosophers since.

Almost to a person, philosophers form their biographical creeds in a quarrel with the heritages they try to inhabit, and in that I take some comfort. Socrates so entwined his destiny with Athens-city that he left most of life unexamined; his biography ignored biology. "You see, I am fond of learning. Now the country places and trees won't teach me anything, and the people in the city do." (*Phaedrus*) Quarreling with Socrates, I found that the forest and landscape taught what city philosophers could not. So I found my biography took a natural turn, away from culture. The political animal still had an ecology. Aphoristically put, I was a philosopher going wild.

Of course, I could be simply acknowledging the roots that had nurtured me. My childhood years were spent in the Shenandoah Valley of Virginia, where my father was a rural pastor; my first residence was among trees in a country place. Jump Mountain and Hogback were on the skyline; the Maury River ran in front of the house. There was no electricity; we trimmed kerosene lamps. Our water was a cistern pump outside and another cistern on the hill behind the house that flowed by gravity to the kitchen inside. Dad kept a large garden; there was a chicken yard, a wood pile. My mother was from an Alabama farm, and I spent a month each summer there, prowling the woods and swamps.

But formal education had its way, as it will in this country, and I entered Davidson College in the mid-1950s eager to learn the mysteries of physics. That seemed the science of fundamental nature, and I was and still am attracted by the physicist-philosophers probing nature in the very small and very large, microphysics and astrophysics, and the cosmology that results from philosophizing over discoveries at these ranges. My college mentors had studied under the seminal physicists of the 1910s and 1920s. *Physis* is the Greek word for nature, and I needed a physics and, with it, a metaphysics. Perhaps there was nothing to learn from trees and rustic places, but there was everything to learn about matter-energy from cyclotrons and Geiger counters in town. This wasn't wild nature; it was mathematical nature. At the bottom of it all, there was ordered harmony, symmetry, universal law, beauty, elegance.

As an added boon, besides understanding how the world was made, the same physics gave us power to remake it. Was not the era of nuclear power, electronic wizardry, and computerized information at hand? In the 1950s, the humane city, fueled by science, was still a dream. So I set out to be a physicist, to understand and to remake the world; I applied and was admitted to some prominent graduate schools.

Still, I seemed to get lost—lost out there in the stars, lost in the mechanics of quantum theory. In the 1950s, cosmology dwarfed and mechanized humans; Earth was nothing but a speck of dust in galaxy after galaxy, a universe 20 billion years old, 20 billion light years across. The metaphysics that seemed demanded by the mathematical microphysics of matter reduced humans to less and less until they were nothing but matter in motion. I wondered. In those days physics had no "anthropic principle," little or none of the insight that it has subsequently developed about how even the microphysics and the astrophysics are remarkably fine-tuned for life at our native ranges.

In college, though a physics major, I had gotten entranced in a biology class taught by a first-rate entomologist. The other students considered him a buggy freak, but he saw things nobody else was seeing. I learned that you could see things in a binocular microscope that you did not catch in cloud chambers. Twice, over spring break, several of us went on extended field trips with him to the Florida Everglades. He kept vials in his shirt pockets, and instead of swatting the bugs, he popped them into formaldehyde for later examination. He could name the birds, the plants; I couldn't. Maybe I wasn't getting it all in physics; maybe, foundational though it was, physics wasn't really getting at the nature of nature. *Physis*, with the root "to generate," is not the only Greek word for nature, especially if such genesis knows only matter in motion. The Latin *natura* is from a Greek root "to give birth," to be native. Life. That was the problem with physics; it had none.

Still, I did not yet move into biology. Or philosophy. I took a turn into theology. Lost in the stars, lost in mechanics, I was indubitably a Cartesian mind-inhabiting-matter, a spirit. So I went to Union Theological Seminary in Virginia.

The trouble was that I had to fight theology to love nature. I finished seminary, went to the University of Edinburgh, and wrote a Ph.D. thesis in historical theology. The Reformers were terribly archaic, but the first generation of Reformers did have one thing right. Life was a kind of gift.

So I had grace and still a hankering after biology, when I set out to be a pastor in southwest Virginia, even though nobody who was anybody thought that these two would make a respectable combination. Biology, even more than physics, was an impossible science to reconcile with religion. Nature was red in tooth and claw, fallen; Paley's argument from design (a watch and its watchmaker) had fallen before evolutionary random mutations and survival of the fittest. There was neither creation nor Creator, only cold, fortuitous nature. I performed my roles as pastor, but inwardly I was searching. I remember once stumbling on a whorled pogonia in a secluded glade to exclaim, "Amazing grace!"

Partly to relieve the pressures, I took two days off each week, one to prowl the Southern Appalachian mountains, and one to sit in on biology classes at nearby East Tennessee State University. Graciously, the science faculty there welcomed me. I spent nearly a decade being a pastor, but becoming a naturalist, bringing in the Kingdom five days a week, going wild the other two. I learned the mountain woods in splendid detail. After the botany and zoology, came geology, mineralogy, paleontology. Now in my late twenties and early thirties, I was for the first time free of mentors telling me what I should study; I could figure it out for myself. I loved it! The trees and country places did have something to teach.

And I began to become alarmed; the natural world I had so long taken for granted, that once seemed so vast, was now vanishing with the surge of development. The sense of wonder turned to horror when I found favorite forests reduced to clearcut wastes, mountains stripped for the coal beneath, soils lost to erosion, wildlife decimated. I worked to preserve Mount Rogers and Roan Mountain, to maintain and relocate the Appalachian Trail. The natural world didn't seem so graceless, and no sooner had I learned that then here we were, treating it disgracefully.

As yet I had read no philosophy, save for a few physicists turned philosophers. For the most part, I had been warned against it. But I began to wonder. Just as I earlier had needed a metaphysics to go with my physics, I needed a philosophy of nature to go with my biology. Denied a theology of nature, I took a philosophical turn. Though I had never formally taken even one course in philosophy I applied to graduate schools. Most turned me down. The University of Pittsburgh accepted me; and I was attracted there because of their strong emphasis in philosophy of science.

But now I had to fight philosophy as before I had to fight theology. Philosophy of science was one thing, really the only kind of philosophy that was reputable; philosophy of nature was disreputable. That seemed the consensus of the logical positivists, then in vogue. The best philosophers of science insisted that natural history was the worst kind of science. For my interest in it, I had to apologize. These hard naturalists were worse humanists than the theologians. Nonhuman nature was value-free, nothing but a resource for the satisfaction of human desires, abetted by the skills of science. Value was entirely in the eye of the beholder, assigned by the preference of the valuer.

In the moments when I could escape the philosophers and the theologians, there were the mosses. I had developed a particular interest in them because they are so luxuriantly developed in the Southern Appalachians, and also because nobody else seemed much to care about them. There they were, doing nobody any good, yet flourishing on their own, not listening at all to the philosophers and the theologians. Indeed, there the whole natural world was—forests and soil, sunshine and rain, rivers and hills, the cycling seasons, wildflowers and wildlife—all these timeless natural givens that support everything else, all prior to these arrogant humans who thought that "man is the measure" of things. That valuable world, that world that humans are able to value, is not value-free; to the contrary it is the genesis of value, about as near to ultimacy as we can come.

My teachers all said I was all wrong. Almost the first lesson in logic is the naturalistic fallacy; there is no implication from descriptive premises to axiological or ethical conclusions. But in the wilderness, hearing a thrush singing to defend its territory, maybe even singing because it enjoyed it, seeing a coyote pounce on a ground squirrel, spooking the deer who fled fearing I was a hunter, searching for signs of spring after winter, even peering through a hand lens at those minuscule mosses, I knew they had to be wrong. There was life abundant in the midst of its perpetual perishing. These creatures valued life, each in their own way, regardless of whether humans were around. Indeed, we humans were part of that history. Philosophers have to reckon not just with the *polis*, culture, but also with the *anima*, inspirited matter, by which they become philosophers. Something of the meaning of life does lie in its naturalness. Forgetting this nature is that for which we need to apologize.

No one can really become a philosopher, loving wisdom, without caring for these sources in which we live, move, and have our being, the community of life on Earth.

From Logic to Art

"But 'glory' doesn't mean a 'nice knock-down argument,'" Alice objected.

"When I use a word," Humpty-Dumpty said, in a rather scornful tone, "it means just what I choose it to mean—neither more nor less."

"The question is," said Alice, "whether you can make words mean so many different things."

"The question is," said Humpty Dumpty, "which is to be master— that's all."

LEWIS CARROLL, *Through the Looking Glass*

Where the Argument Led

PETER CAWS

The George Washington University

When I was fifteen or so I greatly irritated my family by drawing their attention, excitedly and insistently, to what seemed to me a remarkable discovery about colors. It was that I had no way of knowing whether what I called red, or blue, or any other color, *looked* that color to *them*. I could not know this because as long as they *said* "red" when looking at something I saw as red they satisfied the only criterion I knew for the correct identification of colors. Under these conditions they could be seeing it as any color at all; as long as they called that color "red," whatever it was (my green or blue or some color entirely unknown to me), I would naturally assume that what was happening to them was what I called "seeing red." But in fact this assumption was quite unjustified. My family did not get the point of this; they were, as I said, irritated, so I soon stopped insisting. But the example stayed with me because it was clear that I had to be right; it was the first case I'd come across of something quite unshakable that could be established just by thinking.

Perhaps a year later the headmaster of my school, who had been using the one hour a week devoted to "Scripture" in the sixth form timetable to talk to us abut Egyptology, decided to turn the class's attention to philosophy, a term I knew only in its biblical use: " . . . philosophy and vain deceit." He gave us thumbnail versions of Locke's distinction between qualities and ideas, of Berkeley's "to be is to be perceived," of Kant's phenomenal world pre-determined by the forms of the understanding. I recognized these as belonging to the same class as my color problem—they were complexes of thought that could be explored and challenged in one's head, in which moves followed, or were blocked, with an immediate certainty the experience of which was almost viscerally satisfying. You could try to worm out of a block by thinking of supplementary conditions or alternative meanings, but you couldn't cheat. The whole point of the activity was to see where the argument led, as it were, of its own accord.

It soon occurred to me that the kind of reflection I had begun to try out on abstract problems like color perception could be applied to more practical issues like religious belief. In my family, which belonged to an obscure fundamentalist group known as the Exclusive Brethren, such matters were *intensely* practical. Belief had consequences in the form of parental and social approval or disapproval. (To show how seriously these things were taken: when my father died recently at nearly ninety he had refused to have anything to do with me for thirty years because I could not share his belief in the necessity of redemption by the blood of Christ.) But applying critical methods in this domain led to tremendous battles. My parents believed that the Bible was true, because inspired; when I asked why, they quoted a text from the Bible that said it was true, because inspired. This looked like an illegitimate self-referential move to me, but if I said I needed better grounds than that, they accused me of doubting the word of God and became angry.

It took me a long time to realize that my parents' anger on God's behalf was really anxiety on their own. It must have been unsettling to have the basis of a whole life challenged by the son they had, like all evangelical parents, dedicated to God's service. That such a challenge might, under a suitable interpretation, have been seen as serving God, was a thought that could not possibly occur to them. I never became an atheist in the strict sense—for a finite being to make a positive assertion of cosmic nonexistence seems arrogant—but I couldn't stomach agnosticism. It isn't that we don't know; we know a lot, and none of it as far as I can see supports the hypothesis of God's existence. So if there were a God he would, I think, have a poor opinion of anyone who believed in him on the available evidence, and be well served by those who argued against such a belief.

Simone de Beauvoir remarks somewhere that one never altogether escapes the God of one's childhood. No doubt that is why, in the course of a life devoted to theoretical work, I have rarely been as pleased by any discovery as by the philological speculation that the name of the Athenian *theoros* (the observer whose presence at the consultation of oracles made the oracular word official) was derived from *theos*, god, and *ora*, care: the one who had the word of the god in his care. Theoretical work, for me, springs from a care for truth. The ideas are perhaps not so different.

One thing that followed from the very idea of truth was this: of two inconsistent claims (due attention having been paid to their formulation, so as to remove ambiguities) one had to be false. But another thought came close behind: they might *both* be false. This was a suggestion, not a demonstration, but a most powerful suggestion. It seemed clear on reflection that of the many alternative religious accounts of the origin and meaning of life and the bases of morality, held passionately by conflicting sects, any pair taken at random *would* probably both be false. In spite of elaborate doctrinal proofs of their own election, it seemed implausible to me that the Exclusive Brethren had been vouchsafed the only truth with such certainty as to justify the cruelty they visited upon dissent.

The Brethren had lots of other bad arguments on which to practice philosophical criticism. But seeing through arguments was one thing, leaving the faith quite another. There was a long and painful struggle before the final break with my family. The break was made easier by the opportunity I sought out, and took, to leave England for the United States. But in the meantime I had gone to the University of London to study at the college where T. H. Huxley had lectured a century earlier. Huxley became an exemplary figure for me: if I had to identify one text as decisive in my rejection of religious belief in favor of science and philosophy it would be Huxley's letter to Charles Kingsley on the death of his own infant son. My degree was in physics—I might have been better suited to history or even, had I thought of it as a possibility, to philosophy, but these courses would not have been approved. Science was all right, especially astronomy (and physics was the nearest thing at the University), because "the heavens declare the glory of God, and the firmament showeth his handiwork." On the other hand, using physics to make bombs wasn't so good, so the thing was to become a science teacher, a career for which I duly qualified.

Leaving England solved several problems at once. I didn't have to start teaching science (I had found that I didn't like, and couldn't control, obstreperous schoolchildren). I could also at least postpone another tricky confrontation that was about to arise from the fact that, although at the age of eighteen I had (as expected of a young Exclusive) registered for military service as a conscientious objector, my conscience, when consulted in private and not under the influence of the Brethren, showed me that this was inauthentic. I had accordingly withdrawn my conscientious objection and begun negotiations with the Royal Navy for a short service commission as an instructor in navigation, which might lead to an eventual career in astronomy. I knew that the family situation would become intolerable as soon as this decision was made known, and, having seen posters advertising Fulbright scholarships and the like, I wrote letters of inquiry to a number of American universities. Yale offered me a one-year fellowship, which I accepted.

Physics had reinforced another philosophical interest that had been sparked earlier on by reading some books of my father's, notably the popular works of Sir James Jeans and Sir Arthur Eddington. My father took these as evidence of the wonder and mystery of God's creation. I took them as posing conceptual problems about space, time, matter, causality, and the like. So at Yale I read philosophy, especially the philosophy of science, and through the recognition and generosity of Henry Margenau was able to stay for three years and complete the doctorate.

All thought of professional astronomy was given up—philosophy had captivated me completely. I had a three-pronged attachment to it: my original analytic passion, the light philosophy could throw on human belief systems, and technical problems in the philosophy of science.

A fourth attachment was created when I started teaching the subject, and filled out a profile that is still recognizeable today. At the University of Kansas I was the youngest member of a four-man department, and some very bright undergraduates wanted me to read existentialism with them. They had asked the older members and had been refused; I as a newcomer was their only hope. "But I'm here to teach logic and the philosophy of science," I said. "Please," they urged. "We'll buy the beer." So we had an informal weekly seminar in a student apartment and read an anthology of Kierkegaard, Hazel Barnes' translation of Sartre, and a little Heidegger and Jaspers. The experience was a revelation, and I realized that the scorn some well-known philosophers had expressed for Continental philosophy was often based on ignorance.

I have worked, since then, on both sides of the divide between analytic philosophy and phenomenology, between Anglo-American and Continental philosophy. On reflection it occurs to me that duality has been the pattern of my life: religion and the secular world, science and the humanities, Europe and America, English and French. The disadvantages of this have been ambiguities of identification: I have sometimes been regarded by phenomenologists as an unregenerate intruder from the analytical establishment, and by analytic philosophers as a woolly Continental. The advantages have far outweighed such inconveniences; I have been free to follow my own line, to feel at home in widely divergent disciplines, to take a synoptic view.

I still agree with my fifteen-year-old self about the idiosyncrasy of the subjective, though I have better conceptual tools than he did for dealing with the problem, which has vastly broadened in scope. And I still recognize him in myself: every new insight seems to me as striking and as exact as that first conjecture did to him. I realize now for the first time, in concluding this brief account of becoming philosophical, how much I owe to his ingenuity and his insistence, which led me out of a doctrinal trap into a life of free thought, with its unending rewards.

Life and Logic*

WILLARD VAN ORMAN QUINE
Harvard University

I was very young when my mother came to get me from my crib and I volunteered that 64 and 64 were 128. I had been counting up from some intermediate starting point, perhaps fifty and fifty, adding ones on this side and twos on that. I had stopped where I did because I was shaky on the next move, getting out of the one-twenties. Clearly no infant Gauss was I. Clearly, moreover, I had learned early to bank on generous applause for slight achievements. Little ventures in humorous verse, embarrassingly flat and feeble, were praised and recorded by my mother. I even wondered, for all the tenderness of my years, what was so good about one of my touted creations.
. . .

Uncle Dan's was the scene of an early memory. His farm was only three miles from home as the crow flies, but, unlike crows, my parents and brother and I made a six-mile journey of it by street car and train. While there I amused myself below a grassy bank, pretending to dig a tunnel to Europe. By evening, I am told, I was so homesick as to cause an untimely end to our visit; Uncle Dan hitched up his horse and drove us home.

This early incident illustrates a tension between the lure of the remote and the drive for the familiar. On later occasions this tension has been good for an agreeable thrill: I am in an unfamiliar place and choose an unfamiliar road toward familiar territory, intent on seeing just where it joins up. I have dreamed this of Akron, and I have contrived it in other places. This thrill of the strange way home is a paradigm of the thrill of discovery in theoretical science: the reduction of the unfamiliar to the familiar.

My mother, and consequently my father, belonged to the Congregational Church. My mother considered herself deeply religious, but she got to church only irregularly. My father was a silent partner. My brother and I were sent

*Excerpted from *The Time of My Life: An Autobiography*, The MIT Press (Cambridge, 1985), pp. 8f., 11–12; 13–14; 31; 32; 37f; 51–52.

to Sunday school about half the time, and seldom to church. In later life my mother did indeed become a deaconess and engage in good works.

I did my schoolwork and got good marks, but the work seldom aroused my interest. Sitting in school, I would long for a trapdoor under my desk through which I could slip into the cool basement and out to freedom. Such reading as took my fancy was unrelated to school, as was my passion for geography. Schoolwork was duty and dullish *ipso facto*. This was the fault neither of the curriculum nor of the teachers so far as I am aware, and I resented neither. . . . It was due rather to an odd and deep-rooted trait of mine: a mild resistance to instruction. Throughout college and beyond, I have listened only restlessly to lectures, and with flagging attention, unless the topic was exceptionally absorbing or the speaker exceptionally skilled.

I may have been nine when I began to worry about the absurdity of heaven and eternal life, and about the jeopardy that I was incurring by those evil doubts. Presently I recognized that the jeopardy was illusory if the doubts were right. My somber conclusion was nonetheless disappointing, but I rested with it. I said nothing of this to my parents, but I did harangue one or another of my little friends, and I vaguely remember a parental repercussion. Such, then, was the dim beginning of my philosophical concern. Perhaps the same is true of the majority of philosophers.

The air I breathed was mildly anti-Semitic. I think of Bob Goldsmith, Al Green, and Herb Rose, schoolmates of mine and kindred spirits in stamp collecting. . . . I liked these boys. What a pity, I thought, that they are Jews. Then I had a flash of philosophical insight, as memorable as the one that had put paid to my religious faith some years before. Why, I asked myself, is it a pity that they are Jews, rather than its being a credit to the Jews? It was my first implicit appreciation of the principle of *extensionality* by which I have set such store down the decades: the universal is no more than the sum of its particulars.

My mother's revered brother Willard had liked Poe, from whose stories she recoiled with a tolerant shudder; so it was commendable and indeed manly to like Poe. I read all of Poe. I was enthralled by some of his poems, but I suspect that my taste for his tales was somewhat self-induced. Anyway, a summer midway in high school found me effortfully writing, trying to evoke a mood of horror in a style yet more pompous than Poe's.

An interest in philosophy, foreshadowed slightly perhaps by the two insights already noted, was abetted by Poe's "Eureka." Then, at the end of high school, I acquired two philosophy books from my brother who was studying at Oberlin. They were Max Otto's *Things and Ideals* and William James's *Pragmatism*. I read them compulsively and believed and forgot all. Also I read Swami Vivekananda's *Raja Yoga*. It was not a notably philosophical phase; I was also doing other pretentious reading, including Ibsen, Edward Young, and Samuel Butler.

Thus, when I finished high school in January 1926, my interest in philosophy was partly spurious and partly real. "Eureka," for all its outrageousness, fostered the real thing: the desire to understand the universe.

But I conceived a new interest at about the end of high school: word origins. It did not issue from school; my enthusiasms seldom did. My source was George H. McKnight, *English Words and their Background*, which I borrowed from the public library, I do not know why. Naturally the subject proved fascinating. An interest in foreign languages, like an interest in stamps, accorded with my taste for geography. Grammar, moreover, appeals to the same sense that is gratified by mathematics, or by the structure of boundaries and road networks. Etymology, more particularly, was a bonanza. Here one can pursue scientific method without a laboratory, and check one's hypotheses in a dictionary. Each etymology is a case, in miniature, of the strange road home.

Must youth rebel? Perhaps it is human nature and has had some subtle survival value for the species. Or perhaps it is regional and plays no part in coming of age in Samoa. At any rate it is endemic in the West. In the late 1960s it assumed a horrid air of stalwart self-righteousness, in consequence perhaps of an era of parental indulgence of the whims of childhood. Earlier the paradigm of youthful rebellion was sly naughtiness; the culprit when caught was rueful but not resentful. Greater nonsense was itself no doubt rebellious in spirit, though not mischievous. Similarly for the mockery, in my coterie, of school spirit and the Y.M.C.A. Similarly perhaps for my antireligious harangues, though these were reasoned; and here I must even confess to a touch of self-righteousness. But the virulent form of youthful rebellion in my college days was drunkenness. It was fostered, paradoxically, by national prohibition, by college prohibition, and by prohibition on the part of mothers such as mine; for these invested it with glamour and bravado.

So much, just now, for vice; what of studies? As a freshman at Oberlin I met my science requirement with G. D. Hubbard's geology and my Bible requirement with a term on the Bible by the college preacher and a term on the philosophy of religion. My other freshman courses included intermediate French, differential calculus, and literature. At first I pictured creative writing as my likeliest career, with journalism as entering wedge. But when the time came to choose a field of concentration, I found myself torn three ways—and English was not one of them. There were mathematics, philosophy, and what I called philology, which would have meant a classics major. The glory motive intruded a little: I could not invest philology, or linguistics, with the profundity of philosophy or mathematics.

The decision was eased by Bill Bennett, a knowledgeable senior in English. He told me of Russell, who had a "mathematical philosophy." Mathematics was a dry subject, and stopped short of most that mattered, but the link with philosophy promised wider possibilities. So I majored in mathematics with honors reading in mathematical philosophy, mathematical logic.

A Philosopher Remembers

BERNARD GERT
Dartmouth College

I am a philosopher; that is how I list my occupation on my income tax form. Most of my income comes from teaching philosophy at Dartmouth College, but I give lectures at other places, for which I am sometimes paid. I also make a small amount from writing philosophy books, but I am not paid for most of my philosophical writings. Recently, I have started to use philosophy, primarily moral philosophy, to help non-philosophers deal with practical matters. For some of this I am paid; most often I am not. But none of this payment really matters, for I have never wanted to be anything other than a philosopher.

It began at Walnut Hills High School in Cincinnati, Ohio. It was a public high school, but you had to take a test to get in and almost all of the students went to college. I was not an outstanding student. I found most of the courses boring. I was interested in thinking things out for myself, not in learning what someone else had thought or discovered. In our senior year we had a home room period in which faculty members from various departments at the University of Cincinnati came to talk to us about their disciplines. We had a succession of faculty members from Cincinnati, none of whom I remember except for Howard Roelofs, chair of the department of philosophy. When he finished telling us about philosophy I was quite enthusiastic and I remember saying to myself, "I can imagine doing that for the rest of my life."

The next fall when I entered the University, I went to see Professor Roelofs and told him that I wanted to major in philosophy. He asked what year I was in at the University and when I told him that I was a freshman he said to come back in a year or two. That did not discourage me at all. I started taking philosophy courses in my freshman year and took so many of them that by the time I was a senior there were no more undergraduate philosophy courses for me to take. So I took some graduate courses.

I do not remember the content of many of these courses very well, but

I do remember a course in intellectual history in which we read Hegel and had to write a paper on him. I remember the passage in the *Phenomenology* in which Hegel talks about empirical truths going stale. He said something like, "Write on a piece of paper 'Now it is daytime.' Wait twelve hours and pull out the paper and you will see that your truth has gone stale." I thought this was absurd and wrote my paper proving that this passage showed an elementary misunderstanding of the use of the term *now*. The teacher was outraged and said to me, "You make Hegel look like an ass."

I also remember the time when I lost my faith in reason. I was standing in front of the student union with Richard Brashears, a person whom I do not remember from any other occasion. We were talking about reason and I remember concluding that reason, as we had taken it, had no special authority. My experience at that time resembles what some other people describe as losing their faith in God. One of my major goals in philosophy since that time has been to provide an account of reason that would have the kind of special authority philosophers have traditionally assigned to it (i.e., holding that no one ever ought to act irrationally).

In my first semester at Cornell we had a discussion of reason in which all of the faculty and students accepted the view that it was perfectly rational for two tribes to continue attacking each other even though all of them knew that the sole result of such battles was that many of them would be killed and wounded. When I objected that it was irrational to risk injury and death if no one was to gain any benefit from it, the universal response was that if that is what they wanted to do then it was rational for them to do it. I continue to be amazed that this is still the dominant view of rationality, not only among philosophers, but also in the social sciences.

In a course on social contract theory, John Rawls made the statement that Warrender's book on Hobbes was the first correct account of his moral and political views. Given my view of philosophy, that one should never accept someone else's position unless one cannot show it to be wrong, the thought immediately occurred to me to show that Warrender was mistaken. I was attracted to Hobbes, in part, because he was the only philosopher I read who explicitly stated that it was irrational not to avoid death, pain, and injury. I was impressed by how honestly and straightforwardly Hobbes put forth his philosophical views, and by the fact that he intended them to make a major impact on society. I was also impressed by how seriously he was taken, even if he did not have the kind of impact that he intended (e.g., the Roman Catholic Church put his books on the Index of banned writings and Oxford University not only prohibited his books from being studied, they fired people for being Hobbists). He had that kind of impact, in part, because he wrote in the standard literary language of his day and wrote so well. At the present time, it seems to me philosophers write in a special philosophical language and only other philosophers take what they say seriously. I was and am interested in the kind of audience that Hobbes wrote for.

In my third and final year at Cornell, someone asked me what I was going to do when I finished my thesis. I had not thought about this at all. Someone suggested I should look for a job teaching and writing philosophy. I was amazed that anyone would be willing to pay me for doing philosophy.

Many years have passed and my daughter, Heather, has just received her Ph.D. in philosophy. I remember how she first demonstrated philosophical talents around the age of six. We were taking a walk on a bright moonlit night and she said, "Look at the full moon!" I replied, "If you look more closely you will see that it is not quite full." She answered, "No, not if you look more closely, if you look more carefully." However, when she was in her first year at Kenyon College and asked me if she should take any philosophy courses, I told her to wait until her junior year. She, of course, did not listen to me and by her junior year was a philosophy major. When she talked about going to graduate school in philosophy I tried to discourage her and suggested several alternative careers. Her younger brother, Joshua, said that he majored in philosophy and math so that he could join our conversations. I remember the perplexed looks on the faces of many of their friends when they came over for dinner and heard us get into a philosophical discussion.

When I talk with my daughter about her career I become aware of how much less I knew about what I was doing when I embarked on my career. In most cases, I did not even make a choice, since there were no alternatives open to me. I can see very clearly how easy it would have been for my career to have gone wrong and how little I had to do with its going right.

At the very beginning of my interest in philosophy I thought that it was the only activity I could imagine doing for a whole lifetime. I still think so. In fact, my conception of heaven is to be able to have philosophical discussions with all of the great philosophers. I would like to show them where they went wrong.

The Practice of Philosophy

JAMES GOUINLOCK
Emory University

Happily for me, I did not receive sufficient exposure to philosophy as an undergraduate to sour me on the subject. I was at Cornell from 1952 to 1956, and at that time it was the most analytical school west of Oxford. Philosophy in this manner has never engaged my interest; and had I supposed that what they did at Cornell was all there was to it, I wouldn't be writing this essay today. I came to be engrossed in philosophy naïvely and by other means.

I don't wish to conceal the fact that I did take courses in philosophy at Cornell. There was an introductory two-semester sequence. The first term was devoted to Plato, and the second term, taught by Norman Malcolm, focused on Hume. What I remember from the course is Malcolm holding out his hand, as if it were in a fire, grimacing intensely, as if in excruciating pain, and asking through his feigned agony how he knew whether he *really* had a hand and whether it were *really* in a fire. The effects of such dramatics were no doubt diminished by the very real howling of the huge black dog that Professor Malcolm used to bring with him to class. In any case, the theorizing of scepticism had no appeal to a young man who knew well enough when his hand was on fire.

Through circumstances unrelated to my academic work, I had the good fortune in my senior year to come to know Norman Thomas, the great American socialist. My association with him inspired me to read political philosophy in great earnest. So I started again with Plato—this time on my own—and took up Aristotle, Cicero, Rousseau, and many others in turn, confining myself to acknowledged classics, but staying away from empiricists, who seemed rather bloodless. I quickly became infected with fits of divine madness and haven't been the same since. I unambiguously owe my *beginnings* as a philosopher to Norman Thomas. But *becoming* a philosopher is a more attenuated process.

I was obliged to enter the U.S. Navy after graduation, and I was on a ship whose home port was Charleston, South Carolina. While on active service I did my best to continue my readings. I studied as would any auto-didact—following the passions wherever they led. My understanding of the books I tackled was extremely uneven. On the other hand, I was free to meditate on them without constraint or obligation; I virtually lived in im-aginative dialogue with philosophers. It was an absolutely invaluable and irreplaceable experience.

For those who might be curious about the *truly* practical applications of philosophy, I must also recount the following: early on in Charleston I met an extraordinarily attractive girl. When I asked if I could call on her the next day, she answered that it would be impossible: She had to work on a term paper on Plato's philosophy of education. I replied that I knew the subject inside and out and would be happy to advise her on it. The strategy worked; and we have been happily married for more than thirty years. More-over, her professor, a retired classicist from Oxford, said it was one of the best papers on Plato he had ever read; so my fate with respect to both philosophy and matrimony was sealed in one stroke.

All the same, one's love of a discipline can easily subside. Any devotion requires sustaining experiences, and not all of us have them. Many an academic has realized on some unhappy day that he or she is not, after all, engaged in something that one really loves. The joy and the purpose have dried up. If I had pursued philosophy along orthodox lines, this would surely have happened to me, but I had the luck to acquire a sense of inclusion within a great tradition. This was imparted to me in my graduate education at Columbia, especially under the tutelage of John Herman Randall, Jr. As I look back on it, that experience has been integral to my enduring love of philosophy.

One cannot speak helpfully about the practice of philosophy without addressing the question of just what it is that one is practicing. One tries to become a philosopher of a certain sort. By the happy coincidence of natural inclination, education, and reflection I have come to embrace a certain conception of philosophy and the philosopher. For both our thought and action, the world—including humans—is difficult, complex, perplexing. It is demanding, threatening, exceedingly interesting, and sometimes deeply rewarding. It is not altogether resistant to our understanding and aspiration. A richly and honestly orchestrated vision of the nature of things can be of genuine help in the pursuit of wisdom—and it is in any case delightful to entertain such visions. Many thinkers have undertaken to characterize the nature of things in its contingencies, necessities, intricacies, limitations, resources, promises. These views of things provide *maps*, if you will, of the terrain of human existence; such maps have moved us to specific efforts and aspirations. Philosophic cartography is treacherous business, and it often goes wrong. But I am persuaded that the endeavor is neither vain nor useless; sometimes, it is beneficial and even potent.

Two of the main pitfalls of philosophy are to engage, on the one hand, in irresponsible speculation (commonly devoted to wish fulfillment and apologetics) and, on the other, in scholastic argumentation just for its own sake. Epistemology, for example, is too often a pursuit of the latter sort. It is crucially important, of course, to determine whatever assurances we can of what constitutes a reliable claim to knowledge; epistemologists are right to say that their work is a necessary part of philosophizing.

Too many philosophers, however, never do anything else. They ponder the question, say, of the generic relation between language and the world; and that is *all* that they do. They *never* get around to the ever-present world itself in its singularities and uniformities, its promises and perils. It's hard to believe that they think there is anything helpful a philosopher can say about it. But the world does not wait upon the final verdict from *Mind*; and reflective persons can't either. There is much to be confidently learned with the resources and tests we already possess and use effectively in every other context of our lives. Philosophy as I understand it takes our worldly condition itself as its primary subject matter. Academic philosophers, by contrast, are overwhelmed with the obsession to take the analyses in the latest journals as their primary subject matter, let the world transpire as it will.

When I was a young man, I was intoxicated by Emerson, with his heady exhortations to personal integrity and excellence. I later came to see him as just a sentimental mystic. More recently I have come to regard him with renewed reverence. What I treasure in him is his call for intellectual courage and independence. Such a condition is much harder to achieve than Emerson supposed, and it must be accompanied by a logical rigor unknown to him. Disciplined intellectual independence is indispensable to philosophy, yet it is almost nowhere to be found. Fashion becomes master. "Not for me," each of us says. But, truth to tell, academic philosophers, like most intellectuals, tend to be imitators and followers; we venture to be "bold and innovative" only after an uneasy glance to be sure we are garbed with the same ideas as our peers. We need a good dose of Emerson.

Cybersage Does Tai Chi

MICHAEL HEIM
California State University–Long Beach

A Tai Chi teacher who consults on Virtual Reality technology for the computer industry? What kind of job is that? Does some unity tie the work together, some hidden calling?

I cannot pinpoint an exact autobiographical moment when the job(s) seemed to make sense, but I do recall two occasions when everything came together so wonderfully that I treasure them in memory as moments of illumination.

One was during a coffee break at the 1991 Washington, D.C., Virtual Reality conference I had organized. I sat down to chat with Randy Walser, director of the Cyberspace Project at Autodesk Corporation, a Fortune 500 software firm, and I asked him a question often posed by aspiring graduate and undergraduate students: "How does a person prepare for a career in Virtual Reality technology?"

Randy answered without hesitating, "Study philosophy." He went on to explain how computer breakthroughs require a breed of people fluent in logic and epistemology, able to synthesize psychological, ethical, and historical knowledge. Randy had just finished a presentation in which he cited Mark Johnson's *The Body in the Mind*. Computers of the future will draw the human being further into cyberspace, body and all. Not just the eyes, but the hands and feet too will move through an environment of computer-generated simulations. Philosophers are at home in virtual worlds, Randy said.

Another occasion also stands out, this one a moment when mind and body savored a wordless unity. The pre-dawn air was pale gray and the ocean breezes cool near Venice Beach in Los Angeles. Every morning for the past several months, I had opened the same rickety wooden gate to walk into the backyard of Master Tung, Tai Chi man and Taoist teacher. Quietly I took my position among ten or fifteen human figures standing like statues under the fragrant eucalyptus trees.

Feet parallel, knees relaxed, spine straight, weight sunk into the balls of the feet, arms outstretched with hands open but relaxed, eyelids nearly shut. Begin letting go of all thoughts, forgetting everything, listening only to the inhale and exhale of the breath. Sink down, letting go of muscle tension, releasing worries and desires, gradually merging the attention with the body. Every few minutes, teacher Tung makes the rounds to adjust the posture, and each time a burst of energy shoots from foot to crown of head. The attention wedded to a relaxed body generates a feeling of inner power, of expanding, radiant energy.

By the time the hour is over, the sun's patterns are flickering through the eucalyptus leaves onto the grass with an incredible but gentle brilliance. Sounds of birds and lawnmowers emerge slowly in the distance. Other students are stirring and moving about in the slow martial movements of Tai Chi Chuan. Awareness of the clock returns gradually.

Later that morning, driving on the freeway, or sitting at the computer, or lecturing in the classroom, I feel the sudden pull of body/mind unity reclaim my nervous system: unnecessarily taut muscles let go, clenched fingers release, breath comes full and supportive.

Or I catch myself in a moment of haste moving as if I were no more than a bundle of competing mental intentions, the body twisting with one limb this way and one limb that, without coordinating breath with action, and without making the most of my center of balance. The memory of Tung's garden adjusts me.

These two slices of life—cyberspace consultant and Tai Chi adept—both grew from idea seeds planted by a book that nourished me in my late teens. It was the early 1960s, just before the video screens took charge of the Truth. I was browsing in a library and quite by accident began reading Henry G. Bugbee's *The Inward Morning.*

In the journal of this American philosopher, I found surprising connections woven into a tapestry of personal reflections. Here was Heidegger's "fundamental grounding" connected with D. T. Suzuki's Zen Buddhism and Taoism. Here was H. D. Thoreau's pristine, fresh America juxtaposed with existential ruminations about the "forgetfulness of Being" in the age of technology. This heady brew, concocted by a bold and honest mind, set me on a series of journeys.

The first trip was to Freiburg, Germany, where I needed to pick up Heidegger's trail. I needed to learn how Europeans think about the reality shifts driven by technology. Much of my three years of Fulbright study remained theoretical, without the shock of recognized experience. That shock of recognition came years later when I used a laptop computer to write my first book.

In 1984, I toted a Radio Shack Model 100 notebook computer to Greece.

Sitting on the steps of the Parthenon, I put into the computer the first chapters of *Electric Language: A Philosophical Study of Word Processing.* Old and new flowed together as the ancient *logos* swam in electrified data. My chapters traced the course of language technologies, from chisel and pen, to printing press and computer.

By then, writing books had become my main link to the philosophy profession. I had fallen in love not with academic philosophy, nor with historical philosophers, but with the writing of philosophy. And now the computer as word processor became a seismograph for measuring ontological shifts, the changes in our awareness of what is real. The word processor created a new relationship to symbols, to language, and, by extension, to reality.

But even though my speculations on word processing found several signposts pointing to future turns in reality, my research could never have prepared me for what was coming just around the bend.

My reflections on the computer screen shattered abruptly in 1989 when I first entered Virtual Reality. Instead of sitting before a screen with keyboard or mouse, I donned a helmet and glove and felt immersed in a computer-generated environment. No longer outside the computer, I walked through the looking glass. My philosophical seismograph went crazy.

The Virtual Reality system I tested was still a primitive prototype, like arcade games and amateur flight simulators, but its implications seemed enormous. The shifts in reality awareness I had found in earlier computer use were subtle by comparison. The ontological shift to digital symbols became in VR a full-fledged, aggressive, surrogate reality.

Another book emerged from this journey into cyberspace and it treats the metaphysics of Virtual Reality. It blends a philosophy of technology with Taoist teachings and warns of the ways we can forget the body and lose our balance when we consciously build a technology to "incorporate" our bodies.

Virtual Reality installs the human body in the computer interface, but the technology can impose the same techno-stress on bodily awareness that we feel outside the virtual environment. Modern life in the West, even when glorifying "the body," often subverts what David Levin called "the body's recollection of Being." The body can become just another computer peripheral.

While living much of the time with computers, I still research and teach pre-technological, non-Western ways of moving and being. This strategy operates far from the main campus of Western philosophy, which remains largely verbal and conceptual. Most Eastern sages do not separate theory from practice. As Asia continues to influence America, I think we will see growing interest in unified experience, a future challenge to the Cartesian split of mind and body—and the challenge will not be exclusively verbal.

Artists tend to catch the first waves of the future. As a frequent philosopher-in-residence at the Banff Centre for the Arts in Canada, I have counselled groups of artists who are building Virtual Reality systems. I notice that many of these artists feel a gap closing. Science no longer stands opposite to art, nor does aesthetics oppose technology. Computer algorithms and imaginative freedom are learning to get along.

As more computer science students take to Virtual Reality, the world of science too will close the Cartesian split of mind and body, techno-system and expressive movement. The beginnings exist already in pioneer thinkers like Myron Krueger, the "father of Virtual Reality."

Maybe this, then, is the unity of my job(s), the essence of the vocation? A certain kind of uncomfortable unity arises from spreading oneself over a cultural disjunct, from stretching oneself over an abysmal fissure.

Self-justifications aside, we must span the gaping Cartesian wound that makes education and culture suffer. A life in the gap indicates a certain amount of healing taking place.

Fifty years ago, the Pragmatists looked to relieve the same chronic cultural affliction. For me, like them, the impulse for fresh philosophizing is crucial. We have in our American tradition—in the New World, as Bugbee would say—some notable forerunners who, as members of the New World, tried to respond to the industrial-technological system created here in the U.S. and then exported to the rest of the world. The Greek, French, and German influences in philosophy must be balanced with American self-awareness.

In his preface to Frederick Matthias Alexander's *The Resurrection of the Body*, John Dewey wrote:

> "In the present state of the world, the control we have of physical energies, heat, light, electricity, etc., without control over the use of ourselves is a perilous affair. Without control of ourselves, our use of other things is blind."

The bad news is that Dewey's theories proliferated while the Alexander Method of body alignment never went beyond a tiny cult of devotees. The transmission of Western wisdom seems inveterately verbal.

The good news is that computers are changing our attitude toward knowledge. They have already shown us graphically things that once only mathematicians could conceptualize.

The advent of Virtual Reality might switch on other modes of thought. Neither Pragmatism, with its bias toward scientific method, nor Phenomenology, with its imported vocabulary, were able to find that switch. Where Western culture had ears for Far Eastern culture, it listened only for familiar concepts. D. T. Suzuki introduced many new Buddhist-Taoist texts to the West, but his Zen came clothed in Hegelian abstractions and spoke of a "nothingness" which echoed Sartrean existentialism. The profound background of Oriental practices went unspoken. Some Westerners learned to speak a slightly different language, but their Buddha-speak never sprang from inner body experience. Only a very few readers eventually traced the abstractions back to Yoga, Aikido, Tai Chi. Western scholarship welcomed the concepts but kept the door shut on any direct involvement with transformative disciplines.

Back in 1958, Henry Bugbee sought a switch to other modes of thought by writing a metaphysical journal based on his walks, fishing trips, and automobile rides. He sought ontological significance in the human bodily stance and motion. In *The Inward Morning* (1958), he wrote:

> "It is all very well to image our proper independence as responsible beings by talking of standing on our own feet. But this image, by itself, leaves us hanging in the air. Let us not neglect to think of the ground being under our own feet; and let us not talk as if we placed the ground under our own feet. A ground which our *feet* do not *discover* is no ground.
>
> At this point I am moved to consider the possibility that we must rethink our idea of feeling precisely in connection with our mode of being grounded. I must put the matter cautiously: It seems as if our being grounded, our discovery of ground upon which we may stand, in standing upon our own feet, is a matter of feeling. Somehow, feeling and having a footing need to be thought out together. . . . " (p. 111)

Here Bugbee connected high metaphysics with biofeedback. He dug out the concrete language underlying the abstractions, and he found there the felt earth and the élan of physical movement. Outside of a few somatic pioneers like Thomas Hanna, no one followed up on Bugbee's language, and his remained a small voice crying in the philosophical wasteland.

Virtual Reality may soon amplify that voice. VR systems will soon demand from us, from our whole culture, a total rethinking of our idea of feeling. Biofeedback will confront us in ways we cannot evade, in ways as direct as television. We will view our bodies imaged before us on real-time monitors as we move in virtual worlds of work and play. We will not only act in virtual environments, but we will directly perceive our own biological and neurological states displayed in real-time on our virtual bodies. These cyberbodies may lead us back to Bugbee's "imaging our proper being." A century of metaphysics awaits us.

In the process we might discover the vestiges of our instinctual knowledge. We might find a synthesis of Eastern body wisdom and Western objective science. One fine morning, the cybersage and the Tai Chi player might wake up and greet each other in the same (virtual?) world.

Surrealism, Schubert, and Socrates

EVA H. CADWALLADER
Westminster College, New Wilmington,
Pennsylvania

Both my mother, a Hungarian research chemist, and my father, a German engineer and artist, joined the anti-Hitler underground shortly after I was born in Cologne, Germany, in 1933. We escaped from Germany in December 1937, moving from there to Budapest. Staying with my grandparents in Budapest while my parents emigrated to the United States one by one during the next year, I learned Hungarian as my second language. I was barely six by the time I was learning my third "native" language in a Manhattan public school, my aunt having brought me and my younger brother across the Atlantic in March 1939. My memories of the next few years focus mainly on two "theaters": public school and the neighborhood, and the Ethical Culture Society day care I received after school and during the summer. I loved every minute of being at the latter, which was almost across the street from our apartment. If you have read or seen *Auntie Mame* you will know why. These two years were exciting though often bewildering as I struggled to sort out the American language and customs from the ones so recently left behind.

I think that this is when I first started to become a philosopher. Comparing, contrasting, trying to communicate, puzzling over the seeming contradictions of my changing environments became as natural as breathing. "Why?" questions seemed an inescapable part of this. Standing outside of myself as an observer, consciously scrutinizing my current reality, questioning its assumptions—all this seemed necessary for daily functioning. My lifelong interest in metaphysics, value theory, and value conflict surely began here.

The contrast between life at home and in the outside world was, for me, considerable. It was decades until I would realize that much of what seemed ordinary to me at home was hardly common anywhere. I always thought that the difference between our lifestyle and that of our neighbors was entirely cultural. I didn't realize until after I went to Europe at age twenty that both of my parents had been extreme individualists even in their own countries.

Nor did I know until I had been teaching awhile that my parents' habit of encouraging me since childhood to ask questions to my heart's content was unusual. They almost unfailingly rewarded me with loving patience, interest, and the very best answers they could manage. If this required a look into the encyclopedia, a trip to some museums or a scientific demonstration by my mother, so much the better. Even my many "why's" were perfectly acceptable. "What's the difference between five pennies and five cents?" "A girl at the playground said her name is 'Penny'; how can a girl's name be money?" "What makes the moon shine?" "Why don't the Black children at school come to my birthday party?" "Why do the Irish kids beat up the not-Irish kids on St. Patrick's Day?" Surely, one reason I have become a philosopher is that I cannot remember ever once being scolded for asking questions, or for being told that I was asking "a dumb" or unanswerable question. I came to believe that all questions are answerable, and that question-asking is inherently good.

I slowly learned which parent to ask certain questions. My mother loved answering the "what makes this happen?" and "how does this work?" questions. My father, a Lutheran and Free Mason whose occupation was that of engineer but whose all-consuming hobby was painting, was my favorite bedtime storyteller. He was the one who knew all about people and places long ago and far away, about non-Christian religions, astronomy, and many other mysterious and wonderful things. His stories were like his paintings that hung all over the house: rich with color, design, and incredible imagination. They were often spun out of his own sheer fantasy. At other times (as I found out later) they were his renditions of myths and folklore from all over the world. He was especially good at creation myths, romantic or heroic adventure stories, and fairy tales, sometimes of his own devising. There were Norse and Grimm's tales, Homer, Aesop, Kipling, *Gilgamesh*, *Arabian Nights*, and all sorts of German poetry recited by heart at long stretches. (I never forgot my German, although the Hungarian receded from memory almost as quickly as I learned English.)

These stories were rivaled only by what he told me when I questioned him about his huge "metaphysical paintings," as I called the ones that were neither landscapes nor portraits. Depicting the most profoundly cosmic subjects in a way that was at once representational, abstract, and surreal, they were about life, death, God, creation, heaven, world history, eternity, and human fate. Many included skeletons and nude human figures intermingled with geometric patterns in a "logical" way that might be called existentialist today. Possessing a unique style, they expressed his own peculiar answers to the perennial "why's" of philosophers.

My mother's two greatest heroes were Prometheus, who stole the fire from the gods, and Marie Curie, who was both a scientific and a social pioneer. She said she had named me Eva because Eve had courageously chosen independent knowledge above all values. I liked best the bedtime stories she told about her girlhood. On their big farm in Hungary her father shocked everyone by allowing her to ride astride her own horse at a time when "ladies" rode only side-saddle. In 1910, her tenth birthday gift from him was her heart's desire—a pair of Austrian *Lederhosen,* which she had begged for in order to climb trees. While all Europe was starving in 1917, her father gave her oats and sugar from the farm when she went to study chemistry in Heidelberg and Leipzig. When I was twelve she told me that I would be the third generation Ph.D. in the direct line from her father, and that perhaps my daughter or son would be the fourth. It was always taken for granted that I would have both a doctorate and children, in that order. I recall pondering the dual meaning of my name from the sixth grade on.

On my sixteenth birthday my father presented me with a beautiful copy of Goethe's *Faust* in German. I read and reread it, almost hypnotized with wonder. That year my Austro-Hungarian grandfather, still an excellent pianist at seventy-nine, came to live with us. He opened another whole world of delight by teaching me to sing the Schubert and Schumann *Lieder.* Every evening after dinner as I sang the words of the great German romantic poets— Heine, Schiller, Goethe, and others—the *Weltschmertz* of German philosophical poetry moved me deeply. I almost wonder how I could *not* have become philosophical.

Then something decisive happened. In my parents' bookcase I discovered Plato's *Five Great Dialogues.* This volume electrified me with excitement. "Know thyself." That was it! Certain that I had to read more philosophy, I also found Will Durant's *The Story of Philosophy.* After reading that I knew still more surely that philosophy was what I wanted. Innocently, I went off to the library to check out Aristotle's *Metaphysics.* That cooled my ardor for a while! "Well," I thought, "when I get to college I will learn how to read such things."

But when I enrolled in college in 1950 absolutely no one would permit me to pursue a philosophy major. My mother was heartbroken that I was not planning a career in science, even though physics had been my favorite subject in high school. I was universally informed that philosophy is a useless endeavor, especially "for a girl," and that I had better take a major that would enable me to earn a living after graduation. So "like a good girl" I became an education major and taught in the public schools for six years.

While an undergraduate, I took only three philosophy courses, the first of which was logic. Instantly falling in love with logic, I wondered whether the universe itself is logical or only our thoughts about it. My logic teacher, however, was not interested in discussing this with me. I resolved that some-day I would study whatever was necessary to answer that question for myself. Meanwhile, I kept finding that, in almost every class I took, especially psychology and sociology—both of which especially fascinated me—my teachers consistently dismissed my questions as irrelevant because they were "merely philosophical." Everybody, even my usually supportive parents, laughed at or otherwise discouraged me from pursuing as a career the one thing that interested me most.

Meanwhile I had married, dutifully delivered the regulation two children, fortunately a boy and a girl, and made a fairly standard middle-class American home for them and my husband. But neither this nor teaching in the public schools gave me the fulfillment that I knew I needed. I became deeply depressed. I could not convince myself that life had meaning in its present form. One day, at age twenty-nine, I felt that I had only two choices: commit suicide or become a philosopher. This was a simple, literal fact. That evening I told my husband that I was going to enter graduate school to pursue a Ph.D. in philosophy.

The rest is history.

Moving Between Places

EDWARD S. CASEY
SUNY, *Stony Brook*

I

"Just *why* do you like that painting?" When Dr. Karl Menninger, an acquaintance of my parents, put this question to me at a local art exhibition in Topeka, Kansas, I suddenly realized that a line of questioning had been opened up that was quite different from anything with which, as an aspiring young artist, I had previously been acquainted. I was only ten or eleven years old at the time, and before this moment the only questions I had taken seriously were: "Do you like it?" "How would you make it better?" These latter were questions of personal taste or artistic technique, but the prominent Topeka psychiatrist was calling for reasons, perhaps even for reasoning. The order of discourse had changed, and I was left speechless.

Several years later and now at an "art camp" at Kansas University, I found myself reading philosophy in a small library in the Student Union. Perhaps I was motivated by Dr. Karl's provocative question, yet I was not reading philosophy of art—I did not know it existed—but basic texts by Plato, Aristotle, Nietzsche, and Kant. I was captivated by H. L. Mencken's semi-popular book, *The Philosophy of Nietzsche*, which opens with the arresting sentence: "There is no escaping Nietzsche." (This proclamation, written in 1908, has proven to be prophetically true for several generations of philosophers in America and Europe.) But if there is no escaping Nietzsche, then there was also no escaping my literally ambivalent activity at art camp, where I painted during the day and read philosophy at night— thereby enacting the converse of Karl Jaspers' dictum that "the night is for passion and the day for lucidity." I could not seem to bring art and philosophy together in any meaningful way. This split was to haunt me for a long time; it still does.

It also worried my parents, who opted for the lucidity of the day by sending me to a monastic establishment called the Asheville School for Boys that made no provision for painting. I painted on the sly, but my primary energies went into academic work. I read Santayana's *Skepticism and Animal Faith* and his *Three Philosophical Poets* with intense interest. At Asheville, I came to realize that writing is a difficult skill that requires assiduous application and much revision. Art was gradually edged out in favor of writing. I began to assume that there was no way in which two such disparate activities could coherently connect.

Two subsequent experiences were to prove this assumption wrong. Paul Weiss, one of my first teachers of philosophy, sponsored Friday evening "at-homes" that combined art and philosophy in a unique way. Weiss would paint portraits of Old Testament prophets with his right hand while gesticulating wildly with his left hand as he discussed metaphysics with earnest students. Although I took issue with Weiss' own doctrine of art, the image of him painting-and-philosophizing was to linger with me for many years. It may have precipitated a crisis in my senior year in college, when I suddenly considered re-entering painting as a profession. My senior thesis of "Freedom in Psychoanalysis" was not going well. In this impasse, Nietzsche's apothegm came to mind: "We have art so as not to perish from truth." Stefan Körner, whom I consulted in my distress, told me not to enter philosophy "unless you have to—unless you are compelled to do so."

The second critical experience occurred soon after this encounter with Körner. I was back at Kansas University, this time to learn German. Seeking relief from the summer heat and from the rigors of German syntax, I was reading Suzanne Langer's *Problems of Art*, a book that treats cogently and with utmost clarity such themes as "expressiveness," "creation," "imitation," and "living form." Langer's discussions made so much discursive sense of what she herself called "non-discursive symbols" that I could not put the book down. It brought together in an elegant but unprepossessing synthesis my own two strongest interests: art and philosophy. Reading *The Problems of Art* I realized that one of *my* lifelong problems was how to link art with philosophy. By the end of that steamy summer, it had become evident to me that the choice was not simply between art *or* philosophy. I could continue art by other means—by doing philosophy—and I could pursue philosophy by writing about aesthetic experience. My decision was made, or rather "compelled": Philosophy was to be my *métier*. I could not do otherwise. Ananké had spoken.

II

Just as there is more to art than painting, so there is more to philosophy than aesthetics. I have spent the intervening years searching out these receding horizons. At Northwestern University, I worked closely with William

Earle, who was actively engaged in filmmaking and still photography as well as painting and philosophy. With his congenial support, I explored combinatorial aspects of the arts—above all, the sign and the image. I became preoccupied with how images become words, and words images. What is imagining, I wondered, and how can one *write* about such an elusive and ephemeral activity? How is imagining to be distinguished from perceiving and remembering?

I also asked myself: What is *between* image and word? One answer is: Fantasy. From Surrealism (which I took to be an extended commentary on fantasy) I was led back to psychoanalysis, which was just then beginning to reassess the role of "unconscious ideation." Lacan—whose Wednesday lectures I attended in Paris—helped me to explore Freud's considerable philosophical depths. In teaching and writing (and also in psychoanalytic training) I was especially influenced by Freud's "Project for a Scientific Psychology" (1895), a condensed treatise in the philosophy of mind. In the "Project" Freud showed that the various modes of mentation—above all, imagining, fantasying, hallucinating, and remembering—are intertwined in one concrete psychical whole. To investigate one form of minding is perforce to examine the others as well.

III

Still another horizon—one encompassing both art and mind—began to loom large. This was the horizon of *place*. At mid-life, I suddenly found myself *between* two places—two somewhat distant places between which I had to move myself bodily every week of the academic year. Such commuting was not just disruptive (it was literally a *via rupta*); more importantly, it occasioned unaccustomed reflection on what it means to exist and dwell in a place, and to be *out of place*. I began to wonder why the very concept of *place* had been superseded by *space* in Western thought of the last few centuries—as well as overshadowed by an ongoing obsession with time. I also became increasingly concerned with how place comes to be represented in verbal descriptions (e.g., ethnographic accounts and travel narratives), maps, and works of art (especially landscape paintings).

When I have thought through the complexities of place, I will have come full circle in philosophy as in life. For I will have returned to the topic of artistic representation through my new-found passion for implacement. Image and word—now as bearing on, and illuminating, place—will be on the agenda once again. But I doubt that I will be able to answer Dr. Karl's pointed question even now—some forty years later. Why do I like a work of art, or, for that matter, a certain philosophical text, a given person, or a particular place?

To answer such questions adequately, a treatise on taste would have to be composed. For the moment, I am content to have made my way between distinctively different places, which include Kansas and North Carolina, Chicago and Paris, Connecticut and Long Island. It has been a long way between these various places: a long day's journey into philosophical night. Nevertheless, aided by the auspicious ambience of the places (and persons) I have known, it has seemed a short trip indeed between art and philosophy and psychoanalysis and topoanalysis. These several stations on my life's way were all adumbrated in Dr. Karl's portentous question. I have profited most from the movement—from what Wallace Stevens calls "the pleasures of merely circulating," moving between places held apart both in geography and in disciplinary practices as well.

What Made Me Philosophical

VIRGIL C. ALDRICH
University of Utah

The first time I was called philosophical by anybody in this world was when I was a junior in college (1924) taking a girl for a moonlit ride in a borrowed model-T Ford roadster. Some cattle were peacefully grazing in a pasture on the left, with the moon above them. I said to my lovely date, how remarkable it is that even after thousands of years of being fattened for human consumption, cattle were still so unconcerned about their future. After an ominous silence, she burst out with an exasperated, "You're most too philosophical to live!"

But *was* I philosophical? I graduated without a single course in philosophy, not even introduction or logic. My major was in the English department, where I spent most of my time writing short stories and winning the literary prizes. During my senior year, I did catch myself occasionally wondering about space and time, but in a quite chancy way, not pinning anything down in favor of such curiosity. The day after I graduated, I was wandering free as a lark through an unfamiliar part of the library stacks and chanced upon a thick volume, *The History of Materialism* by Lange, a translation of a two-volume work in German. My first philosophy book. I read it through—which I hardly ever did for philosophy books later on when I had become a philosopher.

Did Lange's book make me philosophical? Was reading it the experience, a seductive epiphany, that resulted in my becoming a philosopher? Shortly thereafter I read Bradley's *Appearance and Reality* at Oxford with even more excitement than I felt over Lange, and I wrote a dissertation on what was wrong with it at the Sorbonne. Clearly, these sophisticated experiences made me *ostensibly* philosophical, but did they make me philosophical? Not so. T. S. Eliot was made ostensibly philosophical by reading, and writing on, Bradley for a degree, but this was for him only a (fruitful) diversion. He was, from the ground up, literary. He became a poet, not a philosopher. The reverse of this is true of me. I was ostensibly a literary person at first, but showed my true nature by eventually becoming a philosopher. Indeed, my early philosophical essays were reactions against the literary potential. The first book manuscript I wrote as a teacher of philosophy was an introduction to the philosophy of science that Ernest Nagel recommended to the University of Chicago Press, but which another reader said had positivistic leanings. That, of course, doomed it. The University of Chicago at that time—in the 1930s—was the knight in shining armor against positivism. I buried the manuscript.

But my perplexity is over the difference between being ostensibly philosophical and being philosophical. The preceding remarks show that one can be ostensibly Φ without being Φ such that the experiences that spark being ostensibly philosophical—like reading Lange—do not have the deep force of epiphanies in the root sense. In short, there is an important sense in which the experience(s) that made me philosophical was (were) recurrent, formative, and pervasive, beginning early in my life. The following is the story of that.

For more than half a century—my adult life—I've had the conviction that what one takes space to be, determining what "really" can and can't be in it, is a function of the kind of person one is, fixed by the character of his experience of the environment or the so-called "external world." I was born in India, and brought up there through high school in the Himalaya Mountains. The boarding school was perched on top of a mountain with a blue-green lake in the valley below, the home of a goddess, Naini. It was a spacious situation, a field of views meant for viewing. So I began early to live, move, and have my being in the visual field. I would lose myself in it, visually in touch with things remote from my body *qua* native organism. Of course, this could not happen in the dark, so for me the visual field was also part of the field of light or illumination. Later, I used to amuse or irritate my philosophical associates by saying I touch with my eyes what I see.

The main point is that as the body of a picture—pigmented canvas—effaces itself for the beholder in favor of the scene shown in pictorial space, so, too, does my native body efface itself in favor of what it revealed in perceptual space. This sort of experience has been for me the most influential philosophical epiphany from the beginning, revealing space as a field that is not just physical. In a conversation with my friend Fred Dretske, a (very intelligent) physicalist, I asked why "physical space" is so often naturally used if that is the only space there is. Why the distinguishing adjective "physical"? (This reminds one of the story of O. K. Bouwsma, looking at the sign "Women's Panty Hose" in a department store, and asking where he could find the men's panty hose. On being told by the flabbergasted female clerk that there aren't any such things Bouwsma asked then why "Women's" in the sign.) Fred answered my question about the use of "physical" by saying it had always irritated him to see people using it in talk about space as if it made a real distinction. (Like another physicalist, who said that "perceptual space" conjures up images of "a ghostly space outside the brain.") I became more philosophical under the impact of such remarks.

Anyway, visual experience revealed to me that vision may be a way of being in touch with things not *out there*, but *over there* in the world. The world for me was not *outside* me, access to which would be from *inside* as through a window to what is *out there*, but a field that I inhabited, occasionally using indexicals like *over there, here, now*, not necessarily pointing with a finger at what I had in view. Sometimes my companions could tell by seeing in what direction I was looking, my visual stance thus doing the pointing . . . like putting an invisible finger on what is in view . . . and I noticed that such contact between people can make them blush. It can be bold, but should be polite in civil situations. As a matter of fact, sight is more like touch than like the other senses. Reaching in the dark to grasp— or just explore—something with the hand, one ascertains its surface texture and temperature, its size and shape, too (if the thing is not too big), and its precise location and motion (if any). This description also fits what is revealed by *visual contact*—an aviator's term—with the thing, where *color* replaces *temperature*. And even a color is naturally thought of as warm or cool, which testifies to its logical affinity with the temperature revealed by manual contact.

However, what I mean to be doing here is not arguing, but confessing. I'm reporting the sort of inclusive experience that made me at home in the world, present with things in it. Not at all the imprisoning "external world" of traditional philosophy. Of course, intimacy with things in the world is not a blessing *per se*. It can be hurtful because there are hurtful things in the world. My intimacy was widespread, so I got hurt and took to thinking philosophically also on this count. (Sometimes I think that philosophy issues from a deep sense of something profoundly wrong, not just of theoretical problems. Remember Boethius, who took to philosophy for consolation.) Anyway, I have been reporting the experience that, somewhat as an epiphany, moved me to become a philosopher, concerned to propagate the vision of an accommodating, colorful reality, adventures in which may be hazardous.

This, finally, brings language into the picture. I noticed that, in maturing into a language-user, I could continue to be with perceptually experienced things in their absence (recall John Dewey's "present-as-absent"); and not only with the things *I* had experienced. They were embodied in the words for them as the meaning of the words. Wittgenstein was so right when he said the meaning of a word is to the word as a soul to a body. Of course, this loosens things from their purely perceptual status, and presents them in logical space. So I could still be with things in the world when using language.

Thus was my notion—and experience—of space enriched by ramification into logico-socio-perceptual space. My experience of the world (reality?) has long shown that, if one is to understand "how things hang together" (Sellars), one must consider them in a spatio-temporal order or field of that accommodating sort, in which nothing has to be reduced or elevated into something it isn't. Better, in which the variety of things hanging together, either actually or possibly, are all at home, including the ways they hang together, making room for all of them. Such "room," of course, will be overall logical. The "moves" that a language-user makes are not just movements of bodily parts in physical space. Remember the moves in a chess game, or in an argument, or in the courtship of a lover.

Consider the great variety of values that can be given the words "things" and "fall" and "support" in: "Things fall when their support is removed." You can begin with cannonballs and cabbages, and end with kings, gods, and theories. The remark is true of all of them, *mutatis mutandis*. You may distinguish literal from metaphorical senses here, but you will go wrong if you give ontological preference to either. Reality (re-ality, thinghood) is neutral with respect to such preferential ontology, since the latter polarizes traditional philosophy into its mighty opposites. For me, the field of things has always been of this accommodating sort, thanks largely to language. My experiences in the field have been trips through it, in all its multi-dimensionality. It was this experience of the world that inclined me to consider action, perception, memory, anticipation, imagination, feeling (contact), and thought as modes of being in or going to places in the world, actual and possible.

All this, in addition to physically moving or being in "physical space." What, then, is added by this remark? It is a reminder of another coordinate of the field (world) of things. Reality is the logico-socio-physico-perceptual field of things. Space has been said to be the possibility of motion, but we have seen what a spread "move" has. Almost any occurrence is a move in some sense. When is it just physical? The quick and correct answer is: when it is least life-oriented, which is when the *values* in its description are primarily numerical (exact science). Then the move (or thing) is in "physical space," defined by extensive abstraction from the matrix field.

What I mean to be saying is that my philosophical epiphany made me *find* myself among things on middle ground, metaphysically speaking. So instead of focusing exclusively on *physical objects* at one end of the spectrum of being, or on *rational beings* at the other, I have tried to understand *bodies* across the board: bodies as just moving (physical objects), or also as growing (plants, organisms), or also as acting (sentient things capable of locomotion), or as capable also of conduct (persons, the only "somebodies"). In short, my philosophical epiphany has from the beginning lured me into an enigmatic (because pervasive) use of *bodily behavior* that makes it applicable to just about anything, shading into the *just physical* at one end of the spectrum, and *just mental* (spiritual) at the remote other. It has no opposite.

The spin-off of this philosophy has been, for me, playing tennis (a bodily demonstration of being in touch with what one sees), painting, and writing an occasional short story. Also playing the piano by ear, since even what I hear shades into the field of what I see and feel. Best of all, however, is conversation with thoughtful people, oral or written. Such liberated, participatory use of language takes me with them on trips through the universe of discourse, which is the universe in logical space. Those are field days.

This whole account makes a shambles of a traditional notion of the *self* or *core person*, hermetically sealed in "the audience-chamber of the mind" (Locke). My philosophically compelling experience—again, the epiphany—has been of occasionally having "the same experience" as others with whom I am companionable, or when we were simply in the same situation. In this respect, a self has no numerical identity fixedly distinguishing it from other selves. Selves are not countable entities. In short, experience reminded me that *self* is a term concocted by theory. In reality, the viable terms are only *myself, yourself,* and so on, and whether even they are denoting terms is an open question. They may show something without referring to it. As for persons, remember even they can be "absent-minded." Where is a person when absent-minded? And is one always one-self? *Sei was du bist!* makes sense when addressed only to persons.

The Good, the True,
and the Beautiful

KATHLEEN MARIE HIGGINS
University of Texas

When I was in grade school, the Catholic church I attended offered a wide array of literature at the end of every Mass. Sharing with my artist brother a love of paper in all its manifestations, I found the display a source of tremendous temptation. "One of every kind" was my ambition, but it was usually impeded by my mother's insistence that church was an inappropriate place to be greedy. At least I knew my priorities. The most important acquisition to make as I passed the table was a Catholic children's comic book, (appropriately) called *Treasure Chest*.

Treasure Chest often featured serial stories, spanning twelve issues or more, with sagas like "The Life of Pope John XXIII." But the one that most captivated me was "This Godless Communism." Many of the images from that series are well-etched memories. The one of signal impact in my becoming a philosopher depicted the young Karl Marx and several blonde young men attentively listening to a philosophy professor. The professor was denying free will, and the blonde students were all thinking something like, "That can't be right! God wouldn't allow that." Karl Marx, however, distinguished from his fellows by a scowl as well as by his dark brown hair, was thinking, "Good! So they don't believe in God."

Of course, I was convinced that communism was evil incarnate, as did most other Americans during the Cold War period. Aiming to ally myself with the Good, I told a number of my playmates about the dangerous doctrines on which my comic book focused. But I remained intrigued by the influential role of Marx's philosophy professor. The result of this initial vision of the philosophy professor was that I spent my youth convinced that philosophy was fascinating, daring to the point of danger, and the secret behind world history. I enjoyed fantasizing that some of my teachers (my favorite ones) had majored or at least minored in philosophy. As an adolescent, my interest in any member of the opposite sex was catalyzed if I heard that he planned to major in philosophy. (This fate was reserved for a very few of my contemporaries.)

I did not envision myself majoring in philosophy. My true loves were music and literature. I considered my interest in philosophy a part of my identity, but more a fantasy life than a career plan. The fantasy was stimulated in high school by Mr. Mabbott, my sophomore English teacher and the first person to direct my interest by suggesting readings. This liaison was one of the most fortunate accidents of my education. Mr. Mabbott had ascertained my interest in philosophy when he read my assignment, an essay on "something that had recently caught our interest." My interest had been caught by an evening news story which featured a zoom lens enlarging a building inscription that read, "You shall know the truth and the truth shall make you free." I found this maxim thrilling, and I wrote a veritable manifesto for Mr. Mabbott, announcing my intention to find the "total truth."

I was not aware at the time of the building's identity. Only when I encountered it face-to-face many years later did I discover what it was. I was touring the campus of The University of Texas at Austin, contemplating whether or not to accept the philosophy department's job offer. The chairman, who was conducting the tour, pointed to the tower in the middle of campus and said, "This is our Main Building." In fact, it was *déjà vu*. Pondering my earlier discovery of the maxim, I concluded that the news show I saw must have been covering the incident in which a sniper named Whitman went to the top of the tower and shot down thirty-three passersby at random. Learning the truth about the building did not, however, dampen my enthusiasm for its inscription.

By the time my final year of college arrived, having chosen to major in music, I was sure that I wanted to go to graduate school. I wanted to teach. In fact, throughout my life I think I had always wanted to teach people "like me," whatever age and circumstance that happened to connote at the time. In a moment of enthusiasm for the future and its potential for adventure, I applied for the Rhodes Scholarship. Just before fall semester finals, I went to the state interview and received the Missouri nomination. The Rhodes competition is fast and furious. Two days after being nominated, I was in Minnesota for the final round of judging. I didn't get it. My euphoria gave way to a feeling of deflation—and also to practical worries. Finals were imminent and I had little time and no energy to devote to studying. Returning home the night before my first final, I mustered my diligence and planned to hit the books.

And hit the books I did, as soon as I accomplished some minimal discussion of my trip with my family on our ride home from the airport. I mentioned my plan beyond finals, which was to apply to graduate school at "interesting" places like the Ivy League, as one of my judges suggested. But for the most part, I did not want to discuss the Rhodes Scholarship just then. Thus, I had a complicated reaction when I discovered that my best friend's family had sent me a dozen roses when they heard about the state nomination. "They thought you won," my mother said.

Curled in a blanket with a music text a few hours later, I gazed at the flowers and thought, "They are beautiful." I suddenly realized that my favorite thing to think about was beauty—that that was really what most motivated me in my music and English and philosophy courses, my passion for thinking about why beautiful things are beautiful. That's what had fascinated me about music. That's what had intrigued me about poetry and literature. So there, exhausted and engaged in some rather plodding study of terms in music analysis, I realized what I would do. I would go to graduate school in philosophy because I could then pursue what really interested me in all the other fields I loved—consolidated in the study of aesthetics. I had already applied to some schools in music and in English, but that didn't matter. My course was suddenly obvious. The next year I went to Yale and put the plan into action.

Backing into Philosophy

ARTHUR C. DANTO
Columbia University

When I entered the graduate program in philosophy at Columbia University in 1948, it was as a probational student. This compromised status reflected the fact that I had had no philosophy courses as an undergraduate, but it could just as well have reflected my overall attitude toward the subject. I had no great interest in philosophy and certainly no intention of becoming a philosopher. Rather, philosophy seemed a good way for me to draw the benefits of what remained to me from the GI Bill, enabling me to be in New York while I pursued my real ambition, which was to become an artist.

I had applied to NYU as well as to Columbia, and would even have preferred NYU had it admitted me, since I had read some works of Sidney Hook, who seemed dazzlingly learned and acute. But NYU would accept me only on condition that I take sixteen hours of remedial undergraduate work in philosophy, which struck me as a waste of time. Columbia, to its credit, was impressed by students who knew something other than philosophy, and even had a requirement that competence must be demonstrated in some non-philosophical subject. I had had a few exhibitions by then, and, probational or not, official acceptance in a proper department was to enable me to get a foothold in the New York artworld. Anyway, in those days the idea of becoming a professor never occurred to anyone. Obviously, people did get to be professors, but in ways too mysterious to imagine means to such an end. It seemed a lot clearer how to become a successful artist, as far as a career went.

I had graduated from Wayne University (now Wayne State University) without taking a course in philosophy, primarily because the head of the department, a dry stick of a man, required that his course be taken as the price of taking any other. I ached to study aesthetics with Raymond Hoekstra, a legendary presence at Wayne, but I had done four years of military service and had no further patience with what used to be called chickenshit. I had two years of the GI Bill left when I finished Wayne, and my decision to study philosophy was based on the idea that of all things I could go into, it would leave me the most free time for painting (I did not want to study painting any more). Literature and history, I thought, demanded too much reading; science required too much time in some laboratory. Art history would put me in just the wrong sort of relationship to art. Philosophy, I believed, was contained in a bare handful of texts it would take no great amount of time to read. Mostly, I thought, it would require a fair amount of thinking, which I could do while painting. So I backed into philosophy by making a rational calculation—perhaps a sign that my mind really was a philosophical one after all.

The department at Columbia was not an especially stimulating one. There was no sense of philosophy being something that was happening. I wrote papers, got reasonable grades, won a Fulbright to France and, by what I think of as a fluke, got a position teaching at the University of Colorado. I was one of three taken on that year (and one of two let go the following year). One was a student of Ryle, the other of Norman Malcolm. They considered my Columbia training hopeless, but I found what they did enormously exciting. It was through them that I found out about analytical philosophy, and that philosophy might be something as interesting to do as art. When the following year, I got a job, again through a fluke, back at Columbia, I was fired by a missionary zeal to blow the dust off the philosophy curriculum and to reveal to students that philosophy was something one could do rather than merely study. There was an immense ferment in philosophy in the early 1950s, everywhere but at Columbia, which was still caught up with the formulations and controversies of an earlier era. It was a dull Tibet in a world of revolution.

I was not able at the time to bring together the two sides of my life. As an undergraduate, I had taken (in the German department) a course on Nietzsche, taught by Marianna Cowan, who went on to do the beautiful translation of Zarathustra. I was inspired to do a series of woodcuts, but these were illustrations of Nietzsche's text rather than applications of his philosophy. As a graduate student I took a course with Suzanne Langer, in which, as I later recognized, she was working out *Feeling and Form*, in every way her masterpiece. Her enthusiasm for an essay I wrote on Kant meant a great deal to me, but I did not find much connection between her philosophy—or Kant's for the matter—and art as I practiced it. The canon of aesthetics struck me as laughably remote. So I did philosophy on one track and practiced art on another, and as these never intersected I felt like a very divided person. One year my income as a painter pretty much equaled my salary as an assistant professor of philosophy, and the sense of dividedness started to become acute when I had to deal with the problems of being a *successful* artist—sending things out for exhibition, matting and framing and storing. Up to a point it was fun living in two worlds, but I also knew that one day I would have to clarify my life.

This happened in an unusual way. I remember with great vividness the moment when, working on a very large print, the thought formed in my mind: "I would rather be writing philosophy than doing this." This was now the early 1960s. In truth philosophy had taken hold of me, and I was writing it with great intensity and conviction. Surprised by my thought, I responded as if in an internal dialogue: "Well, if you really feel that way about things, it's time to quit." And that is what I did. I broke up my studio, stored my work, and have not so much as doodled since then. Nor have I regretted the decision. The artworld took a sharp turn just about then, and moved in directions I had no interest in as an artist. But I was driven by philosophical ideas, and was able to put into my writing a lot of the feeling and energy that had driven me as an artist. I was reasonably successful as an artist, and gained more by way of recognition than comes to most individuals who go that way. But I enjoyed the fact that I could through writing reach many many more readers than I could reach viewers as an artist. And I also think that I had limits as an artist that I do not have as a writer.

The ironic fact is that a few years later, the internal changes in the artworld which would have beached me as an artist, reached me as a philosopher. I have often written about the immense impact made upon me by the Warhol exhibit of 1964 at the Stable Gallery in New York, where he showed the notorious Brillo Boxes. The question rose with the force of a revelation of why these should be artworks while their plebian look-alikes should be mere things. Nothing in the history of philosophical aesthetics would help with the question, which was on the other hand the deep true question for the philosophy of art. I presented my response to this in a paper, "The Art World," delivered before the American Philosophical Association that year, and I always take a certain wry satisfaction that Warhol was discussed in the Journal of Philosophy this way, before he was widely noticed by the world of media. From the mid-1960s on, art became increasingly conceptual, and so the world that I had left in order to do philosophy met me from a different direction, since art and philosophy now seemed deflected forms of one another.

Apart from "The Art World," and one or two papers, I did not settle into the philosophy of art. I was not really ready to write at length on art, and when, in the late 1970s, I did complete *The Transfiguration of the Commonplace*, I was able to draw on a great deal of philosophical analysis I had done in the interval—on the theory of history, of action, of knowledge, and of representation. And I found a looser, more allusive style. Since 1984

I have been the art critic for *The Nation* magazine, and so find myself once more leading two lives. There is not, this time, the tension between them that I felt in the 1950s. That is because philosophy has changed, art has changed, and, though I have no gift for extended introspection, I have changed as well.

Of Places
and Passages

"After a little while I am taken in and put to bed. Sleep, soft smiling, draws me unto her: and those receive me who quietly treat me, as one familiar and well-beloved in that home: but will not, oh will not, not now, not ever; but will not ever tell me who I am."

JAMES AGEE, *A Death in the Family*

"The history of the world is none other than the progress of the consciousness of freedom."

G.F.W. HEGEL

Philosophy—A Lifeline

LINDA A. BELL
Georgia State University

Almost everyone in academe seems to know someone who majored in psychology in order to work through personal hang-ups. I have heard it said, in fact, that such individuals are not particularly exceptional among psychology majors. Other disciplines do not have a similar reputation, and philosophy is probably least likely to be thought of this way, given that it is generally seen as quite abstract and removed from what is designated "real life." One of my favorite used bookstores in Chicago, where I lived in the 1960s, reflected this common observation by including all used philosophy books under the category "Esoteric." At any rate, philosophy for me has been anything but esoteric. My initial reaction to it and my continued involvement in its study have touched me to the core and enabled me to work through many issues into which my earlier "real life" had propelled me. It continues to inform most of my decisions and my outlook on many of the important aspects of life.

Understanding my initial reaction to philosophy no doubt requires some appreciation of what it was like for a white, middle-class girl to grow up in the southern United States in the 1940s and 1950s. Though I was not always (or even frequently) aware of the broader picture, this was a time of segregated schools, churches, water fountains, waiting rooms, and seating on buses and trains. Jim Crow voting restrictions flourished throughout the South. Throughout the country there was frequent harassment, even terrorism, of blacks by groups of whites. It was a time when media, politicians, preachers, and educators told middle- and upper-class white girls and women, in no uncertain terms, that they were suited for nothing so much as for the care of men and children.

While I cannot say exactly when, in what form, and by whose teaching these ideas entered my awareness, I somehow managed to imbibe a considerable number of rather perverse notions; but most of all I was infused with an enormous fear of change. Even challenging the status quo in any way was, I believed, anathema.

Since I connected questioning the way things were with blasphemy, I was even less prepared to question anything about religion. Even two years of college and the completion of almost all the mathematics courses needed for a major had not made too much of a difference. Granted, I probably knew a good deal more than when I began, but nothing had made me really think critically about my ideas and about the way things were until I took a required Bible and religion course at the beginning of my junior year. I was almost spellbound each day in class as I was told that archeological evidence disputed many of the Bible's factual claims. I was constantly challenged with a number of conflicting interpretations of what I had been led to believe was unproblematic and unchallengeable.

My head still spinning from witnessing such disputation of what I had thought beyond dispute, I took a philosophy course. Jack Wilcox was the professor, and the course was an introduction to philosophy. He infuriated me as he took on the persona of the philosopher under consideration and refused to budge an inch, meeting all challenges leveled by the class from the point of view of the philosopher himself (and that, of course, is an appropriate pronoun since all the philosophers studied were male).

Furious or not, I was excited and almost overwhelmed by Professor Wilcox's demand that *I* argue. He made very clear that he expected each of us to do what I had thought was unthinkable. And he communicated this in such a matter of fact, quiet way, as though people did things like this every day and as though there was absolutely nothing threatening, fearsome, or even particularly remarkable about it! I was giddy; I had never felt such a sense of freedom in my life.

I was hooked on philosophy. I had found a discipline that would help me sort through what I had been taught or what I had just osmosed from my culture. I no longer just had to accept it all, regardless of whether it made sense and regardless of whether one part of it conflicted with other parts. Best of all, I realized that convention is not particularly hallowed and that nothing becomes right or good or true simply by virtue of being somehow enshrined in the status quo. I could challenge whatever victimized or oppressed myself or others just as I saw others throughout history questioning and challenging the accepted "truths" of their respective societies. I gradually became less tyrannized by the faceless, nameless "they" whose opinions and gossip I had been taught to respect, to heed, and to fear without ever inquiring into their correctness. Later I was delighted to find John Stuart Mill characterizing such enforcers of the status quo as "Mrs. Grundy" and dismissing them as the moral imposters they are.

Though I loved the idea of the examined life, I found, as Peter De Vries has a character say in one of his novels, that "the examined life is no bed of roses either." I discovered that it was painful to challenge accepted "truths," both in myself and others and in society. As I began and continued my very difficult, frequently demoralizing, and very nearly disastrous struggle to become an academic philosopher, I quickly learned that many of my professors and colleagues, some of whom were giving me the most grief about being out of my "element" as a woman, were, to say the least, not particularly enamored with or concerned to live the examined life themselves. While this recognition came as a hard blow to me, I nevertheless persevered. After all, no matter how much they tried to discourage, no matter how much they used convention and authority against me to show me that I had no place in academe, I had philosophy on my side since I knew (as these professors and colleagues supposedly also knew) that convention and authority are not sacrosanct and that they can and should be subject to rigorous scrutiny.

While women have made great strides in striking down academic barriers, I find myself, after two-and-a-half decades of teaching in colleges and universities, still to a considerable extent on the outside looking in. Although I am now in a position to determine in some measure the academic degrees of a few and the academic futures of some others, I am bemused by various colleagues' self-assuredness, their sense of belonging and of being, as my father would have said, "to the manor born." I am frequently appalled by the arrogance, the pride, and the sense of authority and entitlement manifested by individuals who have read enough philosophy to know better.

Generally drawn to unpopular causes, questions, and even philosophical positions, I have no doubt that when I retire some ten years from now I shall still be in an anomalous position vis-à-vis academe and academic philosophy. It is not a comfortable position, and I sometimes envy those with a sense of entitlement and belonging. Maybe, though, it is an appropriate position for one whose original attraction to philosophy issued from a concern to be free from the tyranny of unquestioned convention and authority, and whose continuing dedication to philosophy has led to a determination to disrupt as much as possible the oppressions embedded in the status quo. It also seems a peculiarly fitting stance for one whose quest for truth has always brought her back to an awareness of freedom and a conviction that values must be forged rather than discovered.

Philosophy, Chocolate Ice Cream, and the Weight of the World

KENNETH SEESKIN

Northwestern University

For some people philosophy is an acquired taste. One learns to appreciate it in the way one becomes a connoisseur of rare port: slowly and over a long stretch of time. For example, Plato argues in the *Republic* that philosophy should be put off until a person reaches maturity, the apex of one's development coming around the age of fifty. For others the first exposure to philosophy is like one's first bite of chocolate ice cream: The pleasure is both immediate and intense.

My own experience puts me in the second group. Around the age of eight, when I still held out some hope of becoming a professional baseball player, I discovered that everyday events can take on enormous significance if one looks at them philosophically. It was summer, and workers had just finished constructing a garage behind our suburban Chicago home. My father, an electrical engineer, was putting in the switchbox and noticed that he left some important tools back in the house. He asked me to watch over the switchbox when he was gone because the current was on, and if someone were to touch the exposed wires, they would surely die. Although I normally liked helping my father, I sensed that there was something odd about this request. Instead of agreeing to help, I bolted out of the garage and told him to get someone else.

Puzzled, my father said I was acting like a baby; in one respect, he was right. It would have taken him no more than two minutes to get his tools and return to the garage. But in another respect, he was profoundly wrong, *for it had quickly dawned on me that in those two minutes, I would have the weight of the world on my shoulders*. The problem was not that a stranger would walk in and start poking around in the wrong place, but that I would do something foolish. All it would take was a moment of frivolity, a spontaneous urge to touch the wires and see whether my father was telling the truth, and I would be dead. There would be nothing standing in the way of death save ten feet and the will not to cross it. Unfortunately, that will was contingent and could be overcome by an even more powerful desire to taste forbidden (and lethal!) fruit.

The danger of the situation became even more manifest when I ran to a vacant lot and began to reflect more deeply. There are plenty of things in the world to strike fear into the heart of an eight year old: big dogs, the neighborhood bully, the principal at the local elementary school. Yet all of these are external threats, things over which one has little or no control. What made staying in the garage so frightening is that *I* would be the threat— the ultimate threat—to myself! If for some crazy reason I did get the urge to touch the wires, there would be nothing to stop me.

I regard this episode as my first encounter with philosophy because as I would learn much later, it is a good example of what the existentialists call *anguish*. As Sartre wrote in *Being and Nothingness*: "A situation provokes fear if there is a possibility of my life being changed from without; my being provokes anguish to the extent that I distrust myself and my own reactions in that situation." It is, however, in the experience of anguish that we become conscious of our freedom. While freedom was something that I, like most children, wanted more of, *this* kind of freedom was too much for me to bear; hence the desire to run away.

One result of this experience was that I developed a strong dislike for any situation that forces me to confront freedom in so radical a fashion: mountain tops, roof tops, narrow, winding roads, fast cars, and yes, electrical outlets. The other result was that I learned the world is never simple, finite, or obvious. Nothing in the realm of human affairs just is the case. Behind every event is the will of the person who brings it about. Thus *in* every event is the possibility of tragedy or heroism, suffocation or transformation.

When I got to college, there was never a serious question about what I would study. I wanted a subject that would provide a high degree of abstraction, that would enable me to look at all of existence from the standpoint of self-awareness, that would enable me to discuss freedom, existence, and contingency in the starkest terms. I was interested in history and literature; but when it came to the questions that really mattered (e.g., "What is it like to be free?"), they could not hold a candle to philosophy.

Needless to say, my first great love was existentialism. When I found that Sartre had the same experience on a cliff that I had with the switchbox, I felt that wonderful exuberance every college student feels when he or she discovers that a great thinker came to exactly the same conclusion. In its own way, it is like winning an Oscar or being awarded the Nobel Prize. Although I no longer consider myself an existentialist, I have never given up my commitment to, and fascination with, the idea of freedom. I am committed to it because the many attempts to deny freedom or to define it as resignation into necessity never persuaded me. The world would be much easier to understand if freedom were an illusion, but such a world is not the one we inhabit. I am fascinated with it because freedom is both our most precious gift and our gravest responsibility. As Kant says, we must make ourselves into what we are to become.

Philosophy is intriguing because it often requires one to hold contrary propositions before one's mind and see a bit of truth in each of them. Freedom is both a boon and a burden. The experience in the garage was both terrifying and liberating. It could be said, therefore, that rather than end my life at so early an age, from an intellectual standpoint, I had just begun it.

Philosophy as Flash and Character Flaw

MARGARET P. BATTIN
University of Utah

If you really want to know how I became a philosopher (though it seems pretentious to use this grand term) and whether becoming a philosopher can be traced to a specific, irrevocable moment, let me repeat a little story:

> If you live in the West, as I have for over a dozen years, you begin to treasure a curious form of recreation: long, long drives through the basin-and-range country, 200 miles in one direction, 400 miles in another. It is empty country: dry lunar valleys ridged every 100 miles or so by arid, unused mountains, inhabited only by the thin strip of the highway and an occasional crossroads: two or three bleak wooden houses and a couple of rusting gasoline pumps. What you see out the window, after conversation in the car has exhausted itself and the radio stations you can trust are long out of reach, is a country of almost nothing: utterly empty land, only sparsely stubbled with sagebrush, with a few isolated cattle and maybe, perched on a random fencepost, a hawk.
>
> There is a reason for treasuring such drives. Unlike the more vivid, sophisticated and teemingly peopled parts of the world, where there is always something to attract one's attention, this bare landscape is good for thinking. It is where rumination begins, where a train of thought is measured in miles, where ideas for which one would never have patience in a busier part of the world strike without warning. That is how this book was born: It began with an instantaneous idea, like the proverbial light bulb turning on, which occurred four or five hours into a drive somewhere out in nowhere, hundreds of miles beyond anything that might pass as a town.

This passage opens the preface of my book *Ethics in the Sanctuary*. Except for a little innocent exaggeration in the huge number of miles and the bleakness of the towns, it is a true story: This piece of philosophic work really did begin in a classic flash of discovery—an instant of insight, an inchoate but enormous seeing of what appeared to be a whole new subfield of philosophic reflection, all at once. Like falling in love, this insight was accompanied by that quivering, weak-kneed feeling that something is happening to you, that you have stumbled onto something, that it won't let you go, that you are irrevocably changed. It knocks the breath out of you. Is this the quintessential philosophical moment? I don't know; but it is the way philosophical ideas sometimes happen for me.

Of course the philosophical labor comes next. For *Ethics in the Sanctuary*, the labor began with endless jottings of component ideas, together with objections and counterobjections, on hundreds of random little scraps of paper. It meant hours in libraries. It meant days of thinking, staring vacantly into space. And, since it was an applied-ethics project looking at the moral issues raised by actual religious practice, it meant reading countless religious pamphlets, quizzing religious missionaries, making endless calls on the telephone to a huge variety of religious practitioners, and sometimes interviewing disaffected church officials in discreet little restaurants or arranging clandestine rendezvous with church members who believed they'd been mistreated. Of course, it wasn't all adventurous ethical sleuthing; it also meant hours staring into the blank screen of the word processor, forcing oneself to face the methodological issues, to pursue rigorous argument, and trying to refrain from cheap, easy answers to a problem you know is more complex and subtle than you will ever fully recognize.

You wanted to know how I became a philosopher. This peculiar question might tempt one to construct a legend of oneself—you know, the susceptible, sensitive individual, the extraordinary experience, the blinding flash of insight, the moment of transformation from ordinary mortal to *philosopher*. Sure, I've had flashes of insight, like the one out there in the desert. But I think these flashes of insight are merely something that being a philosopher permits, not what it is to become one. Becoming a philosopher is a lot less glamorous: It's more like becoming old or overweight than like religious conversion. Becoming a philosopher is something that happens gradually, barely perceptibly, through the accumulations of continuing excess and inexorable degeneration: more like developing a character flaw or succumbing to a chronic illness than it is like having a cataclysmic transformation. No legend here: Little by little, bit by bit, one's habits of mind grow "philosophical," though at the beginning you cannot understand what is happening to you or diagnose your disease.

It must have begun in adolescence, maybe earlier. The first symptoms probably appeared in childhood, as a kind of stubbornness, recalcitrance, a careful disobedience coupled with irreverence for the pronouncements of adults: *Listen to what they tell you, but you don't have to obey.* It was surely compounded with never wanting to take *no* for an answer, whether practical or disciplinary in character: *Find a way around the problem, especially so they don't notice.* Skepticism crept in, too; a kind of defense against shame over my own gullibilities: *Don't believe what they tell you, and don't believe what you read.* I developed an allergy to authority. By the sixth grade, I learned to worry, enough so that my parents and teachers were alarmed; but I now like to think that what they saw as worrying was really an elaborate mental exercise in entertaining possible causal outcomes of current states of affairs. My seventh grade art teacher complained that I was "too changeable": I'd see a project one way, and then lump up the clay or paint over the canvas and recast the whole project another way. But what I was learning, I think, was the use of alternative conceptual schemes, and how to practice differing canons of evaluation.

Of course, many adults, including some teachers, made heroic efforts to expunge these dangerous traits of character from me, but the best teachers reinforced them. And so I developed: stubborn, recalcitrant, irreverent, disobedient, unwilling to accept no for an answer, skeptical, anti-authoritarian, resolute in getting around problems, changeable, and capable of extended worry. All this was fortunately packaged as a nice little girl with a happy disposition who did well in school. So I survived.

And I went to college. Bryn Mawr *required* philosophy of all students, in those old golden days, and so there I was: class 1, day 1, year 1, my first moments in college. A slick, crafty (and, I later discovered, famous) Spaniard named José Ferrater Mora sidled into the room, sat on the edge of the desk, and looked around the room. "You know," he mused, "I've been wondering what all these things really are." He patted the desk, touched his sleeve, gestured to the students staring at him. "It seems like wood, cloth, flesh. But if you look a little closer . . . ," and he went on to persuade a roomful of innocent freshmen that all was water. The next day he was back. "You know," he said, patting the desk again, "I think I was wrong. It's really fire that's at the basis of all things," and in rapid succession persuaded us of all four of the Presocratic hypotheses. In the process, he reinforced an abiding suspicion of the cleverness of argument, and an eagerness to play the same game. Formal philosophical training was wonderful: it allowed you to perseverate over a single idea or clump of ideas, and even reinforced you for doing so; it took challenges to what they told you not as disobedience or disrespect, but as symptoms of intellectual growth; and it regarded asking provocative questions not as disruptiveness, but as a contribution to the world. Somewhere in these early courses I learned to think of philosophy as a way of *making trouble*, a way of raising conceptual, epistemological, and ethical issues where there did not seem to be any before. Being duped by the

Presocratics four times in a row was as close as I came to a transforming experience, but what it really did was to activate all those early character traits still more.

Occupying an academic, professional position as a philosopher is even better: not only are those early character traits tolerated and reinforced, but you get paid for having them as well. Of course, there are Presocratics around every corner—or rather, silly arguments you still fall for—but it keeps all those traits of stubbornness, recalcitrance, anti-authoritarianism, and skepticism going: all those things that began for me when I was a child. In retrospect, it seems a direct path (despite its many painful detours) that has led from those early character flaws straight to that single, instant, lightbulb-flashing-on idea out in the middle of the desert. The moment that a legend of oneself might count as the quintessential philosophical event—that flash— is not *becoming* a philosopher; rather, it's what already being a philosopher permits, a chronic, life-long—probably incurable—condition.

Being unto Death

JAMES W. GARRISON
*Virginia Polytechnic Institute
and State University*

BANG! The report of the rifle faded like a slowly dying C-sharp struck on a piano key. Damn! The bastard had struck first. I WAS DYING.

In 1967 my favorite escapist fantasy asleep or awake had been about a war that I had been waging with the assistant principal of the junior high school to which I had just moved. Well, actually, it wasn't all just a fantasy. When awake I *really* was waging a war with the bastard. Mr. Mac, as we called him, was a large, heavily mustached and tatooed ex-sailor with a deep belligerent voice, no neck, pug nose, and a snarl where most people normally speak. Our real war was fought on several fronts, though he always had the same stupid weapon: the paddle with holes drilled in it. There had been several paddlings for fighting on the school grounds. It was like getting my butt beat twice. Once, I got paddled because of a teacher I had hit. I felt bad enough about that one. It wasn't right, but how was I to know it was Mrs. Roberts? I had been fighting this creep, and every time I pinned him his buddies would pull me off. Each time I would just pop them one and get back to business. It was nice to be winning one for a change and I meant to enjoy it. But then she grabbed me. I didn't realize what I had done till it was too late. The entire playground was silent; and it stayed that way until Mr. Mac came ten minutes later. (Even today I still wonder why she, they, and I all waited so patiently, almost eagerly, for him to arrive and reestablish the natural teacher–student order.)

Now the real war between Mr. Mac and me was very vivid, and I always lost. The escapist fantasy was that I was winning. You see, the thing was that in my dreams I had sorta started a revolution at the school, and the revolution had started getting newspaper, radio, and—best of all—TV coverage. The girls all thought I looked good on TV. Most of the students and even some of the parents and PTA people were on my side. Strangely enough, apparently no one had ever led a revolution at a junior high before, especially one like this, with guns, pitched battles, and even tanks. It was a shooting war, sure enough, and people, the staff, parents, and everybody almost everywhere had taken sides. Justice stood a chance if I could just hold out.

My command post was outside "Twines." It was the perfect place for a revolutionary command post. It was where all the "hoods" and "whores" hung out: the tough guys and not-too-tender girls. Some of them had already dropped out of school and maybe even had their own car. It was where those, who like myself admired the "hoods and whores," went when they skipped class. Exactly how I had become their leader wasn't clear even to me except maybe because it was my dream and not theirs.

Well, anyway, Twines was where I was (in the dream) when that b————Mr. Mac shot me. He shot me right in the head. Well, I didn't see him do it, he shot me from the back, the coward. But I knew it was him. I had been sitting on the hood of a car getting high on a beer, "smoothing out" and "seeing the sights" when the sharp sound of the rifle arrived only slightly after the round entered my head.

The note was dying and so was I. Eerie! It wasn't at all as I had imagined it would be, this act of dying. It hadn't hurt at all, and now my soul was just sorta hanging over where I had been hanging out. That's when I saw Macgosline with the rifle in his hand. Then the scene blurred; things got further and further away from me and events moved faster and faster. The last I could see it was spring and almost time for school to end, and everyone had forgotten about the revolution—and about me.

Meanwhile my mother was downstairs in my grandmother's house in Norfolk. I knew she was there because she had called out her soft "I love you" as she always did when she came up to make sure I had turned off the light. Maybe I wasn't dead after all; maybe it was just a bad dream and she would just wake me up in the morning. Nothing happened. Nothing happened for a very long time. Being dead wasn't at all painful, but it was a horribly horrible, boringly boring way to Be. The blackest blackness, no sensation, no feeling, nothing but nothing, except that same constantly sustained note that no one alive had ever heard. Actually, I didn't hear the note anymore either. I was the note! Then, I became nothing.

Something suddenly seized me, an animating something, a spirit, a very cold and uncaring spirit. But this "whatever-it-was" loved nothing as much as my mother loved me. This lifeless spirit next to which a passionate demon like Mr. Mac appeared magnificent was on my case! (After all, anything is better than nothing.) We arose from wherever we were, which sure hadn't seemed to be anywhere.

Whatever "it" was, it was within me and we did what it willed. First we went flying. Together we drifted over the Christmas party I had been to a year before. I could see, and even more fortunately feel, myself kissing Pam.

Wow, that had been my first "tongue" kiss, and reliving it was great! The scene shifted. Suddenly it became something different from Pam and Passion. Much different. (In fact, even now after twenty years, and as many equally horrifying *déjà vus*, I can't write about it.) Eventually, we drifted out of town and out of sight to some countryside I had seen in a Wordsworth poem we had done in English class, and even to a church that also had been in the poem. In the churchyard an open grave demanded that I descend. The thing left me and my body began rotting away. All I remember thinking about was that funny little third grade ditty, "the worms crawl in, the worms crawl out, the worms they crawl all about. They eat your eyes, they eat your nose, they eat the goodies 'tween your toes."

Suddenly, out of nowhere "whatever-it-was" spoke. I understood then that I was saved. What? I remember thinking. "I must crawl out of the earth on my own if I wanted to live badly enough, before it was too late?" As I was really used to living, and often badly so, I started crawling. Then I awoke and repeated out loud what the spirit had said. I understood. I was alive.

Or was I?

I knew I needed to pee like a race horse and that that was a good sign. Yet what if I tried to get up and couldn't? Well, when you got to go, you got to go. And that's when I learned how great it is to be alive.

My story is as true as I can tell it. Later, when I took my first philosophy course we read in Plato that lovers of wisdom—philosophers—wanted to die. When I learned what that meant I knew that I had found home. Only, I remember wondering then, as I still wonder now, what *really* happened? This has, of course, been a major philosophical question from the ancient Chinese sage Chuang-Tzu (who dreamt he was a butterfly; until he awoke. Then he didn't know if he was Chuang-Tzu who had dreamt he was a butterfly, or a butterfly dreaming he was Chuang-Tzu) to the modern French thinker Descartes (who analyzed his dreams while dreaming). For me, this confusing question of what is fact or fancy, reality or dream, is haunting. Some people to whom I have related this story think my account is a bit Dickensian. Others have heard reverberations of Ambrose Bierce and James Agee. Whether or not there are incidental echoes of such literary themes in my experience, my life and my commitment to philosophy have been inextricably intertwined with hesitant thoughts toward why I am not DEAD.

Becoming a Philosopher in Mississippi

ROBERT G. SHOEMAKER
Hendrix College

In 1946, when I was five, my family moved from New York to Mississippi. That should explain a lot right there. I grew up in Mississippi, had friends who fed me grits and greens, cornbread and okra, blues and Bible verses. I knew its voice, breathed its air. But I was never a member, never a true communicant. I talked funny, after all. I did not especially care which water fountain was which, and ate really strange stuff at home like sauerkraut and pretzels, scrapple and pizza. Being a Yankee meant that I was forever on the outside, looking in. Life was full of questions, asked either of or by me. Such circumstances practically guaranteed that I would develop a "philosophical bent." Bend or break. Philosophize or go mad. For those who in some sense live apart, alienated, disconnected or uninvited, philosophy provides at least a fulcrum, a viewer's box, an Archimedean platform.

When I was eleven, however, things really got interesting. A sixth-grade teacher had praised my work, and for the first time I learned how satisfying it was to understand things. I was good at math, good at art, good at reading, and good at remembering things generally. I decided to apply myself to a Sunday School lesson one time. The subject was Moses crossing the Red Sea, and I did some homework in order to impress the teacher. I discovered, somewhere, that the "Sea of Reeds" was the more likely route for the exodus. When I duly reported this to the group, however, I was admonished to keep my strange opinions to my still stranger self. I learned much that day that had nothing to do with Moses.

The summer of my eleventh year contained probably the crucial watershed that shaped the rest of my life. My hormones were going off like pituitary popcorn, and I was growing nearly an inch a month. My bones hurt, my muscles ached. It was seasonably hot and humid, and the house was not air conditioned. I could not sleep. I had an odd fixation on illustrated female anatomy, and drew pictures that I hid under the mattress.

I was agitated, and felt like getting out and *doing* something. But I was also feverish and fatigued, and so lay in bed a lot, reading, thinking, and complaining. My throat was sore constantly, and my neck felt stiff. A doctor was called to the house more than once, but nothing specific was ever diagnosed. One night, however, when I should have been asleep but was not, I overheard my parents talking in another room. Their tones were hushed and the words mostly indistinct, but I became convinced they were speaking about me, about my illness. As I strained to catch their drift, I was certain I had heard the word "polio." I listened even more intently now, for even children understood in those days the ugly implications of that word. "Roosevelt's disease." Leg braces, crutches, iron lungs, and even death. Truly dreadful scenes were shown at school assemblies and in the newspapers. Health officials fought to convince city administrators to chlorinate the water in public swimming pools. Unfortunately, in the McCarthy era, chlorination was widely believed to be a liberal–pinko–Communist plot, so the pools remained hazardous. (Which was convenient, a few years later, when health and public safety was used as the excuse for closing all public swimming pools rather than integrate them.)

"Polio!" That was what I thought I heard—in fact, apparently did hear. Never mind that the rest of it, which I did not hear or else chose to ignore, included the phrase "very mild case," and in any event was nothing more than one among several diagnostic straws that the doctor had been grasping at earlier that day. So, I decided, it was curtains for me! I was going to die! Everyone knew it, but they were keeping it a secret from me, sparing me the ghastly truth.

I did not cry. I knew, after all, that death happened. To the old, to the young, to animals. A classmate had died the year before. Death was, to be sure, a bit of a bitch, but there was nothing to be done about it. I felt anger, not so much about dying, but over being humored or coddled. In the following months I lived like a zombie, waiting [as though bracketed], but gradually adjusting to my all-too-certain mortality. I think it took the better part of two years for me to emerge from this paranoid cocoon, but when I did, I had pretty much metamorphosed into a young philosopher.

Meanwhile, there was school, where science, art, literature, track, and football were my interests. There also occurred another conflict with traditional religion. In the Presbyterian Church, to which my family then belonged, a youth "learns the catechism" preparatory to becoming an "adult" member. Since I would become twelve in September of that year, it was my turn. I was willing enough, in principle, but I ran into problems with the first few questions.

QUESTION: "Who made you?"

ANSWER: "God."

I thought that was fair enough, *faute de mieux.*

QUESTION: "Why did God make you?"

Damned if I knew, but I was pretty sure that the vague and question-begging response, "To glorify Himself," was not a satisfactory answer. It seemed to me, at a pathologically introspective age eleven, that God was simply not the sort of Being that needed that kind of applause. Needless to say, my parents were thoroughly embarrassed by my recalcitrance, and shortly thereafter they became Methodists.

My religious intensity weakened after all this, but revived again a few years later when I discovered (real live) girls. There were a lot of good-looking girls at the Methodist church, and most of them seemed impressed with Wesleyan sincerity. Perhaps it allowed them the excuse, as young women then were inclined to need, that any sexual adventures which might befall them were not premeditated, and thus morally outrageous, but were instead forgiveable moments of spontaneous human passion generated by the concurrent tide of profound religious fervor. Dating a "boy from the church" made their parents feel better, anyway, which in turn made it easier to negotiate such thorny matters as curfews.

Methodism, against the background of Calvinistic indoctrination, ultimately embroiled me in a dogged effort to resolve for myself the complexities of free will versus predestination. I entered college still wrestling with Augustine and Aquinas. By the time I had most of that sorted out, it was perfectly clear that I could no more avoid philosophizing than I could avoid breathing. I studied the classics with Robert Bergmark, I inhaled Nietzsche, I was impressed by Dewey, and I eventually wrote a dissertation under David Miller at Texas. Though I had never learned as much philosophy as when I began teaching it, most of my basic notions have fit the same pattern since I was twenty years old.

There are two things a human being must know: (1) *How to live with people,* and (2) *How to die alone.* For me, certainly, but I suspect for philosophers generally, the former has been by far the more difficult undertaking. From the beginning I have struggled with the problem of how to participate smoothly in the grand flow of social life, while also and helplessly captivated by the need to observe it, examine it, and evaluate it. In sports, it is possible to be a player/manager, but can one be a player/analyst? Can one subject human relationships to philosophical scrutiny, yet also, unself-consciously and whole-heartedly, *be* a lover, a parent, a citizen, a friend, a teacher, an enthusiast (of *any* thing), a philosopher? We find ways to split certain differences, of course, and therein lies much of our burden. But on the whole, yes, I think we can.

Becoming a philosopher, while also discovering how to secure a relatively sane, happy, passionate, justifiable, and meaningful life for oneself was probably no more difficult in Mississippi than elsewhere. I cannot be sure. In any event, it was interesting, and ancient Chinese curse ("May you live in interesting times") to the contrary, that suited me just fine.

Interstices

DAVID D. KARNOS
Eastern Montana College

For a seventeen-year-old kid from L.A., marching up and down a football field in full dress uniform carrying an M-1 rifle and singing "What are you gonna do with a drunken sailor..." was a Big Thing. So was Annapolis that summer of 1965. It was Big Time, major league for the kid from the coast who liked to play baseball, cruise Hollywood Boulevard, and watch the girls go by. Unfortunately, the Navy played hardball. The kind that was serious, and not simply a pretense for a game. Later on in my college career I would learn this was called the rites of passage.

My initiation to the Academy began with a haircut. Actually, a baldcut. For the first fifteen years of my life I had had the standard 1950s all American cleancut "look": the crewcut. Then my hormones kicked in and I, like the great tide of surfers and beatlenuts, let my locks flow. Two years later I sat in the butcher's chair, alongside five other shearlings, and stared ashen sullen at the next six plebes standing opposite us waiting to be mowed. I have hated the sound of clippers ever since. But I was going to be made a man (so I had been told, cajoled, whispered to, and promised); matured through the horror-glory, love, and terror discipline where 4,000 pals, comrades, midshipmen, form an elite company of brethren trained to respect insignia, to love decorum, to honor tradition, to revere victory—and to despise the average, disdain the plebian, hate dishonor, and shun the loser. I was welcomed to the clan, the tribe, the battalion, the Corps!

Only, I liked my body and I didn't want to be a corpse. I was also in the wrong ballpark. Granted, we played; that is, we drilled, we marched, we studied, we cheered together. But there was no roaming, no straying from the code or you're o.u.t. The problem was that when I am in fields I tend to wander. Growing up, I found the local sandlot a haven from that hardened womb, the city, where everything is structure and direction, where concrete and asphalt draw all things together—from the home's front door to the porch, to the driveway, to the street that gathers all the outlets unto itself and funnels them into parking lots and skyscrapers. That's why I liked base-ball; especially at night when I would roam the outfield's grassy wilderness and wonder, in-between pitches, of such matters as why things happened the way they happened.

This habit of wandering and wondering in fields got to be a problem at Annapolis. Though I liked the rhythm, the cadence of marching along to the tune of some dinty, sometimes I just would have preferred to stroll, even skip a bit together like the lion, tin man, and Dorothy. Sometimes, I would ponder "what *do you do* with a drunken sailor?" The lyrics provided treatment by prison, sex, and torture. Strange ethics for a trade I was to be undertaking. Then, too, there was the logic of the matter. Marching past politely clapping crowds inside the academy's tradition hardened walls through gates that opened onto the streets lined increasingly with jeering fist-shaking people (mostly of my own generation) was unsettling. I had always been taught "to think for myself"; and even disciplined for not doing so. Now, I was being disciplined "to not think."

Meanwhile, I had another disturbing habit. I liked to read. A lot. Cal-culus, chemistry, naval science, and Italian I fumbled, but English I de-voured. And toward the end of that first semester I read a book by a person with a neat name: Jean-Paul Sartre. *No Exit* was its name, and I would like to think I carried it with me to Sunday morning chapels over the crypt of John-Paul Jones. But I didn't. Here was a book, a play actually, about a guy caught between a rock and tight spot, between two persons whose lifestyles were consistent with, but perpendicular to, his own (mildly put). I would like to think my philosophical nascence began with reflections about his existential philosophy. But it didn't. What held my thought rapt were two rather minor details in the text describing the scene: the room was lit by one light bulb that was permanently on, and the eyelids of the characters were sewn such that they remained forever open.

The wash of time fades recollection of what connections I might have made then between Sartre's play and my situation, but the memory of that event is unclouded. What I saw, unblinkingly, was Routine. The lights went out, then they went on. Taps and Reveille. Just currents and sounds repeating themselves endlessly. Time did not pass; only the clock's hands moved. There was nothing in itself, no significance. Just order and direction; like push-ups: up and down. A staccato existence in which I marched to the tune "turn left, turn right, do this, do that."

I can think now of many reasons, events, and conditions that would presage this epiphany. Twelve years of parochial school provided a regimen of preparatory experience: uniforms, catholic fervor, service before the habits of authority, credos and glorias. Baseball and boyscouts, too, paraded me in style, and taught me chants and secret signs. To be sure, these forces shaped my social psychology, and continue to haunt my everyday existence. But my journey through the gate of philosophy began the day I chose to step out of line with the gold-buttoned paradigm of reality and march to the wanderer's beat. Like some genie released from a bottle, a glass binding contract, I rejoiced in my freedom. I knew then that I preferred shadows to bright lights (and night lifes), and ever since have celebrated both resistance and participation as magnitudes and powers that always draw me toward their center. For from their pull I have always resisted, succumbed, become annhilated, and reborn again.

Yet, somedays I wander over the lifestyles my choices could have effected, and wonder, too, whether if they had had philosophy classes at Annapolis in 1965 (as they do now) would I possibly have become an admiral? Then I smile, knowing I could never have stayed on course.

Transcendental Resonance

MAURICE NATANSON
Yale University

In the first part of the nineteenth century, the *Encyclopaedia Britannica* informs us, "under Russian rule historic Lithuania comprised six provinces: Vilnius (Vilna in Russian), Kaunas (Kovna), Grodna, Minsk, Mogilev, and Vitebsk . . . " My father, Charles Natanson, was born in Minsk. That was in the very early 1870s. After emigrating to New York City, he became an actor in the Yiddish theater when he was about eighteen years old, was among the first to act in Yiddish theater in London, moved to Johannesburg, where his success was interrupted by the Boer War, which forced him to return to New York. I owe my existence to the Boer War. Though he was Russian, my father, for historic reasons, was dubbed a "Lithuanian." The standard history of the Yiddish theater in the Yiddish language, *History of the Yiddish Theater* by B. Gorin, refers to my father as "Natanson the Litvak." My origin trails me, but I remain exalted and enthralled by the mystery of the circumstances of my coming to be in this world. My mother, Kate Scheer Natanson, was born in Galicia, toward the end of the nineteenth century. Galicia was then part of the Austro-Hungarian Empire. Her documents identify her as "Austrian." A few years ago, a visiting Polish scholar, upon discovering that my mother had been born in Galicia, embraced me as a Pole.

The New York City I was born in more than sixty-five years ago has disappeared. The split history of my parentage, the ambiguity of geopolitics, the truths and travesties of nineteenth-and twentieth-century European as well as American history continue to shadow my existence. I can still hear my mother recounting the story of the Triangle Shirtwaist Company fire— the rotted creases in the fire hose, the women jumping from the building, and who must have been paid off. My mother never worked at that company, but the reverberations of the story are sedimented in my mind. I have never recovered from history.

In 1932, my father suffered a stroke; it led to partial paralysis and, finally, to his death in 1934. I was ten years old then. During the year preceding his death, I frequently imagined the world of my experience as though he had died. Without any self-conscious effort or intent, I found myself experiencing elements of a subjunctive reality. Were I to achieve such a mode of experience by a methodical, willed procedure, I would be engaged in phenomenological work. I make no claim to being a phenomenological prodigy; of what use would such a claim be? But the imagining of the present as future and the experiencing of an imagined future state were forceful features of my world, intermittent though they were. I never mentioned any of this to anyone. It was an "alone" experience, not anguished, but presenting itself as strange without being self-labeled or even felt as strange. From my present perspective, looking homeward, I had without self-consciousness entered a phenomenological zone. As I see it now, I had found my first philosophical moment of experience. The imagining I think of is transcendental; I am viewing it in non-causal and essential terms. Moreover, the transcendental experience had a resonance that, in Husserl's language, "appresented" certain images of my past, of what I had heard about as well as witnessed directly, in lastingly powerful form. The theatrical world of my father, for example, pressed upon me and continues to haunt me. When I was five and six and seven years of age, I saw my father act in a number of plays in New York City and Chicago, where I spent several months, when my father was "on the road." Experiences of what I would like to call "theatricality" reverberated in me, resonating for years, and are not done yet. I find that transcendental resonance to be a living analogue of the phenomenological concept of "origin." Without undoing my reports, I would like now to qualify the sense in which they may be taken.

I do not think that Yiddish, the Yiddish theater, or anything connected with that realm has anything to do with phenomenology or philosophy. I do not think that my childhood experience of subjunctivity is a part of an aspect of phenomenology or a philosophical epiphany. What I have written here is itself phenomenologically presented—a non-causal statement of certain remembered states of affairs. The only element of my recollection that, in my judgment, might be challenged is the vividness with which my recollection is saturated. Let us suppose I am wrong about that—suppose intervening experiences over many years have colored what I report. Instead of an imagined "inverted world," suppose what I have taken to be my first philosophical clue to experience is the result of phenomenologically "foreign" forces: the product of looking at stage photographs of my father, for example. Although it has been about fifteen years since I looked at those photographs, they are clear in my mind. In one of them, there is a shot of a scene in Jacob Gordin's *God, Man, and Devil*—a Yiddish theater version of *Faust*. I see my father in a white suit, at the center of the photograph; he is playing

"Man" (it must be Act I). In another photograph, my father, playing a Russian peasant, is shown threatening a famous Yiddish actor, David Kessler (a kind of Marlon Brando of the Yiddish theater) with an ax. The play is *Yankl Boyle* by Leon Kobrin. Am I to say that these playwrights or plays or actors have anything to do with philosophy (for a child or for an adult)? Absolutely not. Transcendental resonance is independent of causal explanations. I have been displaying a fragment of what I take to be an initial part of my career within, not in, philosophy. In the beginning is a release from actuality to possibility: philosophy as origin.

Being Elsewhere

ALPHONSO LINGIS

The Pennsylvania State University

It could be that one discovered something of the nature of philosophical speech years after one had been "doing" philosophy. It could be that what one understood in deep, reverberating, chance encounters are later thought to have been somehow understood from the beginning.

Philosophy is abstract and universal speech. It is speech that is not clothed, armed, invested with the authority of a particular god, ancestor, or institution—speech that does not program operations and produce results, speech barren and destitute. It is speech that is destined for all, speech that subjects whatever it says to the contestation of anyone from any culture or history or latitude, speech that accepts any stranger as its judge.

To speak is to speak to someone, to answer for his ignorance, lacks, destitution. To speak is also to speak in the place of another; when one speaks to someone one formulates one's own insights in his words, one puts one's own words in his mind. When the other is there and able to speak himself, he listens to the thoughts one formulates for him, and assents to them or contests them or withdraws from them into the silence from which he came. Speech becomes serious when one speaks for those who are not there to assent to or contest what one says in their name—the excluded, the silenced, the tortured, the dead. One will have to hear the assent and the contestation of the most remote silences.

I

I had just come back from India, land of destitution and death. I went to the nearby supermarket to get some food. In the hypnogogic state of one still groping for the old coordinates, I heard, as I turned the corner of an aisle, a male worker saying to a woman worker arranging the cans on the shelves: "You'll have to come over . . ." That was all I heard, but, as I was waiting in line at the cash register, somehow the words hung still suspended before me. What did he mean, this young man, working here for minimum wage, without much therefore in the way of possessions, without much in the way of marketable skills, without, probably, much in the way of virility? What did he have in his apartment he wanted her to view? A new VCR? A collection of compact discs? A python in a glass box? A pile of photographs brought back from Florida or Reno, where those who possess much disport and gamble with fortunes? I thought that here, in this fortress-nation where 6 percent of humanity consumes 60 percent of the planet's resources, existence consists in acquiring a compartment of one's own, stocking up some commodities there, and inviting other possessors over for the ceremonial viewing.

I had delayed going to India for many years. First I went, year after year, to the European countries stocked dense with accumulations, with cathedrals, with castles, with museums, with opulent, and ceremonial restaurants. I knew I was terribly afraid of going to India. I thought that there, where millions of people breed and hunger and languish and die in the rotting tropics without any hope of leaving the street for a room with a roof, without any hope of having garments in a closet in addition to the rags on their bodies, without any hope of stocking up any possessions to view, I would lose definitively any sense of the worth of another individual existing on his or her own. I felt deep anxiety about ever again thinking I had anything to say to another individual, at the turns of the aisles in supermarkets and shopping malls stocked full with the uncountable excesses of merchandise, heavy with the incalculable weight of commodities.

But eventually, I went, alone, to India. One day I stepped out of my hotel and there was someone waiting for me, offering his services to me, offering to accompany me, offering me all his time, all his skills and resources, offering me himself. But one quickly sees he is dressed in the minimal rags he has been able to scavenge for decency, covering the most vital part of himself, his sole excess, his organs for orgasm; one quickly discovers he has no idea where the famous temples of his city are, what the names of the conquerors and despots that built them are, when these famous statues were carved or what they signify with their strange multiple-armed gesticulations; he has no idea where the restaurants where one can eat food without microbes or lethal viruses are to be found; one finds his garbled tourist English exhausts one trying to be civil enough to respond. One finds oneself in front of a naked human being, divested of everything. All one's life one has encountered people within the rules and the conventions. One has sent one's precoded messages down the clean and straight wires that conventions string between us; the clerk at the supermarket smiles and asks how you are, but you understand the strict limits and rules that regulate this encounter. Her smile as she says "Will that be all you want?" is not an invitation to suggest meeting her after work. As her hand touches yours when she hands you the change you understand that it is because the marketing research agencies employed by supermarkets have determined statistically that supermarkets where the clerks make contact with the hands of the buyers as they give them back their change are subliminally perceived by the buyers as more friendly than those in which the clerks avoid contact with the buyers' hands as they put the change into them.

That day, every day in India, I found myself faced with another human being without any understanding of the conventions that regulate social intercourse among us, without any sense of the rules and the limits, the contract; a human being who offers you everything without having anything whatever, without having the language or the knowledge or the gear, who offers you himself, insistently, importunately, with terrible urgency: "Let me be your friend!" He is saying, I have nothing to do, no commitments. For as long as you are here I will be with you everywhere, all of me; and when you go your way I will ask nothing of you. I have no address where you can send back in exchange a postcard with an image of your country. One of us, I think, does not understand this compulsion of an individual there manifestly without value offering you his existence, holding back nothing. One finds oneself dumbfounded, thinking what is one to do with this existence of the other? Should one cherish this bare mortality of flesh and blood? Is this what is called friendship?

Then, one day in Varanasi, an orphan youth gave me everything he had. The treasures that the Ganges, which waited for the ashes of his body to wash them to the sea, gave to him. The coins and silver figure that could buy him food for years, and his name, his divine avatar, the god Gopal, the Ganges gave him. It was a vertiginous moment for me. I realized that if I gave him all I had, all my possessions, it would not be the same. For I have a job, and money is deposited automatically in the bank for me at the end of each month, and will continue being deposited after I stop working and until I die. Were I to be stripped of my job, were I to stay on here, in India, I have, deposited in the vaults of my brain, skills, knowledge, languages, experiences that I can market anywhere. He gave me a gift I could not reciprocate, a gift the equivalent of which I could not give him, or give anyone. A nonreciprocatable gift, an absolute gift.

II

Among us, all relations are contractual, and specify rights and obligations. Being a son is a bond; however prodigal one has been, however long one has abandoned one's parents and their directives; if, one day, wasted, destitute, or dying of AIDS, you turn up before them, they will receive you back and take care of you. Being of the same blood is a commitment. Being of the same office, of the same neighborhood is a bond; to be a colleague or a neighbor invests you with rights to solicit assistance from your colleagues or neighbors. Being of the same country is a bond; if, in the airport, another American seeks you out, because you are an American, for assistance, you, because he is a fellow-American, will answer his questions and his anxieties. Being of the same age-group is a bond; a youth abroad seeks another youth for a meal or a bed, and is not refused; an old woman from the United States on a tour will step forth to assist an old Chinese woman in Beijing to cross the street. Being of the same race is a bond; white people turn to one another for support and receive it in the black crowds of Nairobi or in the streets of Lebanon. One knows the bond exists, the contract, with one's blood kin, one's neighbor, one's countrymen, one's age-mates, one's fellow-whites, and that the bond can be counted on when facing the others, the strangers.

One day, in Mahabalipuram, I felt death come for me. I had been bereft, in a single day, of the robust strength that once climbed the cliffs to see the cave-temples of Ajanta; within a few hours a microbe that had entered my veins through some prick too tiny even to locate had drained all my strength. I was a week in the hospital in Madras, too weak to turn my head on the pillow, too delirious to assess my situation. Then one day the delirium lifted, and I fled the hospital, and went sixty miles south, to Mahabalipuram, where I rented a hut by the sea to take my antibiotics and vitamins by myself. In the ten days that followed, I hardly noticed that each day I got sicker, more debilitated. I hardly noticed the paralysis that first affected the muscles of my back, then advanced down my arms, stiffened my hands.

Then one night I awoke from a fever to find my rib-cage rigid, my compressed lungs wheezing and choking. I stumbled out of the hut into the night, collapsed on the brush. Then I felt myself being lifted by firm hands and turned; over me I could hardly make out, in the storm-cloud blackened night, the small figure of a man clad only in rags. He took charge of me. He came with a cart, hoisted me on it, dragged it through the brush, located a rickshaw from someone he roused in the night, pedaled me on the rickshaw through the jungle road, found a boat in the village by the sea, roused the owner, and laid me in it, then paddled it through the sea whose waves roared about us. When lightning began to slash through the night, I saw him, silent, resolute, concentrated, never pausing to rest or rub his arms. I looked at him and understood he would save me, he would do that, if the boat capsized he would hold me at the risk of his own life. When the leaden dawn came, I saw he was half my age. I understood nothing of his tongue; I only understood he was from Nepal. Still more a stranger here than I was. For me it was nothing, secured with credit cards, to fly in a jet plane in eighteen hours from my home to here, on the other side of the planet, in the tropic south of India. But for him, unlettered, dispossessed, not speaking the language of this land, to have come from the Himalayas here was a journey from which he would never return. He pulled the boat through the seas to the coast, where he lifted me onto a bus, and supported my body with his on the seat, and then dragged me to the clinic in Madras. Then he left without saying a word. I would never see him again, no letter from me would ever find him.

We were on opposite extremities of humanity, linked by no culture, language, faith, enterprise, race, blood, or age. Across these most remote distances he had come to put his life in the place of my death. This substitution across the unmediated distances seemed to me to seal a bond of the most extreme kind, an absolute bond, sustained by no kind of contract. What could I do with his existence put in the place of mine but cherish it, cherish his mortal arms, his legs, his frail and vulnerable body, the carnal surfaces of his silent face?

A youth from Nepal who rowed through the storming sea with a stranger, and departed; this seemed to me a kind of nomadism radically different from the nomadism our inordinate excesses of individual value and commodity values makes possible for those who venture forth from the fortress-nation that has appropriated 60 percent of the planet's resources. One thinks, in this age when one can fly anywhere on the planet for $500 or $1,000 that one can have one's breakfast in the Piazza San Marco or the shores of Lake Atitlán, that one can see for oneself all the most sublime canvases in the Louvre or the Winter Palace painted by visionaries, that one can travel one's eyes across the Himalayas and the volcanic chains of Java or El Salvador, that one can revere whatever humans have ever found sacred, in the caves of Bali, in the monoliths of Easter Island, in the Andes walls below Machu Picchu, in the hallucinogenic nights of Borneo, that one can worship oneself in the most sacred sanctuaries of the planet, Begazkoy, Teotihuacán, the Hagia Sophia, the temples of Khajuraho. But everyone gets weary of traveling, after a few weeks or a few months or a few years. I think it is because in this kind of traveling one drags oneself along, and goes everywhere to accumulate still more photographs, experiences, memories, reports, revenue, return. The further one goes one finds oneself only the more in oneself, the more wearied with the weight of oneself. The true nomadism is rather that which drives one, when one goes far, not to find, on each new shore on which one arrives, someone with whom one shares a language, a belief, or practical concerns, but to find someone with whom one shares nothing, the stranger, and, reduced to the solitude in which one has been mired by contracting an existence one's own, one is delivered by the carnal arms of a stranger. If one starts with this access to the other, outside of all contracts, one will then hear the thoughts and see the perspectives and glimpse the visions of another land, without the inevitable deviation and misunderstanding and parody, the unending Western recoding. One would know *depaysment,* one would fine oneself *elsewhere.*

Would not this displacement, without projects in which one projects oneself, not seeking recognition, not seeking to return a value, be the absolute eroticism? One day, behind the Iron or the Bamboo Curtain, or behind the battle lines of El Salvador, one finds oneself in the tender arms of—the enemy. One finds oneself in contact without the relationships of language, belief systems, or practical objectives, held in a contact without relationships, in absolute contact; one finds oneself preposterously cherishing the bare carnal existence of this enemy as much as one has ever or could ever love anyone; one finds oneself overwhelmed by a compulsion to pour upon her or him all one has of kisses, caresses, tenderness and lust, pleasure and torment; one finds oneself holding back nothing in reserve for any subsequent encounter. The compulsion for this separation from oneself is the absolute of eroticism, which is not another avatar of the unendingly wearying concupiscence to convert the weight of one's own existence, mired in itself, into worth.

Events that come to make one understand something of the depths that lie under the abstract and barren word *philosophy.*